THE "DESERVING POOR"

THE
"DESERVING POOR"
A Study of
Welfare Administration

JOEL F. HANDLER

and

ELLEN JANE HOLLINGSWORTH

University of Wisconsin

**Institute for Research
on Poverty Monograph Series**

ACADEMIC PRESS   New York San Francisco London

A Subsidiary of Harcourt Brace Jovanovich, Publishers

This book is one of a Series sponsored by the Institute for Research on Poverty of the University of Wisconsin pursuant to the provisions of the Economic Opportunity Act of 1964.

ACADEMIC PRESS, INC.
111 Fifth Avenue, New York, New York 10003

United Kingdom Edition published by
ACADEMIC PRESS, INC. (LONDON) LTD.
24/28 Oval Road, London NW1

LIBRARY OF CONGRESS CATALOG CARD NUMBER: 78-155543

PRINTED IN THE UNITED STATES OF AMERICA

To Stephen, Adam, and Frances Handler
and J. Rogers Hollingsworth

ACKNOWLEDGMENTS

As is true of many academic endeavors, this study began in a seminar. Several years ago, law and sociology students, in a seminar on welfare conducted by Professor Handler of the Wisconsin Law School and Professor Anthony J. Costonis of the Department of Sociology, decided to interview AFDC recipients in a nearby community to find out what they thought about the system. That student effort was the start of this study.

As the study grew and matured, many other people gave us valuable assistance, but initially, we would like to express our gratitude to the welfare officials who made the study possible. The permission and cooperation of the Wisconsin State Department of Health and Social Services was crucial. From the very first, they agreed with the objectives and goals of the study and had confidence in its execution. At the State Department, many people helped thoughout the entire course of the study, but from the beginning, Miss Cynthia Stokes of the Division of Public Assistance was the most important and energetic person. She encouraged us, advised us, arranged appointments, and ran interference; and all of this was done despite an extremely demanding job of administering a large state program during a period of considerable change. We drew on her experience and wisdom throughout the study. Professor Marygold Melli of the Law School, at that time on the State Board of Welfare, gave us valuable help in these early days. Her contacts with the State Department were important for the initial undertaking, and we frequently drew upon her knowledge of and experience with the state welfare system. The study itself was conducted in six Wisconsin counties; therefore we needed and obtained the cooperation and support of the welfare directors, their staffs, and their caseworkers, as well as the state district supervisors. We gratefully acknowledge their help.

The Institute for Research on Poverty at the University of Wisconsin financed the entire study, but it provided far more than financial support. Its community of social scientists provided intellectual stimulus, criticism, and support. Although from time to time we discussed parts of the study with many members of the staff, we would like to mention the particularly valuable help given by the director, Harold Watts, Professors Robert Lampman, Myron J. Lefcowitz, Glen G. Cain, and William A. Klein, and Mrs. Felicity Skidmore. Other scholars who helped but who are no longer at the

Institute were Professors Theodore Marmor, Robinson Hollister, and Leonard J. Hausman. For us, the Institute was a rich and rewarding place to work; we hope that this study justifies their commitment to us.

The data-gathering process was conducted by the Wisconsin Survey Laboratory. The director, Professor Harry Sharp, and particularly Mina Hockstad and Tracy Lord, in charge of our operation, were especially helpful. Various other members of that staff worked hard and well for us for several years.

We would also like to mention people who helped us, from time to time in different ways. Some taught us a lot of sociology; others provided legal insights; others gave much constructive criticism: Richard Ratcliff, Doug Gurak, and Jerry Turem, and Professors Edward Sparer, David Mechanic, Margaret K. Rosenheim, Gilbert Steiner, and Vincent Blasi.

To Sue Goldberg of Social Systems Research Institute, who worked tirelessly as programmer on the project, we are particularly grateful. In the final preparation of the manuscript, Ann Jacobs was a most helpful editor.

We would also like to thank the Institute's secretarial staff for their able work, often under trying conditions.

A study of this type ultimately stands or falls on the welfare recipients themselves. We asked them to tell us their story, and we think they did. By now most have probably forgotten the interviews, and it is doubtful that more than a handful, if any, will ever see this study. But our initial goal in undertaking this study was to try to understand the welfare system from their point of view and to contribute to the arduous task of making the lives of the poor in this country somewhat easier. If this study does make some contribution, then perhaps we have acknowledged our debt to those welfare recipients who helped us.

Joel F. Handler
Ellen Jane Hollingsworth
University of Wisconsin
Madison, Wisconsin

FOREWORD

Six percent of all American children were beneficiaries of the Aid to Families with Dependent Children (AFDC) program in 1970. By the time they reach age 18, almost one-fifth of all persons in the country have received such benefits for at least a brief time. Although the total benefits paid amount to less than $5 billion per year—or about one-half of one percent of the national income—AFDC is our leading cash-benefit, antipoverty weapon for children, and the largest public assistance or "welfare" program. It has doubled in scope in each of the last two decades in spite of prosperity, the growth of social insurance, and the vast reduction in the number of people who are counted as poor according to the guidelines of the Social Security Administration. It is necessary to understand this program if one is to comprehend what is called the "welfare crisis" and to evaluate President Nixon's comment on August 8, 1969, that "nowhere has the failure of government been more tragically apparent than in the efforts to help the poor and especially in the system of public welfare."

Since at least one-third of the persons counted as poor are in households headed by women, and since this third has been a center of controversy about poverty policy, an inquiry into the working of AFDC takes one a long way toward an appreciation of the dilemmas and ironies of dealing with poverty in the richest nation in the world. Should one regard the increase in number of AFDC beneficiaries as evidence of increasing generosity and an achievement of welfare state goals? It does after all pay a substantial amount of money to desperately poor people. Or should one see it as indicating moral breakdown and rising criminality? Should one deplore the increased willingness of people to accept such benefits as likely to cause permanent damage to their integrity? Does welfare, after all, do more harm than good to its "beneficiaries"? What, then, do the "deserving poor" (as they are ironically referred to in the title of this book) deserve? And what would constitute a "reform"? By running through this tangle of questions, one may well suspect that there are many different changes that will be identified by some as reform. Hence it will come as no surprise to the reader that the authors are against one line of "reform" and for another.

This book joins the company of such other important studies of welfare as Winifred Bell's *Aid to Dependent Children* (New York: Columbia

University Press, 1965) and Gilbert Steiner's *Social Insecurity: The Politics of Welfare* (Chicago: Rand McNally and Company, 1966). Like those two books, this one is written against a background of political and journalistic discussion, as well as professional comment by social workers and lawyers and others, about public assistance. It assumes that the reader knows something about this continuous flow of observation and opinion, but nonetheless it will have great interest to anyone who reads it as his introduction to the field. Since the senior author is a professor of law, it is not unnatural that this book approaches AFDC from the point of view of its "lawfulness." Through the use of modern survey techniques, which were in the special province of Mrs. Hollingsworth, the book affords an inside look at the administration of AFDC in Wisconsin. The authors find that that administration, which they chose for its good reputation, is relatively "benign" and gives results that are "satisfactory" to four-fifths of the recipients. They reject as inapplicable to Wisconsin the generalization made by the harsher critics that welfare is "vicious," "predatory," and "dehumanizing." This would seem to suggest that if AFDC in every state could be brought up to Wisconsin standards, then the authors would find the national program acceptable. However, that is not the case. While the Wisconsin administration is "benign" in the sense that it is free of corruption, pays the full needs budget, and involves minimal variation from case to case, they find nonetheless that it is "intolerably lawless." It is lawless compared to the standard of lawfulness which prevails in the administration of certain categorical assistance programs such as Old Age Assistance, social insurances such as Old Age and Survivors Insurance, and income taxation. In these fields rights to benefits (or obligations to pay negative benefits) are clearly spelled out in legislation and in centrally promulgated regulations which are easily available to potential claimants or taxpayers and their attorneys. Field workers have limited discretion in interpreting the law, and that discretion can be readily appealed back to the center and to the courts. In AFDC, quite to the contrary, field workers have wide discretion and are "out of control," since both legislation and administrative regulation are extraordinarily vague.

The reader may want to consider as he goes along whether income tax administration, which we mentioned above, is a good standard against which to judge welfare administration. Can we expect the same kind of administrative standards to apply when government gives money away to people as when it takes it away from them? Or, turn the question around. Suppose an income tax statute reads: "The administrator shall take an unspecified amount of money away from people whenever they choose to come in and inquire about their liability. The administrator shall set the tax liability of individuals in accord with his judgment of their ability to pay, their morality, and their employability."[1]

The authors have a standard of lawfulness and recommend that certain changes be made by Congress and by the state legislatures to approach that standard. They call for reclassifying broken poor families as "deserving poor" and for the abandonment of all attempts to "reform" AFDC along the lines which Congress stressed in the amendments made to the Social Security Act in 1962 and 1967. This type of reform tightens eligibility conditions, requires efforts by the states to rehabilitate recipients and to extend more social services to them, all with the avowed intent of reducing the number of welfare cases. Presumably, the authors favor other changes which would tend to increase the number of such cases. And this Congress has often done since 1935, when, as an afterthought to the adoption of Old Age Assistance, it initiated federal participation in what was then called Aid to Dependent Children. It has adopted more generous formulas for sharing expense with the states, extended the maximum age under which children could be considered eligible from 18 to 21, broadened the group of persons with whom a dependent child may live and still draw benefits, opened the way for payments to children with an unemployed father present, and pushed for statewide uniformity of administration.

Beyond this, Handler and Hollingsworth would make eligibility conditions clear in the legislation and would make benefit determination subject to self-assessment, just as is income tax liability. Eligible persons would not be subject to any performance standards nor required to accept any services. They might, however, be offered incentive to work or undertake other constructive activity. Field workers' control over supplementary benefits and services would be sharply limited. The job of the caseworker would be closely circumscribed and more clerical than professional. (We are assured by the authors that this is in fact the picture today. The caseworker seeks to avoid confrontations with her clients, tends to minimize her administrative decisionmaking, and delivers virtually no services. Perhaps this means that her potential for harm far exceeds the harm realized.) Services would, for the most part, be delivered by nonwelfare agencies to those AFDC recipients who seek them on their own initiative. Recipients would be encouraged to organize for self-help in providing these services and in assuring a responsive administration of them. These changes are all pro-

---

[1] It is interesting to note that a delegation of authority almost as loose as that is made by the Selective Service Act (see the study sponsored by the Institute for Research on Poverty entitled *Little Groups of Neighbors: The Selective Service System,* by James W. Davis, Jr., and Kenneth M Dolbeare. [Chicago: Markham Publishing Company, 1968]).

posed in the hope that they will produce a more constructive tension between the dignity of the recipients and the risk of their being led into an
unhealthy dependency.

Each reader must, I suppose, try to reach a judgment concerning
the "intolerability" of the administration under review and the likely out-
comes of the changes proposed by the authors. In reaching those judg-
ments, he will be helped by the authors' historical work, which does not lead
them to be overly sanguine about the possibilities for adoption of their
standard for lawful administration. They are most insightful as scholars of
legal history in explaining why AFDC in Wisconsin is as "lawless" as it is;
i.e., why the legislature has delegated so much authority to the state administrators, and why they in turn are content to leave so much authority
in the hands of the county boards and field workers. The basic reason for
this, they argue, is the lack of certainty in the public mind and conscience
of the moral claim to a benefit by the family broken by a cause other than
death, and the general belief that a forthright statement of a right to benefits
will reward irresponsibility and encourage dependency so that the poor
enjoy less welfare rather than more. Thus the lack of clarity in the existing
legislative-administrative arrangement has a functional relationship to the
community's ambivalence toward helping broken families. The community
is not quite sure what such families are deserving of, or what the consequences would be if they were given the kind of treatment they may deserve. Welfare law, which emerged only recently from the criminal law, has
wavered between the desirability of certainty of benefit and the need for
flexibility to deal with the peculiarities of the individual case. The latter need
is seen both to achieve equity and to encourage self-reliance by recipients.
Only a flexible administration can mediate between the public's sense of
obligation and its fear of an unreasonable outcome if that obligation is too
generously underwritten.

What basis do the authors give us for predicting what the outcome
of their proposed changes would be? They do assure us that the mothers
now receiving AFDC benefits are much like others in the state. But their
study is so narrowly drawn that we do not have much idea what people
would apply or would become or would make themselves eligible if their
more lawful and clear entitlement standard were applied. (In this connection, one wishes he had more information as to why Wisconsin has such
a relatively low recipient rate.) The authors leave us unclear as to how they
would draft their statement of entitlement, but presumably they are thinking
within the terms of the category of the broken family and do not give
specific attention to the still harder question of what to do about the
category of "unemployed father." Can we sustain a more generous program
which takes part of its money from poor families headed by men and pays

it to less poor families headed by women? The reader will want to consider whether the authors have based a policy recommendation upon observation of too small a group of preselected recipients without due regard to the full implications of opening wide the doors to the category.

There is then room for argument and need for research concerning the costs and benefits of the authors' proposals, even though many people would agree that, in general, lawful administration is preferable to unlawful administration. (Some information along these lines will be supplied by the several experimental studies of negative income taxation now being carried out at the Institute for Research on Poverty.) The key question is: Would the proposed changes lead to more or less rapid reduction of poverty?

A look backward supplies the authors with sufficient explanation for the existence of unlawful administration. However, they may have overstated this case. Certainly the long trend in welfare legislation and administration as well as judicial review has been to resolve the tensions ever more liberally toward the side of obligation to help and less toward the fear of overgenerosity. The same Congress which leans toward restrictive "reform" from time to time has extended the edges of the category and has accommodated higher benefits.

Similarly, there is basis for disagreement concerning the direction of change heralded by the dramatic departure in welfare legislation proposed by President Nixon in 1969 with his Family Assistance Act. Our authors compare this legislation with their ideal standard of lawful administration and find that it falls far short in that it perpetuates, and even extends, the old administrative discretions and uncertainties. It is true that the President used the "old reform" rhetoric of 1962 and 1967 in sloganizing his new plan as "workfare" and in combining services with income maintenance. And it is not clear that federal and state administrators will actually limit decisionmaking by field workers any more than they have in the past with regard to such critical matters as the "work test," who is or is not "fully employed," what is "suitable work," who is eligible for free day care, and who shall be penalized if he does not accept counseling or training. Congress delegates wide powers to the Secretary of Health, Education, and Welfare to determine such key matters as the accounting period to use in positing the size of benefit payable. Some welfare recipients will find that they have to deal with several administrations at state as well as federal levels.

However, there is another, and perhaps more important, aspect to the Family Assistance Act, and it may help to call this the "new reform" aspect, to distinguish it from what Handler and Hollingsworth call "reform." This "new reform" aspect will add 14 million more persons to the welfare rolls. It does this by making all low-income families with children eligible for federally administered cash benefits and then extending the conditions for receipt of those benefits (i.e., key definitions of family, income, and accounting period) to all those now in the AFDC category. This, along with the withdrawal of federal sharing in AFDC, means in a certain sense that AFDC has been abolished. However, Wisconsin, and other states with benefits above $1,600 per year for a four-person family, are constrained to maintain their present schedule of benefits for all persons eligible for what used to be called AFDC. This complicated arrangement is aimed at achieving lessened inequity with regard to two matters not within the scope of this book: (1) the gross differences in AFDC benefits from one state to another and (2) the difference in treatment of the broken and the intact family. Under the new law, a man will not have to abandon his family in order to get some assistance for them, nor will he have to be fully unemployed to get help from welfare if his income and family size are at certain levels. It can be argued that the gain in equity associated with the "new reform" spirit of the Family Assistance Act outweighs the loss or failure to improve the lawfulness of administration. But some critics, presumably including the present authors, find that their enthusiasm for the Family Assistance Act is quite muted, even though they recognize reasonable classification as the basis of administrative justice, because it will perpetuate a scheme of welfare administration which they find offensive.

This book seems to argue that even if the new national program of Family Assistance were to incorporate the relatively high administrative standards of states like Wisconsin, the possible gains in equity would be marred so long as an administration is informed by the concepts of the conventional wisdom and the "old" spirit of reform. So long as Congress and state legislatures refuse to introduce more specificity into the law; so long as there is a professional bureaucracy with discretionary authority operating at some distance from the central administration; and so long as recipients are passive, ill-informed, and without legal representation and aggressive self-help organization—so long will "welfare" continue to yield some of the undesirable consequences of "ill-fare" that come from "intolerable lawlessness."

I would like to add a personal note of appreciation for the contribution made to the vitality of the Institute for Research on Poverty by Joel Handler and a number of other legal scholars who have been associated with the Institute. This book is a good evidence of that contribution, and I am sure that it will provoke thought and further inquiry, both within and outside of the Institute, into the possibility and consequences of lawful administration of not only AFDC, but of other antipoverty programs as well.

Robert J. Lampman
Professor of Economics, University of Wisconsin
Institute for Research on Poverty

CONTENTS

LIST OF TABLES

INTRODUCTION

The Aid to Families with Dependent Children (AFDC) program is our largest cash public assistance program. It is also the most controversial, the symbol of what is wrong with welfare in America. It is the "crisis in welfare." The crisis is many faceted: the number of families on welfare rolls increases continually and costs skyrocket; elaborately designed programs seem ineffectual; in a welter of claims and counterclaims, recipients, administrators, and taxpayers condemn the system. This study is concerned with describing and assessing how welfare is administered and received. The questions asked in the survey on which much of this study is based are designed to discover what is happening in the AFDC program, not what is supposed to happen. Much of the data for the study is from the usual sources—laws, administrative regulations, documents, reports, statistics, and interviews with state and local officials and with caseworkers. However, a primary source of data is survey responses from 766 AFDC recipients in six Wisconsin counties, with follow-up interviews of those families who left welfare.

Our purpose in interviewing welfare recipients was twofold. First, a client survey would provide a different view of administration—it would be a look at AFDC from the "inside out." Second, the survey would help fill a major gap in our knowledge concerning one of the core questions of welfare policy—what does the welfare system do to and for the recipients themselves. Information about client characteristics is relatively full. What we do not know is how the clients assess the program, how they use it or do not use it and why, and what difference the program makes in their lives.

Even with current welfare reform proposals, such as the Family Assistance Plan, many of the questions raised in this study remain vital. The specific consequences of reform proposals will be treated in other studies— but the female-headed households in poverty, the subject of this book, must be of major concern for any substitute or alternative program. The names of programs may be changed, but many aspects of the present welfare system will continue: a means test, a work test, some form of social services, some measure of control over deviant sexual behavior, problems

1

about chasing absent fathers, etc. The extent to which proposed administrative practices will resemble existing welfare practices is not clear, but previous experience suggests that there will be more continuity of practice than change.

The female-headed household in poverty will remain one of the most controversial groups on welfare. Employment prospects are very poor for this group and costs of training will be high. This is also the recipient group that has raised problems of race, religion, family relationships and responsibility, and illegitimacy. These social and political aspects of welfare are not erased by the impending welfare reform and will continue in some form or another to vex welfare policy and administration. Therefore it is still very important to know how these particular welfare recipients view their experience in welfare and its various administrative components. Since some or even a considerable number of features of the present system will probably survive, in various forms, it is important to see what impact these various components have had on the clients.

Another of our major concerns is the development of welfare policy and administration, especially as that development will influence future directions. Welfare policy and administration are deeply rooted in our value conceptions of the nature, causes, and cures of poverty. These values have had enormous staying power in their fundamental conceptions, and one result has been that in overall approach and structure, the welfare system has shown remarkable stability. On the surface, the welfare system seems to be changing all the time with changes heralded in the most dramatic terms. The impending welfare reform is not the first "new direction" in welfare that the country has been promised. Crises, of course, trigger more promises of reform, and more legislative activity. In this study we examine quite carefully a number of previous changes in the welfare system and how and where old ways of doing things still survive although names and labels change. We try to indicate the nature and intensity of the conflicts and interests shaping welfare policy and to show the techniques that have been used to achieve or frustrate change. Given the stability that has characterized welfare legislation and administration, the lessons from the past may very well not be obsolete yet.

The selection of one state such as Wisconsin has both advantages and disadvantages. Most of the research, politics, and publicity about welfare deals with New York City, the large urban centers of California, and to a lesser extent, Chicago. We often forget that most of the poor are not black and most probably do not live in the largest cities of the country. Welfare reform, as well as other anti-poverty measures, raises special problems in the less populated areas (including middle-sized cities), particularly when one considers that the welfare system is only one aspect of the lives of welfare clients. The availability of other community resources affects the experience of the clients. This study, then, should provide some basis for comparing the experiences of recipients living in middle-sized and smaller communities with those living in a large city.

Our impression is that in many respects Wisconsin administration may be unique. The state has had a long tradition of liberal, progressive social welfare programs. For many years the supervising agency at the state level, the State Department of Health and Social Services, has been outside the political patronage system. Outside professionals view Wisconsin's welfare administrators as highly professional, progressive, and liberal. Wisconsin's top welfare personnel seemingly are committed to experimentation and reform. Until this past year, the state has always met 100 percent of need and at the time of this study had an extensive program of extra grants for special needs. In 1968 the average grant per AFDC recipient was $50 per month (higher than California or Illinois) and the sixth highest in the country. Wisconsin was one of twenty-one states to adopt the extension of AFDC to unemployed parents, although the program in Wisconsin has been quite small. Between 1961 and 1965 the Wisconsin AFDC rolls increased by about 21 percent, considerably less than the national average of 46 percent. Despite this increase, Wisconsin has the ninth lowest AFDC recipient rate. At the time of the survey (1967) there were 51,487 people in 13,010 Wisconsin families receiving AFDC benefits, exclusive of AFDC payments made to foster families and to families headed by an unemployed father.

Despite local variation, at least as compared with other parts of the country, the Wisconsin program seems liberal and moderately benign. The county programs thus far appear to have escaped virulent political attacks and to have avoided the more notorious forms of harassment of welfare recipients. Allegations of chiseling, of fraud, of lax administration crop up from time to time, but as far as we can tell, there have not been widespread efforts to scrutinize the activities of recipients, to conduct midnight raids, or to engage in other practices of harassment reported in some jurisdictions, although these things do occur from time to time.

This study, then, is of a program that by certain criteria has achieved standards which are probably close to what could be expected of a properly functioning public welfare bureaucracy. This is a study of a predominantly decent administration.

The value of studying an administration of this type is that if the AFDC program is a failure even here, then the often repeated solutions to welfare administration are not particularly relevant, namely removing welfare administration from state and local partisan politics and improving personnel. The Wisconsin administration, like all others, could probably be very much improved if all personnel were fully trained, humane, wise, decent people. But that will not come to pass in public assistance in the foreseeable future. The reasons for failure go to more fundamental questions about the nature of welfare bureaucracies, the jobs that they have to do, and the constraints that they face. Phrased another way, a study of a welfare bureaucracy such as Wisconsin's should shed light on the limits of what we can reasonably expect in the administration of public assistance. Reform efforts then will have a better basis for taking account of one of the "givens" in welfare. Although there are many proposals for changing the functions and discretions of welfare bureaucracies, it is extremely unlikely that they will be dispensed with. Clearly, though, a central thrust of current welfare reform proposals is reduction of the role of discretionary administrations.

In evaluating and describing administration, how reliable are data collected from clients? Although the client survey responses are only one source of our information, they are a most important source. In order to give the following discussion more meaning, we will present one of our major and most controversial findings concerning client attitudes: most of the recipients expressed quite positive attitudes toward their welfare experience and their caseworkers. Two things should be said about this finding immediately. First, there are important and fairly complicated reasons why clients have these attitudes, reasons which we go into in detail in subsequent chapters and which we think validate these answers. Second, this finding, in our opinion, in no way vindicates the present welfare system. The reasons for these client attitudes furnish *additional* grounds for concluding that the present AFDC program is a failure and should be changed radically.

It is a commonly held belief (contrary to this study's findings) that most recipients feel quite negatively about the welfare system and the caseworkers. The argument is that since recipients are dependent and fearful of retaliation, they will not criticize the system or the caseworkers, especially in an interview conducted by a stranger usually of a different race and class background. Why not give the safe answer—"everything is all right"? This is a common but nevertheless critical problem of survey research. Although one can never be sure of the truthfulness of the responses, we can explain the methodology and the reasons why we think the answers are reliable.

The data were gathered by the University of Wisconsin Survey Research Laboratory. The sample was drawn from the state AFDC payroll records for March 1967. Since the primary concern of AFDC has always been households headed by women, we attempted to exclude from our respondents those families in which a father was in residence.[1] Many of the

---

[1] Thus if the payee was male, the case was not eligible for the sample; all families under the AFDC-U program were also excluded.

survey questions centered on quality, quantity, and evaluation of client-caseworker-agency relationships; therefore only women who had been in AFDC at least six months were included. Women in the program a shorter time, although perhaps more sensitive to some problems, would have too little experience with the effect of the program over time to be as helpful in assessing it. On the other hand, the six-month requirement may have dimmed memories of negative feelings that were present during the application stage and the early period of welfare and may have biased the sample in terms of a more "adjusted" recipient, a person who has come to terms with welfare.

The sample was selected from six counties: Milwaukee, containing the nation's twelfth largest city with over a million people and a black ghetto; Dane and Brown, containing two middle-sized cities (Madison and Green Bay); and Walworth, Sauk, and Dodge, all rural. For Milwaukee and Dane counties stratified proportional samples were drawn, reflecting the distribution of the AFDC population into "wed" and "unwed." Within each category a random sample was drawn that met the criteria set forth above. In Brown County a random sample was drawn. For the three rural counties the entire AFDC population that had been in the program six months was approached.

Each potential respondent was sent a letter from the Survey Laboratory, requesting her cooperation in a study of welfare from the viewpoint of clients and informing her that she would be contacted by an interviewer. The letter (which appears in the Appendix) stressed that the interview would be entirely voluntary, that what the respondent said would be kept secret, and that the welfare department would not be able to find out what the respondent said. Respondents were offered three dollars to participate and told that the welfare department said they would not have to report the income. Respondents could refuse by tearing off the bottom part of the letter and returning it in an enclosed stamped envelope to the Survey Laboratory, by calling the Survey Laboratory collect, or by refusing the interviewers when they called to make appointments. Women who refused by mail were asked in another letter at a later date if they would reconsider (the letter appears in the Appendix). Approximately 80 percent of those approached agreed to be interviewed. The interviews, lasting about an hour (the schedule appears in the Appendix), were taken in the summer and fall of 1967 by interviewers trained and coordinated by the Survey Laboratory.

As women left welfare we attempted to reinterview them approximately two months after their exit. Again, they were first approached by a letter (which also appears in the Appendix) requesting the interview, assuring them of confidentiality, and offering a five-dollar fee for the interview. By the time the study was terminated (about two years after the initial survey) 272 respondents had left the program. Only 12 refused to be reinterviewed (although 54 could not be located). These interviews were also conducted by the Survey Laboratory and they lasted about a half hour. The response rates are shown in the Appendix.[2]

An initial question is whether the population that was interviewed, by dint of self-selection, was different from the population that refused. We did have a high response rate, as far as surveys go; still, one out of every five refused to be interviewed. We compared the "face sheet" data of these women with those who were interviewed.[3] On several major variables such as age, race, number of children, time in the AFDC program, and marital status, we found only very slight differences between those who were inter-

---

[2] The "typical" Wisconsin Survey Research Laboratory interviewer (at approximately the time of this survey) was a white woman of northwestern European stock, in her forties, well educated (most had almost finished college), married to a professional man or one who ran his own business, and had three children. She was of relatively high socioeconomic status (in 1965, combined family income was about $10,500 annually), most often identified herself as upper-middle class, was a Protestant and a Republican ("A Profile of Wisconsin Survey Research Laboratory Interviewers—1965," Wisconsin Survey Research Laboratory, University of Wisconsin Extension, Report No. 16, Project 202, October 1965). In our study one of the interviewers was black. She was single, a resident of Milwaukee, thirty-one years old, and an elementary school teacher.

The interviewers on this study underwent a required initial one-week training session conducted by the field staff of Survey Research Laboratory for the basic interviewing technique—e.g., introducing oneself, maintaining rapport, probing on open-ended questions, and the mechanics of recording responses. Each interviewer also did a practice interview during this period, results and experience of which were discussed at a training session. They later participated in periodic retraining sessions.

In addition, for this study, there were study orientation sessions conducted by those members of the Survey Laboratory field staff who had participated in the pretesting of the interview schedule. These sessions dealt with the background and overview of the study as well as an analysis of the content and objectives of each question. The interviewers were also provided with a manual or instruction book which included an analysis and explanation of each question.

Then the first completed interview of each interviewer was checked by the Survey Laboratory field staff and Ellen Jane Hollingsworth and Richard Ratcliff, a graduate student in sociology who had worked on the questionnaire for over a year.

All of the interviewers who reinterviewed the clients after they left welfare had worked on the initial interviews.

[3] Although the case records of those who refused to be reinterviewed could have been made available to us without violating any federal or state law, we felt that these records should not be inspected because it would invade the privacy of recipients who had already indicated that they would prefer to be let alone.

viewed and those who refused. The respondents and those who refused to be interviewed for the three largest counties are compared in tabular form in the Appendix.

An important measure of the validity of survey responses is comparability with the results of other surveys. The results of a survey of welfare recipients in New York City have been published in preliminary form.[4] The New York survey was taken between January 1 and November 10, 1966 (that is, less than a year before the survey for this study was taken), of over 1,500 female heads of AFDC households. The sample was 40 percent Puerto Rican, 41 percent black, and 19 percent white. The field work was conducted by the National Opinion Research Center, and respondents and interviewers were matched in ethnicity and (in the case of Spanish-speaking respondents) language as well.

The New York study was interested in different things and asked different questions than this study did; therefore complete comparability is limited. On several basic issues, however, the results were the same, particularly with regard to positive attitudes that welfare recipients had toward the caseworker.

The New York respondents were asked these four questions about their caseworker (called "investigator" in the survey): How fairly does he treat you? How freely can you talk with him? How much do you trust him? How well does he understand your problems? For each question, the respondents could answer: very; somewhat; not at all. For *all four* questions, more than 80 percent of the respondents said either "very" or "somewhat." Over 90 percent said that they were treated very fairly or somewhat fairly by the caseworkers. Moreover, these positive responses were related to the *duration* of the home visit. Satisfaction with the caseworker, on all four indicators, increased with the length of the home visit.[5] There were no dif-

---

[4] The New York City study is under the direction of Lawrence Podell (principal investigator), Harold Yahr (project director), and Richard Pomeroy (project associate). The titles of the reports issued so far are: "Families on Welfare in New York City"; "Professional Social Workers in Public Social Welfare"; "Effects of Eligibility Investigations on Welfare Clients"; "Effects of Caseworker Turnover on Welfare Clients"; and "Reactions of Welfare Clients to Caseworker Contact" (mimeo., Center for the Study of Urban Problems, Bernard M. Baruch College, City University of New York).

[5] The New York authors point out there is a problem of causality—whether longer home visits contribute to a "positive" relationship or are the result of them. However, one should not get the impression that an extended amount of time is spent with clients. The New York City Welfare recipients experienced very high turnover in caseworkers (two-thirds of the sample had two or more caseworkers in the ten-month study period) and short visits (for 80 percent the visit was thirty minutes or less, and for 30 percent it was fifteen minutes or less). But when the caseworker does manage to stay longer, clients approve.

ferences in these results in terms of ethnicity. Blacks, whites, and Puerto Ricans alike reported a high degree of satisfaction with the caseworkers, and for all, satisfaction increased with caseworker contact.[6]

There were several other important areas where client attitudes in this study and the New York one were the same. For example, we found far less negative feeling toward the intake process than we expected. In New York City only 12.8 percent of the recipients said that they disliked having their eligibility checked "very much" and 58.4 percent said that they didn't mind it at all. For these responses there were no differences between blacks and whites; Puerto Ricans were more accepting of eligibility checks.[7]

It is somewhat harder to compare attitudes toward the welfare experience in general. The Wisconsin recipients were asked to evaluate their experience in light of what they needed. The New York recipients were asked whether or not they agreed with several possible perceptions of welfare. Sixty-five percent agreed that the New York Welfare Department *"really cares* about Welfare clients and their problems" and 80 percent agreed that the department *"tries* to help anyone who really needs it."[8]

There were other points of similarity between the New York results and our results which we will discuss shortly, but on the issues of positive client attitudes toward the caseworker and the welfare system, the Wisconsin respondents are not unique. Nor do ethnic differences in interviewers seem to make a difference in the responses.

Aside from comparability, the other major test of validity of survey responses is the internal consistency of the responses themselves. For most recipients the quantitative statistics dealing with caseworker visits dispel the basis for the belief that AFDC recipients suffer under the regulatory heel of caseworkers—or conversely that they gain much from AFDC social services. Caseworkers see clients three or four or perhaps five times a year for about thirty minutes a visit. For most recipients, then, there is no time for regulation or service; and this is true for New York City as well as Wisconsin. Nor do caseworkers have the inclination to regulate the clients. The vast majority of public assistance workers are not professional social workers, are not particularly interested in that career or their job, and soon leave. Those who are interested in social work find public assistance work frustrating and also leave. The caseworkers discuss superficial things, stay away from sensitive subjects, and do not enforce troublesome rules. The

---

[6] Podell *et al., supra* note 4, "Reactions of Welfare Clients to Caseworker Contact," at 37–45.

[7] Podell *et al., supra* note 4, "Effects of Eligibility Investigation on Welfare Clients," at 7.

[8] Podell *et al., supra,* note 4, "Effects of Caseworker Turnover on Welfare Clients," at 68.

home visit, then, is not threatening to the recipient. The recipients know these things. They like the home visit because it is mostly just a friendly chat. They expect little from the caseworkers and get little.

The quantitative data on number of caseworker visits, amount of time spent per visit, caseworker turnover, and caseworker training and orientations, determine both the regulatory and service features of the AFDC program. Neither feature will be present, as we found in this study, if the bureaucracy lacks the resources. For example, we found that most clients were not very upset by eligibility determinations conducted at intake. Questions for the most part were restricted to basic financial matters, and there was little prying. This pattern continued once on welfare—short home visits with little or no regulation of eligibility or other financial matters. The New York study reached basically the same results. Most recipients were not upset by eligibility determinations, and these attitudes were not affected by the home visit (this was true for all three ethnic groups). The New York authors also stressed the pressure of caseloads and the demands of the financial aspects of AFDC—that is, the core business that has to get done—as conditions which prevent both regulation and service.

Lack of regulation explains one of the reasons for client satisfaction with welfare. The other reason is economic security, even though at a low level. In contrast with clients' situations before welfare, AFDC provides security and not much bother. As we shall see time and again, the respondents, in open-ended questions, stressed the economic aspects of the program—what was good about it was that it gave them a regular supply of money; what was bad was not enough money. There were few complaints about caseworkers or regulations. This is not to say that these AFDC recipients enjoyed welfare. They were pressed by lack of money and would, like almost everybody else, rather have had husbands and jobs than be on welfare. In other words, the positive responses of AFDC recipients toward welfare must be read in the context of what life was like before welfare and within a framework of low expectations.[9]

---

[9] This passive and grateful attitude on the part of welfare recipients was also found by Scott Briar in his study of about one hundred AFDC-U families in California. He found, for example, that:

> The stance these recipients adopt toward the welfare agency is not that of a rights-bearing citizen claiming benefits to which he is entitled by law but that of a suppliant seeking, in the words of a number of recipients, "a little help to tide us over until we can get back on our feet again." Moreover, the "little help" they sought was modest indeed. Of those recipients who were able to specify the amount of aid they expected when they applied for assistance, sixty-four percent said they expected to receive less than one hundred dollars. Since

Similarly, the New York study concluded that the AFDC program is an income maintenance program with a medical-care component and little else; the only other "service" is extra money for special needs. Both knowledge and receipt of social services were low. In examining the lack of willingness to ask for services on the part of clients, the New York study concluded that these attitudes were not based on hostile attitudes toward welfare or the system, but rather on lack of confidence in the ability of the system or the caseworker to deliver.[10] We obtained the same general results. There seemed to be very little utilization of services, but then there were very low expectations. In Wisconsin, too, AFDC was little more than an income maintenance program.

The recipients who were reinterviewed told the same story. They were no longer in the welfare system and for the most part did not expect to return to it. Yet they spoke well of their caseworker and the welfare experience, emphasizing the same points—the caseworker really didn't do anything for them (they were hard pressed to think of specific things other than money), but they didn't expect much. Their evaluations of welfare remained the same—concerning both good points and bad points and suggestions for change.

Finally, it should be kept in mind that although our findings about positive client attitudes toward administration are often based on high percentages—quite often 75 or 80 percent or more—there are still many recipients who do not fit into this picture. It is not much credit to a system if one out of every four or five is getting hurt or is upset by regulatory practices. Indeed, one of the major points that we make about welfare administration is that its flexibility allows the basic nonregulatory pattern to change for a variety of reasons.

---

over fifty percent of the recipients actually were given aid in excess of one hundred dollars, it is not surprising that most recipients were satisfied with the amount they received and that only seventeen percent reported that the amount of aid granted was less than they had expected.

Scott Briar, Welfare from Below: Recipients' Views of the Public Welfare System, 54 CALIF. L. REV. 370, 377 (1966).

The recipients viewed the welfare agency as a "benevolent autocracy" in which the clients had little right or justification to object to regulation as a condition of receiving public money. In discussing the validity of the responses, Briar pointed out that his interviewers were matched in terms of ethnicity. Moreover, the interviewers had expected much different responses and had to be cautioned against expressing their dismay at the attitudes of the clients and advising them of their rights.

[10] Podell et al., supra, note 4, "Reactions of Welfare Clients to Caseworker Contact," at 69–73.

Client attitudes and welfare administration characteristics are strikingly similar for Wisconsin and New York City. Similarly, within the six counties studied in Wisconsin much the same pattern emerges. In some ways this is surprising, for there is a great deal of flexibility in the legal and administrative AFDC structure producing a great downward flow of discretionary authority from the state to the counties. For a variety of reasons, state supervisory and administrative control over county departments and caseworkers is weak. Thus there is considerable local autonomy in administration. This should produce administrative variation at the field level in view of the different political, social, and economic environments in which the six departments operated, but in fact we found considerable uniformity between the six agencies.

Uniformity in administrative practices between the six Wisconsin agencies does not mean that the AFDC program is administered uniformly in the sense that the State Department of Health and Social Services issues standards and rules of operation and supervises and enforces them. Rather, uniformity within the state comes about for the same reasons that the New York study findings are the same as the findings of this study—namely that the principal determinants of administrative behavior are size of caseloads, the characteristics of administrative personnel, and the attitudes and expectations of clients. In other words, although there is a great amount of flexibility, of looseness throughout the system and particularly at the lower levels of administration, in the normal day-to-day operation the dominant pressures are for routinization of administration and exercise of discretion in a nonregulatory, uninvolved manner.

But the flexibility and discretion is there, and this allows for administrative changes at every level of the bureaucracy—the caseworker, the supervisor, the county department, or even the State Department—to respond to demands for more regulation or service. There is room in the system for an individual caseworker to do a variety of things for or against a family or for particular agencies to "crack down" or conduct harassing investigations or to push rehabilitation or day-care plans. There have also been several instances where states have from time to time taken drastic action against recipients in efforts to cut costs or to regulate deviant sexual behavior. This is the other side of the AFDC program. From time to time the rules of the game change, often drastically and harshly, to reflect state and local political conditions or individual caseworker proclivities.

Therefore, whereas the tendencies in the system that push toward a routinized, nonregulatory administration increase the likelihood that the findings of this study are applicable to other states, the built-in, inherent flexibility within the administrative structure push in the opposite direction. In particular times and circumstances it may make a difference which state or county AFDC program is studied. The similarities in findings between this study and the New York study are encouraging but not conclusive. This is still a study of six county administrations in one state; generalizations must be treated with caution.

As to the plan of the book, the first two chapters provide the setting for the discussion of the administration of AFDC. Chapter 1 deals with historical materials. It traces our society's fundamental attitudes toward the poor and conflicts over welfare policy and attempts to show the political and sociological basis for the distribution of authority in the welfare bureaucracy among the federal, state, and local governments. Chapter 2 describes the environments within which the present administration functions—the six Wisconsin counties, their departments of welfare, and their clients.

Chapters 3, 4, 5, and 6 deal with key parts of AFDC administration: intake, budget management, social services, and employment. In each chapter we set forth the legal and administrative structure with an analysis of how policy is supposed to work according to law. We then compare theory with actual administration as indicated by the client responses and other data.

Chapter 7 deals with two special problems often associated with welfare: stigma and privacy. In Chapter 8 we analyze the responses of those who left welfare and compare them with those who stayed (that is, as of the time the data gathering was concluded in August 1969).

Finally, in Chapter 9 we attempt to draw the strands together and set forth a general theory of welfare administration, which we think is indicated by the findings, and discuss the implications of this theory for welfare reform.

PART ONE

The Administrative Environment

Chapter 1

THE FUNCTIONS OF
DECENTRALIZATION

Social welfare programs start with enabling legislation. Legislation is a collective, purposive, and rational attempt to solve a particular problem. In social welfare, the overall problem is poverty. The enabling legislation sets in motion a program, an administrative system. From time to time, legislation amends the administrative system, but the bureaucracy also takes on a life of its own. Officials interpret and apply the laws; they issue regulations and guides for conduct and standards for behavior. They pay out the money. The bureaucracy becomes a political force; it tries to make its influence felt in the arenas of power and in the all-important periodic clash over available public funds. Other factors also influence the growth, development, and shape of the program. A welfare system has ties to other branches of government, the private sector of the economy, other social agencies both public and private, and various classes of people and political groups. In short, welfare systems grow in the context of a broad political, economic, and social environment. They reflect the values of that environment.

In this chapter, we trace the development of the AFDC program.[1] We have two purposes. One is to show how the fundamental ideas about the nature, causes, and cures of poverty were reflected in the growth and the development of the program. The major point is the endurance of these ideas, for the basic legislative and administrative approach to AFDC has remained remarkably stable for over sixty years. Evidently, welfare ideology has great staying power.

The other purpose is to show the importance of decentralization in welfare administration at both the national and state level. Social welfare laws are not self-executing. Legislatures decide how programs within states will be administered, and how much decision-making authority will be delegated. There are a number of possibilities. The legislature may itself

---

[1] This chapter appeared in an earlier version in J. F. Handler and A. E. Goodstein, *The Legislative Development of Public Assistance*, 1968 Wis. L. Rev. 414.

decide the substantive issues by quite clearly specifying in the statute eligibility, amounts and types of aid, as well as other conditions. In this situation, administration of the program will tend to be objective and routine. Or the legislature may delegate major substantive decision-making authority to the administrative unit by couching the legislation in broad, abstract terms. The administrators, then, through the process of applying the statute to individual cases, define specifically the statutory words. Frequently there is a mixture of broad and narrow delegation in the same program; certain substantive issues will be carefully defined in the statutes and others will be vague.

The administration of the AFDC program has always been one of great decentralization. Local administrative officials are delegated wide discretionary powers which they exercise under loose supervision from state and federal bureaucracies. The origins of administrative decentralization reach back into history, when welfare was strictly a local government function. But the survival of local decisionmaking power cannot be explained merely in terms of the traditional American emphasis on state and local government. Relief for the morally blameworthy poor—in an older day, the "undeserving"—has always created severe conflicts in our society. The top-level decisionmakers delegate authority as the principal technique for avoiding the political risks of resolving these conflicts. With rare exceptions, the major policy questions in the AFDC program have been decided at the local level. When moral blameworthiness is not at issue, there are different allocations of authority. Local control of welfare policy can be explained only in part as the result of local interests tenaciously holding on to their traditional powers; it also is the product of the unwillingness of federal and state governments to assume responsibility.

In order to demonstrate our thesis, we reach back into the historical treatment of the poor. Our major concern is with the origins and development of the AFDC program, but it is necessary to contrast that program with the treatment of other classes of poor.

THE RISE OF THE SPECIAL CATEGORIES:
1849–1907

AFDC is one of the public assistance "categorical aids." Technically, the term refers to the five public assistance programs administered under the Social Security Act: Aid to the Blind, Old Age Assistance, Aid to Families with Dependent Children, Aid to the Permanently and Totally Disabled, and Medicaid. Historically, it refers to the nineteenth century process of making special provisions for certain *categories* of the poor. An effort was made to distinguish these categories from the general mass of poor who were covered, more or less, under general assistance or other public programs. The development of the categories reflected different attitudes toward the classes of poor and different treatments.

In the nineteenth century a distinction was made between paupers and others who were poor, and welfare policy was designed to prevent the poor from passing over the line into pauperism.[2] Paupers were recognizable by their extreme state of moral degeneracy, drunkenness, vice, corruption, and criminality. In a society which revered initiative, work, and individual capacity, and which prided itself on its free land and unlimited resources, failure to earn a living could only be due to individual weakness, and people who sank to this level were treated as outcasts and undesirables.

Even the more enlightened reformers were sure that the poor lived in a morally precarious position; pervasive temptation made it likely that the poor would fall into pauperism.[3] The general view was that noninstitutional relief was a dubious, if not a dangerous policy; it would certainly not reduce pauperism and might even further it.[4]

Society was reminded that it had a large stake in controlling pauperism. The links between pauperism and crime, vice, and delinquency were clear. The festering slums of the eastern cities were described as growing cancers, threatening the entire community. It is not surprising, then, that despite some attempts to justify the harsh, punitive provisions in terms of "rescue" or rehabilitation of the recipient, the dominant theme of relief

---

[2] "They have passed over the line which separates poverty from pauperism." D. Matza, *Poverty and Disrepute,* in CONTEMPORARY SOCIAL PROBLEMS 619, 642 (1966).

[3] For example, Hastings Hart, Secretary of the Minnesota State Board of Charities and Corrections, while speaking before the Wisconsin Conference of Charities and Corrections in 1888 approvingly quoted a local administrator's treatment of an applicant for relief: "When a person comes to me for relief for the first time, I sit down and talk with him kindly. I say to him: Do you know you are throwing your family onto the county, and it will be a disgrace to you as long as you live? Now go home and see if you can't get along." Wisconsin State Board of Control of Charitable, Reformatory, and Penal Institutions, ANNUAL STATE CONFERENCE OF CHARITIES AND CORRECTIONS (1888), at 89 [hereinafter cited as WISCONSIN CONFERENCE].

[4] As much as possible, relief was conditioned on the performance of labor. In 1879 the Wisconsin Board of Charities stated that "the greatest service we can do to the poor is to enforce upon them the duty of making themselves useful to themselves and others . . . and one of the ways to diminish pauperism is to keep the poor out of the poor houses as long as they can earn even a partial support." 1879 WISCONSIN STATE BOARD OF CHARITIES AND REFORM, NINTH ANN. REP. 24. Cited in D. Berthrong, Social Legislation in Wisconsin 1836–1900, Sept. 10, 1951, at 238 (unpublished thesis in University of Wisconsin Library).

legislation was the protection of society by the prevention and control of deviant behavior.

The original Wisconsin legislation dealing with the care of the poor stated broadly that, "Every town shall relieve and support all poor and indigent persons, lawfully settled therein, whenever they shall stand in need thereof."[5] Administration was placed in the hands of the town supervisors. Neither eligibility nor budget was defined. It was up to the local authorities to decide what "poor" and "indigent" meant, and what, if anything, to do about such people. Although the statute was amended periodically over succeeding decades, its basic orientation and structure remained the same.

A second strand of welfare policy dealt with the "deserving poor." Immediately after gaining statehood, Wisconsin began to distinguish certain types of needy people from paupers on the basis of moral blamelessness. During the 1850's, state institutions were established for the blind, deaf-mutes, and "curable" insane. Means tests for these institutions were rejected on the grounds that they would require otherwise eligible persons to obtain "certificates of pauperism."[6] Immediately after the Civil War, the state established a separate institution for children of deceased Wisconsin soldiers, distinguishing the Civil War orphans from other dependent children in order to avoid the pauper stigma.[7] In 1887 counties were authorized to levy taxes for the relief of indigent Civil War veterans and their families.[8] These were not to be considered morally degenerate. In the words of the State Board of Charities, needy soldiers are not a "class of professional paupers, but are poor from misfortune."[9]

These classes were the "deserving" poor for whom separate state

----

[5] WIS. REV. STAT. ch. 28, § 1 (1849). This statute borrowed heavily from Pennsylvania, Northwest Territory, Ohio, and Michigan statutes.

[6] State Board of Control, A HISTORY OF THE STATE BOARD OF WISCONSIN AND THE STATE INSTITUTIONS 1849–1939, at 77 (1939). Governor Lucius Fairchild, in commenting on the requirement that certificates of pauperism had to be obtained from county judges, stated:

> Wisconsin cannot afford to be niggardly in her charities. The people do not only ask it, but are perfectly willing to bear whatever small addition to their burden of taxes may be necessary to the proper care of such of their fellow-citizens as are blind, deaf and dumb, or insane. I concur . . . that this law be repealed.

Message of Governor Lucius Fairchild, Jan. 10, 1867, in GOVERNOR'S MESSAGE AND ACCOMPANYING DOCUMENTS OF THE STATE OF WISCONSIN XV (1867).

[7] "These children, to whom we owe so much, cannot be objects of charity from the state." Message of Governor Lucius Fairchild, *supra* note 6, at 15.

[8] Ch. 304, [1887] Wis. Laws 323.

[9] 1889 WISCONSIN STATE BOARD OF CHARITIES AND REFORM, THIRD BIENN. REP. 1887–1888, at 184.

institutions were established. Indigency caused by gross physical or mental defects was not blameworthy, nor could one attribute character defects to Civil War veterans or their families. The county and local administrative systems were for the paupers—the undeserving. When noninstitutional relief was required for Civil War veterans and their families, a separate county system was established to avoid the pauper stigma; aid was to be administered by a board of three commissioners, two of whom were required to be veterans.

The third major direction in social welfare policy stemmed from the Child-Saving Movement. Believing that there was a causal connection between poverty and crime and that city slum life was the breeding ground for deviant behavior, the Child-Savers were particularly concerned with predelinquent children.[10] Children allowed to grow up in ignorance and vice would in turn become paupers and criminals. Accordingly, little if any distinction was made in treatment between the delinquent and predelinquent child; the state had the right to remove *any* child from a bad environment to prevent a career in crime.

By the turn of the century the merger of delinquency and dependency in Wisconsin was complete. Separate juvenile courts, or in some areas county courts, had jurisdiction over delinquent, dependent, and neglected children. Two ostensibly different types of institutions—reformatories and industrial schools for delinquents and the state school for dependents— might receive children in either category. Intervention and institutional treatment for dependent children were justified on the same grounds as intervention for delinquency: to prevent pauperism and crime.

Ultimately, much nineteenth century welfare policy was justified in terms of prevention of deviant behavior. Efforts to assist the poor were often measured in terms of predicted impact on the control of pauperism, which was viewed as a form of deviance. When it was recognized that aiding certain classes of the poor (such as veterans) would not contribute to pauperism, the state provided separate programs for the "deserving poor." Programs for dependent children were viewed in a special light. Dependent children could not be "blamed" for their condition yet, unlike the "deserving poor," they were likely to become paupers and criminals unless treated. In effect, these were crime-prevention programs since the children were considered predelinquent.

The differences between the types of poor people affected the allocation of decision-making responsibility among the various units of government. The central issue of poverty in the nineteenth century was pauperism

---

[10] A. M. Platt, THE CHILD-SAVERS: THE INVENTION OF DELINQUENCY (1969).

and the basic poverty program—general assistance—was administered by county and local governments under very broad delegations of authority. Those units decided who was to get aid, who was not, and who was to go to the poorhouse. Their function was clearly identified with controlling and preventing this form of deviant behavior. When moral character was not at issue, the needy were extricated from the county and local system. Because dependent children were considered predelinquent, that program was given to county judges who also had jurisdiction over crime and delinquency.

THE CATEGORICAL AIDS: 1907–35

The first of the present categorical aid programs, Aid to the Blind, was enacted in Wisconsin in 1907.[11] In addition to blindness, eligibility was established in terms of age, residence, need, and not being an inmate of a state institution or receiving other public aid. Administration was objective and routine, with little delegated discretion. The deaf were added to the program in 1919.[12] The program was amended from time to time, but the amendments were chiefly to raise benefit levels and to refine and clarify the eligibility criteria. The only reference to moral character was that the applicant not be publicly soliciting alms, a provision made in 1923.[13]

The second categorical program, Aid to Dependent Children (as it was then called), was enacted at about the same time as the Aid to the Blind program, but it arose from entirely different considerations and as a result had a very different structure. Although the Child-Savers had envisaged reformatories and other types of state institutions as rehabilitative substitute homes for dependent and delinquent children, institutional care had not worked out that way; institutions were overcrowded and lacking in staff and other facilities.[14] The hard realities of trying to maintain custodial facilities for large numbers of delinquent and otherwise unruly slum children were brutally inconsistent with romantic notions of idyllic country life, and reformers naturally began to turn to noninstitutional alternatives.

Illinois was the first state to enact an Aid to Dependent Children program. Since Wisconsin as well as other states quickly followed and borrowed heavily from Illinois, it is worthwhile to examine in some detail the structure of the Illinois legislation. The Illinois Funds to Parents Act of

---

[11] Ch. 283, § 5721 [1907] Wis. Laws 125.

[12] Ch. 563, [1919] Wis. Laws 914.

[13] Ch. 355, [1923] Wis. Laws 619.

[14] E.g., see 1909 WISCONSIN STATE BOARD OF CONTROL, NINTH BIENN. REP. 365.

1911 was an amendment to the Illinois Juvenile Court Act and part of the overall system for the prevention of juvenile delinquency.[15] Prior to this amendment, the Juvenile Court had the following options for children adjudicated "delinquent," "dependent," or "neglected": commitment to an institution, removal to a guardian family, or home probation. For those who were "dependent" or "neglected," the new ADC amendment provided that:

> If the parent or parents of such dependent or neglected child are poor and unable to properly care for the said child, but are otherwise proper guardians and it is for the welfare of such child to remain at home, the court may enter an order finding such facts and fixing the amount of money necessary to enable the parent or parents to properly care for such child, and thereupon it shall be the duty of the County Board, through its County Agent or otherwise, to pay to such parent or parents, at such times as said order may designate the amount so specified for the care of such dependent or neglected child until the further order of the court.[16]

By 1913, twenty states including Wisconsin had enacted ADC programs.[17] The structure of the Wisconsin program followed that of Illinois. A section entitled "State Aid for Dependent Children" was added to the Wisconsin Juvenile Court Act, which also closely followed the Illinois act. Children under fourteen were eligible for aid if they were "neglected,

---

[15] Incorporating the first ADC statute into the Juvenile Court system was not accidental. For a long time the Illinois Board of Charities argued the Child-Savers' view that dependent children should be considered predelinquent and that additional public intervention was necessary for this class of children to prevent the growth of delinquency. In 1898 the board said, "If the child is the material out of which men and women are made, the neglected child is the material out of which 'paupers and criminals are made.'" 1898 BOARD OF STATE CHARITIES OF THE STATE OF ILLINOIS, 15TH BIENN. REP. 62. At that time the board was arguing for a state school for dependent children such as the Wisconsin State School. *Id.* at 61. The state, however, continued to rely on private institutions. In 1912 the Illinois State Charities Commission criticized this approach and reiterated the view that unless some strong arm is interposed early in the dependent child's career he will surely become delinquent, and that these private institutions should be required to meet a higher standard of care. 1912 STATE CHARITIES COMMISSION OF ILLINOIS, THIRD ANN. REP. 67.

[16] Ch. 23, § 175, [1911] Ill. Laws 126.

[17] Ch. 669, § 2, [1913] Wis. Laws 925. In 1893 Judge Doyle, of Milwaukee, speaking before the Wisconsin Annual State Conference of Charities and Corrections, anticipated the ADC programs. He questioned the value of the Wisconsin State School for dependent children and suggested that the state "may act indirectly by giving aid to private institutions or even to individuals." WISCONSIN CONFERENCE (1894), at 84.

destitute, abandoned, homeless or in any manner dependent upon the public for support, or whose parent or parents, or person occupying the position of a parent, for any reason are unable without aid, properly to maintain, bring up or educate such child."[18] The statute provided that the county superintendent of the poor, the superintendent of the poor in any city or village, the chairman of any town, or a relative or friend could apply to juvenile courts (where established) or the county or municipal courts for aid to the parents or guardians of such children. However, instead of giving aid, the courts could remove the child from the home and place him with another family, commit him to the state public school, "or make such other disposition of such child as it may deem wise."[19]

It is significant that in these original ADC statutes, eligibility was in no way restricted to "deserving" mothers. The legislature authorized, but did not require, ADC for unwed, deserted, separated, and divorced mothers, as well as widows. Assistance was a matter of discretion for the juvenile court judge and would only be given if to do so would further the goals of the delinquency prevention program.[20]

---

[18] Ch. 669, § 2, [1913] Wis. Laws 925. This definition of eligibility was roughly the same as the "dependent" portions of the "dependent" and "neglected" definitions in the first sections of the Juvenile Court Act. WIS. STAT. § 573l(1) (1913).

[19] WIS. STAT. § 573j(1) (1913).

[20] This apparently was the contemporary interpretation. At the 1915 Wisconsin Conference on Charities and Corrections, County Judge Marchetti spoke of the Juvenile Court and the ADC program as combined efforts to combat crime. Judge Marchetti thought it wise to leave administration of ADC in the hands of the Juvenile Court judges. Since these judges had the responsibility of taking the child away from the parent, they should also be able to help the child with public funds if such welfare would best serve his interests. WISCONSIN CONFERENCE (1915), at 14. In the same year the Wisconsin attorney general said that the statute

is, in a sense, supplementary of other statutory provisions providing for the care, protection and maintenance of dependent and abandoned children. . . .

This law was passed in response to a rapidly crystallizing public sentiment that the state should not only take a human interest in the present welfare of children so situated, but that the interest which the state has in them as future citizens justifies it, as a plain business proposition, in doing whatever may be necessary to promote their development into good and useful men and women, saving them from future delinquency. . . .

Cited in 2 G. Abbott, THE CHILD AND THE STATE 303, 305 (1938).

The connection between ADC and social deviance was shown in the uneasiness immediately expressed by those who thought that the programs would

The 1913 Wisconsin statute was recognized by the legislature as experimental.[21] At the next session the legislature passed a new law which established the basic principles for the ADC program and mandated the program for all of the counties.[22] A child was eligible if he was "dependent upon the public for support" and his dependency was caused by the father's death, incapacitation, incarceration, or desertion and refusal to support. The mother or other specified caretaker had to be of "good moral character and the proper person to have the custody and care" of the child.[23] The county court judge determined the extent of need and the level of the grant, subject to a statutory maximum.[24] However, the judge was still not required to give aid, even if he found poverty. He could, in the "best interests" of the child, remove the child from the home.

Shortly after the enactment of the basic program, eligibility was expanded to include the children of divorced and unwed mothers.[25] Both amendments were viewed as correcting defects in the scope of the statute; after all, there was no reason not to consider these children as predelinquent too. Another early amendment (1917) authorized the judges to require mothers to work.[26] At the same time, the program began to take on

---

in fact foster deviant behavior. Moreover, the critics were not only those who fought charity and social reforms. Prominent social reformers protested that giving assistance under these broad statutes would encourage illegitimacy and desertion. It was much more difficult, they argued, to determine the worthiness of deserted and unwed mothers than of widows. *Id.* at 232.

[21] The "statute was passed and the appropriation made on assumption that the need for it existed, instead of upon proof that it actually did." Wisconsin State Board of Control, CONCLUSIONS AND RECOMMENDATIONS ON THE "SURVEY AND INVESTIGATION INTO THE QUESTION OF AID TO MOTHERS WITH DEPENDENT CHILDREN" 3 (1915).

[22] Ch. 637, § 2, [1915] Wis. Laws 976.

[23] There were other detailed provisions dealing with the age of the child, time periods, and other requirements. For example, the period of desertion has to be at least a year and during that time the mother had to have attempted to use the legal machinery to obtain support from the father.

[24] The statutory maximum was $15 per month for the first child and $10 per month for each additional child, up to a maximum of $40 per month per family.

[25] Ch. 589, § 1, [1917] Wis. Laws 1006; Ch. 308, § 1, [1919] Wis. Laws 346. The "divorced" category was included at the urging of the State Board of Control. 1916 WISCONSIN STATE BOARD OF CONTROL, 13TH BIENN. REP. 5. In 1916 the Attorney General ruled that the ADC statute did not include unwed mothers. 1916 WIS. OPS. ATT'Y GEN. 13. In 1919 the statute was amended to include this category. In both instances, the ease with which these groups were included in the *statutory* coverage (as distinguished from administrative coverage) is additional evidence of the original purpose to cover all potentially delinquent children.

[26] Ch. 589, § 1, [1917] Wis. Laws 1006.

welfare administration characteristics. For example, the judges were authorized to appoint boards to assist in making investigations and preparing budgets, and to help recipients in managing the grant.[27]

The statute continued to be amended during each legislative biennium; for the most part, the amendments liberalized the substantive provisions.[28] Then in 1929 the ADC program was revised as part of a revision of the entire Children's Code. Many of the changes were reactionary, with eligibility restricted and greater administrative control introduced into the program.

The legislature rejected a proposal to give the State Board of Control authority to promulgate a standard budget (which would have increased state administrative control),[29] preferring to leave budgetary control at the local level. However, it directed the judge, in conjunction with the county board (or its committee), to prepare a standard annual budget.[30] The legislature also imposed more administrative regularity on the judges. It tried to insure that there would be proper investigations; a home visit and a written report, incorporated in the record, were made conditions for the granting of aid.

The alternatives available to the judge were reduced to either granting aid or not. He was no longer authorized to consider alternative dispositions of probationary supervision, removal of the children from the home, termination of parental rights, or institutional commitment. However, this

---

[27] *Id.*

[28] The overall dollar limit per family was removed in 1921, although the maximum aid per child still remained $15 for the first child and $10 for each additional child. Ch. 86, § 1, [1921] Wis. Laws 155. Public medical aid was exempted from the stipulation that a family could receive no public assistance in addition to ADC. In 1923 the duration of the sentence of the husband to a penal institution was reduced from one year or more to three months or more; and the time period for desertion was reduced from six to three months. Ch. 83, § 1, [1923] Wis. Laws 74. In 1925 maternity aid (in the form of supplies, nursing, medical, or "other assistance in lieu of money") was made available for the six months following birth if the "financial circumstances are such as to deprive either the mother or child of proper care." Ch. 426, § 1, [1925] Wis. Laws 618. No substantive changes were made in 1927 (the name "Aid to Dependent Children" was restored in lieu of "Mothers' Pension." Ch. 374, § 1, [1927] Wis. Laws 459), but the legislature evidenced an uneasiness over local administrative practices. Examination of each ADC application by the county judge was made mandatory. *Id.* Further, the county board was authorized to appoint three of its members to serve as a board of child welfare to assist the judge in making investigations and examinations. The county board was so authorized in the event that the judge failed to appoint such a board of child welfare. *Id.*

[29] Wis. A. Bill 237A (1929).

[30] Ch. 439, § 9, [1929] Wis. Laws 625.

change did not represent a significant break with the social deviant control origins of the ADC program. The program remained as one section of the basic juvenile court act, in which dependency, neglect, and delinquency were the three categories of jurisdiction. The juvenile court proceeded on information brought to its attention. If it found either delinquency, dependency, or neglect, the full range of alternative social control dispositions was available. This same court also received applications for ADC. In practical terms, an applicant failing to qualify for ADC on social conduct grounds would still be subject to other dependency dispositions, if the court felt that these dispositions were more appropriate than relief.

The legislation also established a system of probation officers for the juvenile courts. These officers were charged with investigating delinquency, dependency, and neglect cases, as well as ADC cases, and they were authorized to bring dependency petitions to the juvenile court.[31]

The 1929 statute was the last major legislative change in the ADC program until 1935. The number of people receiving ADC and the cost of the program steadily rose. In 1913 there had been 187 families receiving aid at a total cost of $9632. By 1931, 8058 families with 20,092 children received assistance and the cost was in excess of $2 million.[32]

The third and last of the categorical aid programs was Old Age Assistance, enacted in 1925.[33] In many respects, the legislature viewed this program with as much suspicion and caution as it did the ADC program. In the 1920's the aged were clearly not as "deserving" as the blind. There was both a long residency requirement and a citizenship requirement. The applicant had to have had high moral standards: eligibility would be denied if he had been imprisoned for a felony during the preceding ten years, if he "without just cause" failed to support his family for a six-month period at any time during the preceding fifteen years, or if he had been a "habitual tramp or beggar" within one year preceding the application.[34] The legislature was also concerned about fraud, particularly applicants who divested themselves of property in order to qualify for aid. County judges administered this program, too, deciding eligibility and the amount of aid (which in any event could not exceed $1 per day). The court had authority to require that all the property of the applicant be transferred to the state administrative agency. There were criminal penalties for fraud, which included disposing of property without the consent of the court.

Old Age Assistance was placed in the general assistance statutes. The

---

[31] Ch. 439, § 3, [1929] Wis. Laws 594.
[32] State Department of Public Welfare, General Relief in Wisconsin 1848–1935, at 12 (1939).
[33] Wis. Stat. § 49.22(1) (1925).
[34] Id.

same judges who ruled on commitments to the poorhouses received old age applications. The old age statute, more than any of the others, attempted to exclude the "morally unfit."

The substantive provisions of the old age program were not changed during the subsequent years. After some hesitation, the 1933 legislature provided that the counties could adopt the program if they wanted to.[35] From 1925 to 1933 only eleven counties in Wisconsin granted Old Age Assistance.

SUMMARY: SUBSTANCE AND ADMINISTRATIVE STRUCTURE

The line drawn between "poverty" and "pauperism" during the latter half of the nineteenth century influenced the three categorical aid programs in Wisconsin. The Aid to the Blind program was placed within the statutory framework that dealt with the education of the blind. It was administered by the county board, not the county courts. Moreover, delegated discretion was narrow, with the legislature deciding the means test and the amount of the grant. Determination of blindness was specifically entrusted to a physician.

Moral blameworthiness and crime prevention were key concepts of the ADC program. This program was delegated to the county courts or the juvenile courts, since the prevention of crime and pauperism was thought to be a local not a state responsibility. Despite the growing welfare aspects of ADC, the program continued to be justified in terms of social control as late as 1935.[36] The county judge had broad discretion. Eligibility was very inclusive but not automatic. Only children of "fit and proper parents" were eligible; eligibility was decided on the basis of whether assistance would further the goals of the juvenile delinquency program.

The legislature never prescribed a means test for ADC but did author-

---

[35] Ch. 375, § 1, [1933] Wis. Laws 827. In 1929 the legislature had declared that all counties must adopt the program. Ch. 181, § 3, [1929] Wis. Laws 188. Apparently the counties did not comply with this provision because a 1931 statute provided that the program was to be mandatory in all counties by July 1, 1933. Ch. 239, § 1, [1931] Wis. Laws 372. But in 1933 the legislature abandoned this particular effort and compliance was made voluntary.

[36] According to the Director of the Child Welfare Study Committee of the Wisconsin Conference of Social Work: "Were there no special aid [i.e., ADC], it would undoubtedly be necessary to commit a high percentage [of children] if not to the State Public School then later to some correctional or penal institution. . . ." E. De Weerdt, FIVE YEARS OF CHILD WELFARE UNDER THE CHILDREN'S CODE IN WISCONSIN 1929–1934, at 99 (1935).

ize the judges to require the mothers to work. For most of the period in question the legislature set upper limits on assistance, but the judges had authority to grant less than the maximum. Thus the judge could tailor the amount of the grant according to the economic needs of the family and the likely consequences of various amounts of assistance for the behavior of families.

So far, the allocation of authority has been looked at as a choice between the state legislature and county agencies. Another alternative for the legislature was the use of state agencies to administer the welfare program. For some programs the legislature had no choice. Decisions to extricate the deserving poor, such as the blind, the deaf, and Civil War orphans, from local administration required state institutions and state administration. By 1871 there were six state institutions, each run by a board of trustees and financed by separate appropriations.[37] Despite periodic scandals and constant complaints about lack of coordination and control, it took the legislature several decades to establish a single state agency to run these institutions.[38]

The minimal central supervision over state-run institutions reflected a legislative reluctance to create state administrative agencies. Consequently, when Wisconsin decided to give noninstitutional relief to the deserving poor in the nineteenth century, it naturally turned to existing county administrations to implement the work of the state programs. Similarly, when the categorical aid programs were enacted, the state again used local administration instead of creating a system of state administrative units. When these programs became mandatory on the counties and the state agreed to pay one-third of the cost, the statutes provided that the State Board of Control (which had jurisdiction over the state institutions) had to approve the amounts paid by the counties before they could receive state grants. This potential source of centralizing authority was never used. The board, in its reports to the legislature, continually pointed out ways in which it could help local administration, not necessarily by regulation, but in the form of supervision and technical assistance—for example, preparing standard budgets, conducting investigations of applicants, and so forth— but the legislature always refused the board's recommendations.[39] Thus

---

[37] State Board of Control, A HISTORY OF THE STATE BOARD OF WISCONSIN AND THE STATE INSTITUTIONS 1849–1939, at 2 (1939).

[38] D. Berthrong, *supra* note 4, at 78; State Board of Control, *supra* note 37, at 2–6.

[39] See, e.g., Wisconsin State Board of Control, *supra* note 21, at 32; Wisconsin State Board of Control, ADMINISTRATION OF THE AID TO DEPENDENT CHILDREN'S LAW IN WISCONSIN 9 (1921); 1922 Wisconsin State Board of Control, 16TH BIENN. REP. 18.

there were ample opportunities for the legislature to shift significant areas
of discretion from the county to the state without encumbering the statutes,
losing administrative flexibility, or forming new and complex state administrative systems. These options were not taken.

THE SOCIAL SECURITY ACT OF 1935

The Depression shattered the states' categorical aid programs; they were
revived by federal grants-in-aid under the Social Security Act. Social Security insurance was the New Deal idea of a long-term solution to old age
security, and there was not much enthusiasm in Congress for Aid to the
Blind and ADC.[40] The federal government entered the public assistance
field only to prevent the collapse of the state programs. The dominant
philosophy was states' rights, and the states were assumed to have the
major substantive interest in the content of the programs.[41]

In order to qualify for the federal grants-in-aid, a state had to file a
plan with the Social Security Board. The state plan had to be in effect in
all the political subdivisions of the state, provide for financial participation
by the state, have a single state agency administer the plan or supervise the
administration of the plan, and provide for an opportunity for a fair hearing for an individual whose claim for aid was denied.[42]

The substantive changes made in the three categorical aid programs
as a result of the Social Security Act were minor. In Aid to the Blind the
only significant change was a reduction in the residency requirement from
ten years to one year.[43] In Old Age Assistance the minimum age was
lowered from seventy to sixty-five and the residency period was shortened
to one year.[44] In the ADC program the Social Security Act stipulated its
own definition of "dependent child":

---

[40] Edwin Witte, one of the major contributors to the Social Security Act,
thought that if President Roosevelt had not insisted that the entire Social Security package be kept intact, only Old Age Assistance would have passed.
E. Witte, THE DEVELOPMENT OF THE SOCIAL SECURITY ACT 78–79 (1963).
See G. Steiner, SOCIAL INSECURITY 18–23 (1966).

[41] G. Steiner, *supra* note 40, at 80.

[42] Social Security Act of 1935, ch. 531, Tit. I, § 2, 49 Stat. 620.

[43] *Id.,* Tit. X, § 1002(b)(1), 49 Stat. 645. Wisconsin also allowed a
person otherwise qualified to qualify if he had been a resident at the time his
blindness occurred; this provision survived the Social Security Act. WIS. STAT. §
47.08(2)(a) (1935).

[44] Social Security Act of 1935, ch. 531, Tit. I, § 2(b)(2), 49 Stat. 621;
WIS. STAT. § 49.22(1)(3) (1935).

A child under the age of sixteen who has been deprived of parental support or care by reason of the death, continued absence from the home, or physical or mental incapacity of a parent, and who is living with his father, mother, grandfather, grandmother, brother, sister, stepfather, stepmother, stepbrother, stepsister, uncle or aunt in place of residence maintained by one or more such relatives as his or their own home.[45]

The class of caretakers eligible for the program was therefore expanded from the 1929 Wisconsin definition.[46] The other ADC eligibility provisions were not changed.[47] For purposes of matching funds, the federal government stipulated a limit on aid: $18 per month for one child and $12 per month for each additional child in the family.[48] The Wisconsin legislature, however, retained its prior decision of fixing no budget maximum; aid was to be based on a standard budget prepared by the county court and the county board, and was to be sufficient to enable the person having custody to care for the children properly.[49]

Thus the Social Security Act was relatively indifferent to substantive state welfare policy, and the 1935 Wisconsin legislature enacted only what was necessary to qualify for the federal grants-in-aid. The shape and character of public assistance programs still remained largely the responsi-

---

[45] *Id.*, Tit. IV, § 406(a), 49 Stat. 629.

[46] Ch. 554, § 7, [1935] Wis. Laws 1194.

[47] Thus "continued absence from the home," the federal phrase, meant in Wisconsin lack of a husband, a husband sentenced to a penal institution for at least one year, desertion for one or more years and a legal charge of abandonment, or a husband who had been divorced for at least one year and from whom the wife was unable to compel support through legal means. "Physical or mental incapacity" meant in Wisconsin incapacitation for gainful employment "likely to continue for at least one year in the opinion of a competent physician." WIS. STAT. § 48.33 (5)(d) (1935). Other eligibility provisions also remained. The probability that the aid would be likely to continue for at least one year was required and the person having custody still had to be a "fit and proper" person. *Id.* § 48.33(5)(3). The Social Security Act also stated that residency requirements could not exclude any child, otherwise eligible, who had resided in the state one year immediately preceding the application, or who was born in the state within one year immediately preceding the application if the mother had resided in the state one year immediately preceding the birth. Social Security Act of 1935, ch. 531, Tit. IV, § 402(b), 49 Stat. 627. Wisconsin had a further condition which remained in effect: the child must have legal settlement in the county where the application for aid was made, but aid could still be granted if the person having custody lived within the state the year preceding the application. WIS. STAT. § 48.33(5)(b)(c) (1935).

[48] Social Security Act of 1935, ch. 531, Tit. IV, § 403(a), 49 Stat. 628.

[49] WIS. STAT. § 48.33(6) (1935).

bility of the state. On the other hand, the federal government did press for uniformity in the administration of standards and procedures within the states, and this, as we shall see, did have a significant impact in Wisconsin. Until 1935 the strategy of the legislature had been to delegate broad discretion to the counties, which had resulted in a great diversity of local administrative practices. Statewide uniformity, however, required either legislative decisions on substantive issues, narrowing the scope of local discretion and routinizing local administration (as had been done with Aid to the Blind), or centralized state administration. For the past twenty-five years the legislature had steadfastly refused to adopt either alternative.

THE CATEGORICAL AIDS: 1935 TO THE PRESENT

Substantive Legislation

The most striking characteristic of welfare legislation, from 1935 to the present, is how very little has changed. At least at the legislative level, the basic structure and substantive decisions that were enacted before 1930 remained in the ADC statutes for the next 35 years.

In 1950 Congress passed the NOLEO (Notice to Law Enforcement Officials) amendment in response to political pressures resulting from the rising number of AFDC cases. The statute required that "prompt notice be given to the appropriate law enforcement officials of the county furnishing aid . . . to dependent children in respect of a child who has been deserted or abandoned by a parent."[50] The effect of this legislation was to bring law enforcement officials into welfare administration by transferring the decision to proceed against the deserting father for support from the caseworker to the prosecutor.

Political attacks on public assistance continued, and in the next year Congress reversed a 1939 amendment to the Social Security Act which had required the states to adopt rules restricting the availability of information on applicants or recipients of aid.[51] The purpose of the 1939 rule was to discourage the use of welfare rolls for political purposes. In 1951 Congress amended the Social Security Act to allow disclosure of welfare rolls under certain conditions. In 1953 Wisconsin took advantage of the federal permission.[52]

A 1956 federal amendment required that state welfare agencies pro-

---

[50] Ch. 725, § 10, [1951] Wis. Laws 569.
[51] G. Steiner, *supra* note 40, at 90.
[52] Ch. 185, [1953] Wis. Laws 174.

vide social services plans for AFDC families.[53] In 1962 the federal government authorized the states to establish social service programs with the federal government paying 75 percent of the costs[54] (see the detailed discussion in chap. 5). In 1961 the federal government allowed states to provide ADC payments to intact families if the husband was unemployed (called AFDC-U).[55] This was a major substantive change but it was optional. Wisconsin took advantage of this change in 1966.[56]

During this period there was a series of federally required changes which were interstitial liberalizations of the program. For example, the maximum age limit for eligible children was raised first to eighteen and then to twenty-one if the child was regularly attending school. The list of eligible caretakers was broadened and their needs could be included in the budget. After 1962 the treatment of earned income was liberalized somewhat to increase work incentives. States were required to take into account reasonable work expenses and to disregard income set aside for a child's identifiable educational needs. There was a further liberalization for welfare recipients earning money in some of the War on Poverty projects.

In 1967 there was a decided shift in emphasis. Congress, frustrated over rising welfare rolls and costs, enacted a new work incentive program (called WIN; see chap. 6) under the joint responsibility of the departments of Labor and of Health, Education, and Welfare as well as new taxing rates to increase incentives. Congress also ordered a freeze (since repealed) on the proportion of children under eighteen who could receive ADC.[57]

These then were the more important federal statutory changes in the AFDC program. Most of the changes were at the fringes of the program and did not involve carefully looking into its scope or operation. Other changes turned out to be either authorizations rather than requirements (e.g., Social Service amendment of 1962; AFDC-UP) or else structured in such a manner that the states had wide latitude in interpreting and administering the requirements. The states continued to retain the major discretionary power.

Beyond making modifications required by federal statute, the states initiated few changes. Acting without federal urging, Wisconsin first reduced the various waiting periods in the program from one year to three months and then, in 1965, dropped the waiting periods altogether.[58] Eligi-

---

[53] Social Security Amendments of 1956, § 312, 70 Stat. 848.
[54] Social Security Amendments of 1962, § 108(a), 76 Stat. 189.
[55] Act of May 8, 1961, § 1, 75 Stat. 75.
[56] Ch. 590, § 8 [1965] Wis. Laws 1030.
[57] P.L. 90–248, Tit. 42 U.S.C. § 602(a).
[58] Ch. 585, § 26, [1945] Wis. Laws 1077; Ch. 590, § 7, [1965] Wis. Laws 1030.

bility was expanded to include mothers who were "legally separated," whose husbands fail to support their families, who commenced a divorce or separation action and were unable to meet needs through a temporary support order, or who had obtained a support order which did not meet needs.[59] The residency requirements were changed from time to time, then dropped completely from 1945 until 1957, when the legislature settled on the one-year requirement for the child or for the person having custody if the child was born during the year.[60] (This in turn was declared unconstitutional in 1967.)[61] Other minor changes were made in the foster home program for dependent children, the homestead exemption, and maternal aid.

In 1955 the legislature amended the "fit and proper" requirement by adding that aid could not be denied by the county agency without a court determination that the parent is not fit and proper to have the care and custody of the children.[62] This codified a state administrative regulation that had been in existence for some time.

Federal and state legislation was even of less importance in modifying the other two categorical aid programs, Old Age Assistance and Aid to the Blind. Legislative activity was primarily a step-by-step liberalization of the programs. The major substantive changes in the categorical aids during this period were the creation of two new public assistance programs—Aid to the Permanently and Totally Disabled and Medicaid. Wisconsin initiated an APTD program in 1945.[63] In 1950 the federal government established this category under the Social Security Act.[64] In the same year the federal government agreed to share in the medical costs of the categorical aid recipients. The more embracing Medicaid program was established in 1965.

The Development of Administration since 1935

The Social Security Act required that the states have either a single state agency administering the categorical aids or a single state agency supervising local administration of the aids. This federal requirement proved a real obstacle for the Wisconsin legislature, and it took four years

---

[59] Ch. 505, § 1, [1961] Wis. Laws 535; Ch. 590, § 7, [1965] Wis. Laws 1030; Ch. 483, [1959] Wis. Laws 593.

[60] Ch. 190, § 6, [1957] Wis. Laws 196.

[61] Ramos v. Health & Social Servs. Bd., 276 F. Supp. 474 (E.D. Wis. 1967); Shapiro v. Thompson, 394 U.S. 618 (1969).

[62] Ch. 160, § 7, [1955] Wis. Laws 168.

[63] Ch. 578, § 2, [1945] Wis. Laws 1033.

[64] Social Security Act Amendments of 1950, ch. 809, § 1402(a)(1), 64 Stat. 555.

of false starts and political jockeying before the State Department of Public Welfare (SDPW) was created.[65] Within SDPW the Division of Public Assistance (one of five divisions) supervised the categorical aid programs.[66]

The organization structure of the SDPW closely followed the model plan suggested by the American Public Welfare Association in 1935. The structure was designed to insulate the administration of welfare from the partisan political process. Members of the State Board of Public Welfare were to be appointed for staggered terms by the governor with the advice and consent of the senate and were nonsalaried. The powers and duties of the board were "regulatory, advisory and policy-forming, and not administrative or executive."[67] A director, with important administrative and executive functions, was to be appointed for an indefinite term by the board.

In 1939 the federal government, by amendment to the Social Security Act, insisted that the state establish a merit system for the selection of personnel at the local level.[68] The Wisconsin legislature delegated the task of establishing county merit systems to the state agency.[69] This arrangement had several advantages for the SDPW. Control over the qualifications of county personnel through the merit system would further the gradual shift of power from county to state agency. The state agency would be able to curb the use of welfare posts for local political patronage. The professionalization of the administrative staff would be increased, and personnel chosen on merit would tend to be responsive to the policies emanating from the professionals employed at the state level.

During the next twenty-five years there was little legislation on the structure and functions of the state agency. In 1967, as part of an executive branch reorganization, the SDPW was merged into the newly created Department of Health and Social Services and the Division of Public Assistance combined with the Division of Children and Youth to become the Division of Family Services.[70]

In 1935 the legislature had also addressed itself to the administrative structure at the county level. The result was a compromise. The counties could either administer the categorical aids under the existing county judge

---

[65] State Board of Control, *supra* note 37, at 250, 251.

[66] Ch. 435, [1939] Wis. Laws 705.

[67] Wis. Stat. § 58.33(1) (1939).

[68] Social Security Act Amendments of 1939, ch. 666, § 401 (a), 53 Stat. 1379.

[69] Ch. 533, § 4, [1939] Wis. Laws 928; Ch. 535, § 10, [1939] Wis. Laws 946.

[70] Ch. 75, § 16m(3), [1967] Wis. Laws.

system or they could set up county pension departments. This meant that local administration of these programs remained largely unchanged, with the exception of Aid to the Blind, which had previously been administered by the county boards. Within the next year thirty-eight counties set up pension departments, while thirty-three continued to administer aid through the county judges.[71]

Then in 1945 counties were authorized to establish county departments of public welfare consisting of a county board of public welfare, a welfare director, and supporting personnel.[72] In 1953 the legislature required all other counties to establish county departments of public welfare.[73] The county boards of supervisors (elected bodies) were to select the members of the welfare board and set their compensation, assign "other welfare functions," and approve the annual budget for the department.[74]

But none of these statutes stated clearly whether the state or the counties had the authority to determine who was eligible for public assistance and what the level of assistance might be. The legislature continued to speak in abstractions.

Avoiding the Issues: Delegation and Decentralization

Thus far the legislature (whether federal or state) has been able to delegate the basic policy questions in AFDC through the use of broadly worded statutes. It has avoided getting into the business of resolving the moral dilemmas raised by this welfare program. It is not hard to understand the legislature's attitude. The AFDC programs, in the words of Gilbert Steiner, "introduce problems of race, of sex, of religion, and of family relationships. It is hard to think of four areas most American politicians would rather avoid."[75] The delegations have been successful from the legislature's point of view. A successful delegation is one that stays delegated in the sense that no conflicts arise to demand legislative attention. So far this has been the case with the AFDC program; whether this tactic can be maintained in the face of the present crisis in welfare remains to be seen.

Legislative activity, even of a reluctant nature, may nevertheless have

---

[71] State Board of Control, *supra* note 37, at 15.

[72] Ch. 383, § 3, [1945] Wis. Laws 622. In the same year, the state began to defray some of the costs of county welfare administration through the use of state money; previously the state had granted no more than the federal grant-in-aid. Ch. 585, § 47, [1945] Wis. Laws 1092.

[73] Ch. 513, § 2, [1953] Wis. Laws 478.

[74] *Id.*

[75] G. Steiner, *supra* note 40, at 4.

important consequences for welfare policy. Growth and development, for example, require affirmative legislative approval. Here the legislature plays a key role. The State Department of Health and Social Services cannot enforce its regulations on the counties and supervise their administration unless it has staff, and it has to persuade the legislature to appropriate money so that it can hire personnel. The state agency has the authority to establish or encourage the counties to establish a wide variety of social service programs, but in most instances it cannot move unless it gets state money.

Budget politics in Wisconsin, as in other states, are complex. At least in recent years, they boil down to an intricate negotiating session between an aggressive bureaucracy (the SDHSS); the governor's office, and key, knowledgeable legislators who sit on the Joint Finance Committee, the only appropriations committee of the Wisconsin legislature. The public assistance part of the SDHSS budget is a significant fraction, but is still only part of a large, complex budget contained in a formidably thick document. The decisions reached as a result of these negotiating sessions are generally approved by the legislature and the governor. Not unexpectedly, the legislature, through particular members, maintains a keen interest in the various activities of the Department, including public assistance, during the appropriations process. Program and policy are often decided by a small group of legislators, without a word of law being written. The most important legislative activity in public assistance is, as a practical matter, invisible.

Aside from the appropriation process, the legislature has allowed the familiar, decentralized system to operate much as it has for decades. Wisconsin AFDC *legislation* has not been significantly altered in thirty years. The responsibility of county judges was partially replaced by a more streamlined state supervisory agency and, after a period of years, by county departments of public welfare. But many important substantive matters have not been treated legislatively, and the statutes, despite their length and complexity, have not changed much in the course of a generation.

The fact is, however, that public assistance *has* significantly changed in operation. As pointed out in the Introduction, AFDC has grown enormously and there has been a significant change in the social characteristics of the recipients. Administration has also changed drastically. The State Department of Health and Social Services and its Division of Family Services have become complex administrative organizations. The Division is quite active in attempting to coordinate and standardize county procedures. The state manual contains hundreds of pages of rules specifying, fleshing out, and refining eligibility and budget criteria, and provides guides for social services. State district directors continually consult with county welfare directors about interpretations of the statutes and agency regulations. They also help in the development of local organization and try to stimulate interest in new programs. The Division operates a quality control program (required by federal law) which involves selected reading of case files and interviews with clients and staff development programs for county welfare personnel. It reviews the contents of county manuals, investigates complaints, and conducts periodic audits.

Even welfare administration in the counties has not remained static. Some counties, in the rural sections of the state, have very small, simple organizations and provide a routinely administered program with little emphasis on social services. Other counties, particularly the larger ones, have more complex organizations and more extensive programs.

But the changing character of the recipients and the growth of the administrative structure arose *outside* the legislative process. While the legislature continued to speak in broad generalizations, administrative officials had to decide eligibility, levels of aid, and other conditions. Some county agencies refused to discriminate among those formally eligible; as the populations of poor changed, so did their clientele. Other county agencies went to the other extreme; they adopted general rules allowing aid for certain types of applicants but not others. Some counties, as a matter of policy, would not give ADC to unwed mothers or divorcees.

The increasing centralization of authority in the SDHSS also took place without the benefit of legislation. It was not until the 1950's that the basic conflict between the state agency and the counties began to be resolved. Opinions by the attorney general established that the state agency had the authority to establish uniform standards throughout the state, to prescribe statewide standard budgets, and to disallow a county's reimbursement claim when the county did not comply with statutory requirements or state policies.[76] These opinions gave the state agency significant centralizing enforcement tools. In none was the legislature involved.

The principal effect of the legislative strategy of avoiding the critical substantive and administrative issues in AFDC is to create a very decentralized and flexible administrative system. By speaking in abstractions and by granting authorizations instead of deciding requirements, the legislature expands enormously the downward flow of discretion through the state agency to the county departments and to the field level. In the four chapters that examine in detail the major aspects of the program, we will see just how broad and vague the critical statutory provisions are. In several areas the state agency attempts to detail and make concrete vague provisions by ad-

---

[76] 39 WIS. OPS. ATT'Y GEN. 403 (1950); 40 WIS. OPS. ATT'Y GEN. 190 (1951); 43 WIS. OPS. ATT'Y GEN. 108 (1954).

ministrative regulations, but it can only go so far. In many areas its power over the county departments has not been clarified by the legislature.[77] The result is that most of the conflicts and contradictions in the AFDC program, the political, social, and moral issues that the legislature has avoided deciding, are decided through administration, and further, most of the administrative discretion is exercised at the county level. Accordingly, we now turn to the county departments of welfare. First we will look at the environment within which they operate, and then we will see how they carry out their job.

---

[77] Then, there are real problems in finding out whether the county agencies are following the state regulations anyway. Under present supervisory conditions, much field-level discretion simply escapes detection.

Chapter 2

COMMUNITIES, AGENCIES, AND CLIENTS

Many factors may influence the nature of welfare administration. There is the structure and personnel of the agencies themselves: styles of leadership, professionalization, and attitudes and orientations of the staff. There are factors "outside" of the agency, particularly agencies at the county level: the federal, state, and county governments; national, state, and local politics; the level of the economy, local community conditions, to name only a few. Then there are the clients themselves. They are the raw material, the subject matter of the welfare departments. What the agency can do to them or for them depends to a great extent on their personal and social characteristics, talents and abilities.

In this study it was assumed that social setting and agency structure could make a difference in administrative behavior and client response. For this reason we selected six different county departments of welfare. In this chapter we will describe briefly some of the characteristics of the six counties and of county departments of welfare. Then we will turn to the welfare recipients that were surveyed.

THE COUNTIES

Milwaukee County, covering the twelfth largest U.S. city and a few of its suburbs, is of course unique within Wisconsin. Dane County, consisting primarily of Madison (which is both state capital and home of the main campus of the University of Wisconsin) is a highly professionalized and service-oriented community. Brown County on Lake Michigan covers a fairly industrialized standard metropolitan statistical area, Green Bay. Walworth, Dodge, and Sauk are rural counties—Walworth on the Illinois border, and Dodge and Sauk in the south-central part of the state. The three rural counties are, however, quite different from one another in economic base and even more different in economic growth and prospects.

All six, however, are relatively wealthy in relation to other Wisconsin counties. At the time of the study, not one had been classified as a poverty target area or an area of serious unemployment (as is true for many counties in the northern half of Wisconsin). Thus, although community resources may appear relatively limited for Sauk County, it should be kept in mind that Sauk is but a richer version of the modal Wisconsin county.

Several demographic, labor-force, and wealth indices are shown in Table 2.1.[1] Very roughly, they are indications of resources as well as of need. Whatever the shortcomings of inference from aggregate data, it is fairly evident that the counties differ in many respects other than size.

Milwaukee County, like most metropolitan counties, is experiencing the greatest population growth in its suburbs; moreover, a great deal of this suburban growth is taking place outside the county itself. Consequently the central city and the county face financial problems in trying to harmonize the demands of the deteriorating inner city areas with the available tax sources. Milwaukee has long been known for manufacturing, particularly for the manufacture of heavy machinery, and 41 percent of the labor force is employed in manufacturing. Increasing industrial diversification has done little to alleviate the labor situation; jobs for the unskilled are in short supply, which carries important consequences for AFDC recipients who would prefer to be in the work force.

Basically Milwaukee County is becoming more like other major metropolitan areas in economic base. The days of great population growth, of considerable in-migration, of economic boom are over. Now the city faces the vexing problems of a white ethnic area of poverty pitted against a black ghetto, of fair housing statutes for the city, of securing more state aid for the school system, and so forth. Short of securing massive federal aid or experiencing unanticipated economic growth, Milwaukee, like other American cities, seems likely to remain long on problems and short on resources.

AFDC rolls in Milwaukee County have increased every year for the last decade, and at a rapid rate. Of the six counties described, Milwaukee has the highest percentage of its population on welfare, but even so this amounts to less than 3 percent.

Dane County in south-central Wisconsin, is expanding rapidly. It enjoys a high median family income, high assessed property value per capita, and a well-educated population living predominantly in urban areas. The growth industries, state government and the state university, employ large numbers of semi-skilled and skilled personnel, and provide a talent pool (both volunteer and paid) for assorted social causes. City government of Madison is more bureaucratized than county government, but both are

---

[1] Bureau of the Census (1962 County Data Book) for all 1960 data. State of Wisconsin, Division of State Economic Development, COUNTY ECONOMIC PROFILE SERIES, for all other data.

TABLE 2.1. SELECTED COUNTY DATA (Six Counties)

	Milwaukee	Dane	Brown	Walworth	Sauk	Dodge
1960 population	1,036,047	222,095	125,082	52,368	36,887	63,170
Percent urban (1960)	100.0	75.4	77.7	37.7	30.5	46.8
Population increase 1950–60	18.9	31.1	27.2	25.9	–3.2	9.6
Median family income (1959)	$6,959	$6,518	$6,016	$5,692	$4,589	$5,245
Percent adult population completed high school	43.8	59.6	43.5	45.6	35.3	32.9
Full assessed value of property, per capita (1964)	$6,041	$6,640	$5,859	$8,163	$4,897	$5,444
Percent of labor force in manufacturing (1960)	41	17	28	29	19	34
Percent of labor force in service (1960)	48	65	51	46	42	37
Percent of labor force in agriculture (1960)	0.4	8	7	14	26	21
Percent unemployed (1967)	2.9	2.1	4	3.8	3.6	3.7
Percent population nonwhite	6	1	1	0	0	0

characterized by fairly meticulous planning, and by at least some flexibility and responsiveness. Yet, as Robert Alford has pointed out, the implications of social and political characteristics for welfare administration in Dane County are mixed. He says,

> Because Madison lacked a large working-class base for city politics, the content of public issues revolved far more . . . around the amenities of life and their aesthetics. The goals of preserving views of the Capitol, of getting rid of ugly downtown railroad tracks . . . have historically occupied far more attention, time and energy of public officials and voluntary groups than do unemployment, welfare, poor housing, crime, and other problems which plagued less economically stable and wealthy cities and populations.[2]

In short, there were fewer serious social problems, and there was not much organized support for solving the ones that did exist.

The population of Madison and Dane County is predominantly middle class. Most of its workers are classified as skilled and there seems to be little employment opportunity for the poor and unskilled. However, within the county there are numerous facilities for training people for white-collar jobs, with government, insurance companies, etc. In addition there are a number of services, such as counseling centers, day-care centers, and apprenticeship programs. Some of these are privately staffed and financed; others are community sponsored. The City of Madison is usually fairly quick to take advantage of available federal funds. For example, it has participated in public housing and anti-poverty programs to much greater extent than Green Bay.

Brown County is a much more conservative county than Dane in terms of its political culture, and presumably also in terms of its public policy. Green Bay, which dominates Brown County in much the same manner as Madison dominates Dane County, is a trading center, where businessmen have traditionally played the dominant roles in community activities and government. Local banks also contribute political leaders in Green Bay, where there is not much citizen involvement in most political issues. "Boosterism" has taken precedence over improving amenities over time, and costs are reckoned very carefully. The fact that half the Brown County supervisors are Green Bay aldermen poses the possibility of greater control of county policy by "city men." For issues of social welfare, this situation is more likely to promote spending than the usual arrangement where rural supervisors occupy disproportionate numbers of county board positions. For example, the welfare department in Brown County has a new building, which suggests a fair amount of community support for a

---

[2] R. R. Alford, BUREAUCRACY AND PARTICIPATION (1969), chaps. III, VI.

kind of activity not normally held in high esteem in a conservative political climate.

Although Green Bay's dependence on primary products in manufacturing may pose long-range problems of economic adjustment, so far the city and county have been growing steadily. The influential local "boosters" intend to insure the continuation of growth by keeping costs and taxes down. An active taxpayers' alliance group works on budget review and emphasizes economy. Of the six discussed, Brown County has much the lowest tax rate per capita. The dependency ratio in Brown is very low, although the extent to which parsimony and lack of need are mixed cannot be determined.

Walworth County, the southernmost of the group we are studying, is predominantly an agricultural and resort area, although lately it has been experiencing an influx of electronics firms demanding female labor. Walworth County is only one-third urban, but its population is growing rapidly. It is more like the urban counties described in terms of its residents' educational achievements and median family income than it is like the other two rural counties. However, the full assessed value of Walworth County property per capita far exceeds the values for any of the other five counties. With prosperous farm land, increasing numbers of tourists, and an expanding industrial sector, Walworth County is not short of public monies, despite the fact that one-fifth of its population is in families having an income below $3,000 (in 1960). Though Walworth County inhabitants are more sympathetic to conservative political positions than to liberal ones, public employees do not seem to feel they must scrimp and cut before presenting their programs. Per capita taxes are comparatively high, but prospects for continued growth suggests that the county can probably muster sufficient resources to solve the problems of dependency, within reasonable limits.

The other two rural counties enjoy positions much less favored than Walworth. Dodge County, about fifty miles from both Madison and Milwaukee, had a modest population gain despite a net out-migration. Formerly almost exclusively dependent on an agricultural base, Dodge County has a high percentage of people over 65 (12.8 percent) and an adult population only half of which completed more than a ninth-grade education. However, small industries have moved in steadily. As a result, some employment for women has become available, particularly in the largest city, Beaver Dam. Farm product sales are well above the state average, suggesting that the agricultural sector is not in deep trouble and that the ability of the county to raise revenue is not permanently constrained by the traditional agricultural orientation. On the other hand, with one-fifth of the population having an annual income of less than $3,000, Dodge County must balance carefully the problem of taxing its labor force to provide for the dependent, without establishing a tax level so high that new investment is discouraged.

Sauk County, quite close to Dane, enjoys few of the advantages of the other counties. It is less urban, poorer in terms of median family income and in terms of the percentage of the population with less than $3,000 annual income, low on assessed value of property, undergoing a net population decline and a net out-migration, inhabited by an older population than elsewhere, and dependent, for the most part, on a farm economy. The manufacturing that exists revolves around food processing and textiles, in general, with a little activity in plastics and electronics. Sauk County is the site of the Badger Ordnance depot, which varies in employment depending on U.S. military activity abroad. When the depot is closed or nearly closed, Sauk County must husband its slender resources to meet public demands. When the depot reopens, times improve, but the duration of employment at Badger Ordnance is so problematic that the county can never be confident of long-term consumer demand by employees. Sauk County authorities indicate that the newer industries have brought some jobs for women, almost exclusively in the city of Baraboo. But in general the expansion of the private sector of the economy is sufficiently modest that public spending is greatly limited. However, for the poor the alternatives to dependency are not numerous and the dependency ratio is high. The lack of urban centers and the distances between them make it difficult to develop community resources, such as mental health clinics, programs for teenagers, etc.[3]

The evaluation of the dimensions of the welfare problem for a unit as large as a county is a task of great complexity. Ideally one would seek to know the actual extent of need for welfare support, the extent of coverage, and the impact of coverage for the clients. The extent and impact of coverage are presumably responsive to agency characteristics—to organization strategy, to funding, and to styles of leadership and administration. And the agency in turn is presumably responsive to the environment. For Walworth County, moderately wealthy and enjoying economic growth, client demand should be relatively low and the agency resources rather considerable. Because of employment opportunities, women should leave AFDC rather quickly and very likely without aid of the agency. For those who remain in the program, the agency should have the financial resources and the interest to set up special programs and attempt intensive work. In other words, at least in theory, community considerations shape the role the agency can play, both directly and indirectly, by shaping somewhat the characteristics of recipients as well as their career options. Community characteristics push toward differences in welfare problems and administrative responses. On the other hand, federal, state, and county governments may serve to limit freedom of action of the county welfare agencies.

THE COUNTY WELFARE DIRECTORS

Interviews with the welfare directors in six counties in Wisconsin convey that they have different conceptions of their roles, of the impacts of their agencies, and of the relationships of their agencies to the community.[4] The extent to which these styles make a difference in service will be examined later. It is possible that directors' styles are more important in areas of agency staffing and morale than in services to clients. It may be that the style of the director is not important in contrast with the resources that the community can and will make available. Or perhaps styles are simply expressions of resources—that counties relatively favored economically tend to choose and encourage men who are more likely to be activists.

Each of the directors in the six counties has had many years of experience at different levels in the county departments. Speaking of his most important responsibilities, each gave some attention to his function in securing adequate quarters and resources for workers—the struggle to pay competitive salaries is a source of real frustration in several agencies. Salaries seem to be more of a concern to Brown and Dodge Counties, whereas the Walworth director spoke of trying to insure for his workers the feeling that they had support, that they could take risks or present problems and that there were tools at hand for them to use in solving the challenges presented by their caseloads.

County welfare directors must cultivate, or at least pay attention to, a minimum of four types of relationships outside their agencies: relations with the county board, relations with the community (or with its elites only, in some cases), relations with supportive or auxiliary agencies, and relations with the Wisconsin State Department of Health and Social Services. To a certain extent each of these "outside" groups can threaten or limit the autonomy of the welfare agencies; to a certain extent each group can be conceived as a resource, a support. As a result of these pressures, county directors must spend a considerable amount of time mending fences, being sure that their legitimacy is not called into question, and that they are not threatened with sanctions (at least not obviously threatened). County

---

[4] Directors of county welfare agencies were interviewed in 1967 and 1968. The authors are grateful to Anthony Costonis for his assistance in developing and administering the interview schedule.

welfare directors are understandably sensitive to public criticism and try to allay it in advance. Thus they make it a practice to speak to any interested group and to encourage their caseworkers to do likewise. For the most part, these appearances are occasions for information-sharing: laymen do not always understand what county welfare agencies are charged with doing or how they work. Citizen mobilization about welfare has been slight, although in Brown County a taxpayers' alliance group works through the whole of the welfare budget. Even so, the director did not seem particularly concerned about the impact of that group on his agency.

All of the directors, except in Sauk County, thought they enjoyed considerable community support and endorsement. The Walworth director was one of the most community-oriented men interviewed. In his view, "the more they know the better off we are," referring to the knowledge citizens had about welfare. Brown and Dodge County directors mentioned using radio and television spots to keep the public informed about welfare, to develop interest. Welfare agencies try to work closely with local newspapers and to give them stories on occasion. Perhaps their greatest concern vis-à-vis newspapers is that stories about fraud or misbehavior by welfare clients be checked with the welfare department before they are printed. For the most part, coverage is favorable or neutral in local newspapers.

Concern for community support can, of course, mean many things. It can mean concern for whether the administrative practices of the county agency are approved or whether the concept of a particular aid program is approved, or whether, on a personal level, welfare clients are subjected to criticism or abuse. It is possible, for instance, for a community to approve agency administration and the idea of aid, but to be very hostile to welfare clients who apply for credit or seek to use their Medicaid cards for medical care, the purchase of drugs, etc. Presumably in cultivating community support, county welfare directors and caseworkers would be interested in all three areas, although evaluations of community support tended to be couched in terms of how well what the agency was doing was understood by residents. One director commented:

> The public in general has a fairly good opinion of welfare in the county and perhaps it's because we are active in trying many things together. Most of the Welfare Board and I are members of the Mental Health Clinic Board . . . We have many ways in which we tie the activities together so that these interests overlap and seem to develop a healthy welfare attitude in the county.

Another, more pessimistic about community and elite support, said, "I think there is in Sauk County, just as nationwide this particular election year, resentment of welfare programs, giveaway programs. Most people have a poor understanding of it." But, he added, there had been no local "attacks" on programs.

One of the tasks of a county welfare director is to supervise or coordinate programs with other agencies or authorities having concern for welfare clients. This means working with county counseling centers (mental health clinics), nursing homes, hospitals, special schools, sheriff's departments, juvenile officers, local police forces, schools, D.A.'s offices—in short, with many other service agencies and with law enforcement officials. Directors in Brown, Dane, and Walworth Counties expressed enthusiasm and appreciation for "interdepartmental" cooperation. One director commented:

> We have one of the finest community mental health centers in the state and a very good workshop. We were the first county in the state to have a children's unit in our mental hospital. We have one of the outstanding guidance clinics in the state. We have just about every other service agency in the community.

Similarly, said another:

> We work pretty closely with the counseling center. . . . we work closely with the nursing home. . . . With the hospital I think we have a pretty good relationship. . . We work very closely with the Sheriff's Department, juvenile officers. . . .

In Walworth County a Central Council, which is an interagency group, exists to make members aware of services, prevent overlapping, and initiate new projects. There may also be private agencies that county agencies can draw upon. The directors in Brown and Dane Counties were particularly sensitive to the possibilities of using private resources.

Dane County places great stress on using other collateral agencies as resources. They are more likely than any of the other agencies to turn to other authorities for solutions and assistance with problems—for example, to state government agencies, the university, or a specialized private group. The Dane County department has well-developed programs for routine cooperation with agencies related to the welfare field.

At the other extreme, one county director mentioned only relationships with law enforcement and mental health facilities. He lamented the fact that there were few ties to the schools, that there were difficulties communicating with the people in law enforcement, and that there was no county or city council to coordinate agencies and keep them informed. It is difficult to compare the problems of the Milwaukee County agency experiences in working with collateral agencies. In the large Milwaukee agency, there is probably more stress on internal agency cooperation and coordination than on working with external authorities. Many specialized services are housed within the Milwaukee Welfare Department itself.

The authority of the County Board seems to be uppermost in the minds of welfare directors. State regulations may be promulgated, newspapers may attack or defend, coordinating councils may be created, but nothing is as important to the agency as the level of funding. The customary arrangement in Wisconsin is that the elected County Board of Supervisors has five members who make up the County Welfare Board (Milwaukee has one elected official and four citizens, which is a unique arrangement within the state). For the most part, the members of the County Welfare Board have been in office many years, they have generally been involved with welfare for a long time, and, according to the welfare directors, they are fairly sympathetic.

County welfare directors generally have to rely on the County Welfare Board to present their case to the whole of the County Board (especially at budget time). Accordingly, the directors cultivate their advocates in a variety of ways. The minimum of interaction is for the welfare director to meet with the Welfare Board monthly, and to keep them supplied with whatever details they may require about administration and budget. Other techniques are preparation of annual reports about finances, caseloads, programs; taking board members on calls with caseworkers; and having board members attend special staff meetings. Despite their years of experience, Welfare Board members frequently do not understand the full financial repercussions and legislative implications of new federal and state programs. The introduction of Medicaid, for example, was the occasion for considerable explanation as the county directors tried to keep the boards up to date on the mandates and impact of the new law. A sympathetic County Welfare Board is almost a necessity if a county director is to preserve a floor of security and assurance among his workers. Most of the directors think that quite a satisfactory board-agency relationship exists: budgets are reviewed critically but without rancor; new programs, if well conceived, are approved; and the size of the staff increases, although never rapidly enough.

The Wisconsin State Department of Health and Family Services also affects the operation of the county agencies. The State Department is responsible for enforcing both federal and state legislation in the area of welfare. The Department makes quality checks of county programs; establishes rules, standards, and guidelines for administrators and caseworkers; and conducts fair hearings for clients who have complaints against county agencies. The State Department also provides supportive services, such as in-service training, liaison work, and advice on new programs and personnel. The Department, then, may be both an enforcer and a resource.

Three directors emphasized the positive side of their relationship with the State Department of Health and Social Services, citing the in-service training that the state made available, the workshops that were held at irregular intervals for caseworkers, the existence of a source of innovation, the exposure to professionals caught up in a nationwide welfare network, the assistance received in funding new programs, and the establishment and maintenance of high standards of administration. On the other hand, two directors felt that the State Department was insufficiently sensitive to the kinds of personnel pressures caused by new programs and new regulations. Many changes, for them, were sources of agency strain; they thought perhaps the changes could have been administered so as to cause less disruption. For one rural county welfare director, independence from the State Department was highly prized: he was never reprimanded because he failed to conform adequately, and he preferred to maintain his distance from state personnel. The desire to be somewhat aloof from the State Department was not common to all rural counties, however. In one instance, the director embraced the State Department as a source of information and change; for him, the State Department existed as a desirable pressure for experimentation and flexibility.

There is very little question for an agency the size of Milwaukee about the relationship with state authorities. With half the state's caseload, Milwaukee County needs the resources of the state badly and can reasonably expect to be an area of great interest to the state. There is a great deal of exchange of information and personnel. Dane County, home of the State Department, shares the same direct conduits of information and professional relationships as Milwaukee.

Of the four kinds of resources described, county welfare directors seem to differ only marginally in their evaluation of community support, of collateral support agencies, and of county boards, but rather more in their evaluation of their relationship with the State Department of Health and Social Services.

Asked to indicate the problems they faced and the meaning social work held for them, the six directors give rather dissimilar responses. The directors of the two largest agencies (Milwaukee, Dane) expressed great concern for the creation of better environmental conditions, which would both alleviate the incidence of poverty and ameliorate conditions for those in poverty. Both stressed their intentions of providing the best service possible given the low level of financial support which welfare programs provide. They indicated great interest in and willingness to explore alternative roles for welfare agencies. They thought, for example, that they might eventually serve as auxiliaries to an income maintenance program by acting as referral agencies which would direct clients to the appropriate specific services. Each man spoke of possibilities not only of restructuring his agency but also of restructuring the nature of state welfare programs.

The other four directors were more willing to accept the utility of the present welfare approach, mixing income and services. One director placed his emphasis on broadening the welfare umbrella, so that the agency could be responsive to virtually any problem. The other directors indicated concern with helping the poor through services, through rehabilitation, but did not seem concerned with changing the nature of agency activities. All three of these men would like more intensive services, smaller caseloads, and less administrative work by caseworkers.

The extent to which agencies are supportive of new programs is a matter of some discretion, though not much. For example, if state or federal funds become available for homemakers or case aides, counties usually take advantage of the new options, although with varying speed. The inauguration of the Medicaid program on the other hand, permitted no option: mechanisms and times were rigidly specified. Dane County, probably because of the proximity of the State Department and of the University of Wisconsin, is interested in new programs and able to carry on pilot studies without creating great internal tension in the agency. New programs for Dane and Milwaukee counties usually mean new resources, so they have little quarrel with change. There was unanimous support for case aides to handle administrative detail previously carried by caseworkers and for the simplified declaration form of intake. There is reason to suspect, however, that when new programs mean stretching existing resources, some hesitation exists.

Some agencies, then, are more open to suggestions and change than others; problems differ, and so do resources. Too, pressures for change are unequal—some counties have organizations of welfare recipients, some have young, aggressive caseworkers.

How much of the difference of opinion and style of county welfare directors will be reflected in agency activity? In later chapters we will take up the clients' evidence on this. Here we turn to the caseworker to see how much they differ when they describe their activities and values. As numerous studies of administration have shown, it is the man in the field, finally, who determines what happens.

THE CASEWORKERS

The data for the caseworkers are responses to self-administered questionnaires (see the Appendix) for almost all caseworkers in Dane, Brown, Walworth, Sauk, and Dodge Counties.[5] In Milwaukee, only those dealing

---

[5] Anthony Costonis supervised the preparation of the interview schedule for caseworkers and handled the arrangements of its administration. Interviews were completed during 1967 and 1968.

The Deserving Poor

TABLE 2.2. NUMBER OF AFDC CASEWORKERS
(Six Counties)

	Milwaukee	Dane	Brown	Walworth	Sauk	Dodge
Number	99	27	15	3	3	1

with AFDC and child welfare were surveyed. The analysis below focuses only on those who work with either AFDC or child welfare caseloads at least some portion of their time. In the larger agencies the nature of the caseload is usually specific for any one caseworker; in smaller agencies caseworkers expect to work with all of the categorical programs.

The number of caseworkers who indicated that they worked with child welfare and AFDC, exclusive of supervisors, by county is given in Table 2.2. Non-AFDC cases make up a larger percentage of the total caseload in the rural counties, which is reflected by the smaller percentage of county personnel concerned with AFDC. In view of the small number of AFDC caseworkers in the more rural counties, most of the discussion hereafter will involve only the caseworkers of Brown, Dane, and Milwaukee Counties. Unless there is internal variation, the rural counties will be discussed together. Table 2.3 summarizes some of the characteristics of caseworkers of the three larger counties.

In Milwaukee and Dane Counties, women caseworkers outnumbered

TABLE 2.3. SELECTED AFDC CASEWORKER DATA
(Three Urban Counties)

Characteristic	Milwaukee	Dane	Brown
Age			
20 and younger	31.6%	40.8%	40.0%
21–30	9.2	18.5	6.7
31–40	13.2	7.4	—
Over 40	45.9	33.3	53.3
Education			
Some college	3.0	—	—
College graduate	57.6	33.3	33.3
Some graduate or professional work	32.3	51.8	53.3
Graduate or professional degree	1.0	11.1	13.3
Not ascertained	6.1	3.7	—
Time in agency			
Less than 2 years	55.6	40.7	53.3
2–5 years	32.3	55.6	40.0
Over 5 years	12.1	3.7	6.7
Number	(99)	(27)	(15)

men. As far as age differences are concerned, in all three counties one third or more of the caseworkers were under twenty. In Dane, 59.3 percent were under thirty. Only in Milwaukee were minorities represented among caseworkers, with 7 percent of the caseworkers indicating that they were black.

There were differences in professionalization. Almost every caseworker said she had obtained a college degree. Since both the Madison and Milwaukee campuses of the University of Wisconsin give B.A.'s in social work, very likely some of these caseworkers have had pre-job training. The percentages reporting some graduate or professional work or a graduate or professional degree differed from county to county: only 33.3 percent in Milwaukee as compared with 62.9 percent in Dane and 66.6 percent in Brown County. Caseworkers in Milwaukee County have been in their professions shorter times than those in Dane, but the lack of experience for many is impressive for all three counties: including all welfare work experience, 30 percent of the Dane County caseworkers have been practicing a year or less and 47 percent in Brown and 49 percent in Milwaukee have had only that much experience. In all three counties, about half of the caseworkers said they had been in that particular agency a year or less. Quite a different picture emerges for the rural counties: the workers had more years of experience in their profession and not one had been in the agency as little time as a year. AFDC case workers, then, are often young college graduates, without extensive field experience.

The commitment of these young college graduates to their careers in public assistance is questionable. Although at least two-thirds of the caseworkers said that they did, at some time, intend to get further professional training, only one-third of the Dane workers expect to be in welfare work three years hence, either in county, state, or private agencies. In Milwaukee County 42 percent say they will remain in welfare fields and 53 percent so indicate in Brown, but many do not plan to be in public welfare work. There is in fact a great turnover in public assistance caseworkers. In Dane County several young people said they were planning both to obtain future training and to retire from welfare work. In addition, most caseworkers (64.2 percent) working with AFDC did not belong to any professional group. Milwaukee workers were slightly less inclined to be members of professional groups than were caseworkers in other counties. Perhaps there is no relationship between professional membership and serious intention to seek further training; perhaps caseworkers are doubtful about the benefits of professional organizations. Yet if their interest in social work is sufficiently strong for them to plan to return to school in social work, one would expect reported participation to be higher.

In order to find out what caseworkers said they were doing and their attitudes toward their activity, they were asked a series of questions about (1) how important various areas of discussion were to helping the client to independence, (2) the extent to which they felt the agency should bear the responsibility for initiating such discussions, and (3) the frequency with which they held certain kinds of discussions. The areas that the caseworkers were asked about are:

Budget management (how client-spends the grant)

Child raising (clothing, diet, school problems, social problems)

Home management (cleanliness, cooking, etc.)

Social or personal problems of client (delinquency, drinking, promiscuity)

Involvement in other community social service programs (YWCA, counseling, etc.)

Social life of mother (with family, friends)

Social life of mother (with men including dating, marriage, or reconciliation with husband)

Employment possibilities (supplementary income, retraining, vocational placement)

Religious life of the client

Health problems (medical, dental, mental)

The caseworkers were unanimous in thinking of discussions of jobs as the most important in promoting the independence of clients. Second in importance for achieving independence were issues of child raising. It is not clear how attention to children promotes independence, but here the rhetoric of the AFDC program as stated in the manual and social work training must be considered, as well as the strains of dealing with broken families. Somehow caseworkers, who *have* to deal with children, think of their activities in this area as productive of the ends to which social work is usually directed, however limited these activities may appear to an outsider.

Health, social or personal problems, and budget, were, after jobs and children, perceived as areas of considerable importance for independence. Stress on good health and personal organization are constant throughout society, and in prizing them, caseworkers follow more general norms. The emphasis on budget management is of interest. The State Department's manual stresses counseling on budget matters as an instrument of rehabilitation, and society places considerable importance on the prudent management of household income, particularly insofar as welfare recipients are concerned. However, caseworker youthfulness and lack of experience, as compared to the recipients, cast doubt on how much really valuable counseling they can give on budget management.

Four areas of discussion are regarded by caseworkers as of medium importance: social life, home management, men, and community involvement. Perhaps it is not coincidental that caseworkers cannot do much in any of these areas. Seemingly, caseworkers have a rather low opinion of the value of other community social service programs, which suggests rather little incentive on the part of the caseworker to refer welfare clients to other community resources. Caseworkers were almost unanimous in thinking that discussion of the client's religious life was not important in achieving independence.

In which of these areas do caseworkers think it is appropriate for welfare workers to take the initiative? Caseworkers by large margins approved staff-initiated discussions of budgets, health, children, and community services. They also feel that staff members should take the initiative in discussing social-personal problems and the management of the home. Clients were expected to take the initiative in the areas of social life and men. As far as religion is concerned, many caseworkers doubted that the issue should even be discussed, and if it were to be discussed, it should be at the client's initiative.

To what extent do caseworkers behave so as to emphasize the areas they presumably think are most useful to the client? There are, of course, client initiatives, state laws, and county directors shaping the content of caseworker visits. A caseworker may not be free to discuss, in a brief visit, the issue she thinks is most important. Or more likely, she may be aware of the difficulties of dealing with problems (jobs, for example) so that she spends her time emphasizing areas in which she can be helpful. Nevertheless, as we would expect, health, children, and jobs (in that order) are the areas that the caseworkers says they discuss most often. Budget and personal problems are also treated frequently, with community, social life, men, and the home discussed not so often. Religion is infrequently or never discussed.

In sum, caseworkers say that the things they are giving the most attention to are those things which most promote independence. Circularly, the things they value most (for the sake of the clients) are the things they say they discuss the most.

What are caseworker attitudes toward different proposals for welfare change? It would be expected that they would be most receptive to change in areas they have indicated to be important for client achievement—jobs and children, followed by health, handling of personal problems, and budget. The three areas of health, children, and jobs presumably have a special appeal in that caseworkers' efforts are directed toward those issues more often than toward other issues. Caseworkers were questioned concerning changes in the service program of the agency—whether they thought something "should definitely be done" or whether "they would not mind seeing it done" or "would be against it"—for the following areas:

Provide legal services

Increase vocational rehabilitation plans

Allow clients to add more to budget through earned income exemption

Provide welfare assistance when father is in the home

Support children through completion of college

Provide birth control information to client

Provide a minimum income to all people below the "poverty line"

Intensify service to the client over a shorter period of time

For most items caseworkers agreed that a change should definitely be made, but many caseworkers voiced strong disagreement concerning a minimum income plan or providing assistance when the father was in the home. In general, caseworkers were most supportive of changes in the areas of providing legal assistance, increasing vocational rehabilitation programs, hiring homemakers, and providing birth control information. They were less supportive of changes directed toward providing more intensified service over a shorter period of time and allowing clients to add more to the budget through earned income, and even less sympathetic to supporting families while the father is in the home, or providing minimum income. Among the three urban agencies, Dane caseworkers were most disposed toward change, Milwaukee least.

Other studies have pointed out a host of factors shaping attitudes toward change, or toward actual changes.[6] Professional activity is supposed to encourage change and high job morale to retard it. Milwaukee caseworkers are somewhat less involved in professional organizations, which fits into their lower tolerance for innovation. And Dane County, with the highest turnover in caseworkers, is also the site of greatest sympathy for change.

There is a relationship between attitudes toward innovation and areas of activity. Jobs for recipients, which were evidently highly valued and re-

---

[6] M. Aiken and J. Hage, The Relationship between Organizational Factors and the Acceptance of New Rehabilitation Programs in Mental Retardation, Project Record, Department of Sociology, University of Wisconsin, 1968 (mimeo).

portedly emphasized by the caseworkers, are tied to their support for increased vocational rehabilitation programs. Although caseworkers did not evaluate home care highly, they did endorse hiring of homemakers. Most agencies already have homemakers, who are perceived by caseworkers as supportive of better living on AFDC by clients. Legal assistance for welfare clients means providing an alternate source of authority and aid to which clients could turn and thus reduces the pressure on caseworkers.[7]

Although the caseworkers do support change in a number of areas, their overall position is quite conservative. At least at the time that the survey was taken, they supported most wholeheartedly only those changes in technique that would further the traditional goal of social work—reformation of AFDC families through the personal services of counseling, advice, and guidance. They were less enthusiastic about more fundamental changes —liberalizing the earned income policies, providing aid when the father is in the home, and providing a minimum income for all people below the "poverty line." Interestingly, the first two of these changes have already been enacted, and the third is being pushed quite seriously. The net effect of these three changes would be to reduce the dependency of the AFDC family and the role and influence of the caseworker.

The other striking feature of the caseworker attitudes and reported behavior is the similarity between counties. The counties are very different communities on very important dimensions. The welfare directors also differ in style and philosophy. Yet the caseworker responses are generally similar. The explanation lies in the substantive ideology expressed by the caseworkers. Despite the fact that most of the caseworkers did not have professional social work training, they have been exposed to the standard professional rhetoric and the professional definition of the role of the social worker which is contained in the State Department Manual. In subsequent chapters we will set out in detail the State Department definitions and standards for the activities of the caseworkers. The great emphasis is on producing changes in the lives of welfare recipients through the techniques of counseling, advice, and guidance. This approach stresses the efficacy of the social worker and her personal service techniques, as distinguished from more basic, fundamental changes that would come about from sources outside the caseworker relationship. Social work theory is uniform; the State Department Manual applies to all caseworkers (regardless of training) in all of the Wisconsin counties. The caseworkers in this survey were reiterating the professional position.

---

[7] We do not know what the reactions of caseworkers to welfare client organizations and the use of lawyers by clients to challenge agency practices would be. Both have arisen since the completion of this study.

THE CLIENTS

The popular conception of the AFDC recipient in the 1930's was that she was a middle-class white widow who accepted welfare assistance in order to prevent the breakup of her family until alternative arrangements could be made. We will never know just how accurate was the popular image in all its details, but during the 1930's most AFDC recipients were in fact white widows.[8] After World War II a new stereotype of the AFDC recipient emerged: black, born in the Southeast, she had "moved north" with little education and job experience. Usually unmarried or deserted, she quickly turned to welfare for support. It was frequently alleged that she had even moved into the northern states in order to take advantage of better welfare benefits. She and her presumably numerous children would spend many years on the welfare rolls. Allegations were common concerning the promiscuity of recipients, their unwillingness to work or to better themselves, and their unfamiliarity with the institutions of urban life. The recipients were thought to have come from broken homes dependent upon welfare for support, and they were believed to head families in which the younger members would very likely become the public charges of the next generation. Such a characterization did not carry even face validity for many recipients, but for large urban areas, which make up an ever greater percentage of welfare dependents in most states, it seemed reasonable.

In this section, we will look first at the AFDC population in Milwaukee County to see how apt the stereotype is for one of the nation's largest cities[9] and then turn to an examination of the characteristics of recipients from other counties.

One of the first questions asked about AFC recipients for a major urban area concerns race. The racial distribution of our AFDC respondents in Milwaukee is generally reflective of the total caseload for the county (Table 2.4).

Women turn to AFDC because of various family crises. The marital status distributions (Table 2.5) for all Milwaukee respondents, as well as for the two largest racial groups, help to indicate some of the reasons for dependence.[10]

The striking finding from Table 2.5 is that three-fourths of the Mil-

---

[8] G. Steiner, SOCIAL INSECURITY: THE POLITICS OF WELFARE (1966).

[9] Although the sample of 302 was drawn from Milwaukee County, we found that 294 of the women lived in the city proper. Therefore the findings can be considered applicable for the AFDC recipients of the city.

[10] Hereafter whenever race is discussed, only black and white women are considered. The numbers of women were sufficient for comparison with only those two groups.

TABLE 2.4. RACIAL DISTRIBUTION
(MILWAUKEE AFDC RECIPIENTS)

Race	1965 All AFDC Milwaukee County	1967 sample AFDC Milwaukee
White	47.7%	41.1%
Nonwhite	—	—
Negro	50.3	57.0
Other nonwhite	2.0	1.9

TABLE 2.5. MARITAL STATUS, BY RACE
(MILWAUKEE AFDC RECIPIENTS)

Marital Status	All Respondents	White	Black
Married	20.9%	27.4%	15.7%
Divorced	25.5	34.7	19.8
Separated	27.5	23.4	30.9
Deserted	3.6	2.4	4.6
Widowed	2.3	3.2	1.7
Unmarried	20.2	8.9	27.3
Number	(302)	(124)	(172)

waukee recipients were married, divorced, or legally separated. The percentage of women describing themselves as deserted is very low, although desertion may have been the precipitating incident in many divorces and separations.

The states of birth named by most of those not born in Wisconsin are in the Southeast, where almost half (145) of the women were born. Table 2.6 presents the two major racial groups distributed by birthplace. About

TABLE 2.6. BIRTHPLACE,
BY RACE (MILWAUKEE
AFDC RECIPIENTS)

Birthplace	White	Black
Wisconsin	80.7%	13.4%
Southeast	7.5	79.1
Other	11.8	7.5
Number	(119)	(172)

43 percent of our sample is made up of black women born in the Southeast.

The majority (80.3 percent) of Milwaukee respondents had lived in Wisconsin for ten years or more, and of that number almost half had spent all their lives in the state. Although black respondents had been in the community a shorter time than white respondents, they averaged 10.5 years of residence, as opposed to 21 years for whites. One-third of the respondents had been reared on a farm or in a rural situation, while just over one-third said they had grown up in a city with at least 100,000 residents. But, as Table 2.7 shows, there were rather different distributions of the two major racial population groups.

In terms of long-term urban experience, whites have had an advantage over blacks. However, the blacks did average a decade of residence in Milwaukee County, so one must be wary of making too much of the discontinuities in their experience. Perhaps the significance of the greater urban experience of whites may lie chiefly in their background characteristics: more education for themselves and their parents, for example. But regardless of race, the similarities between the adult lives of rural- and urban-reared women are more striking than the differences.

Over three-fifths of the Milwaukee respondents reported that they had been raised by both parents, although there was a difference in the frequency with which the racial groups reported coming from an intact family: four-fifths of the whites were raised by both parents, whereas only half of the blacks were. Unmarried AFDC recipients were more likely to have been raised by their mothers only or by others, rather than by two parents.

Asked about the occupations of their fathers, the largest number of women replied "farmer," with the second largest group indicating semi-skilled or unskilled factory jobs. Almost 90 percent of the fathers had worked regularly. Sixty percent of the fathers had no more than a grade school education. Just over one-sixth indicated that they had no father (or

TABLE 2.7. SIZE OF COMMUNITY OF REARING,
BY RACE (MILWAUKEE AFDC RECIPIENTS)

Size of Community	Total	White	Black
Farm or rural	32.5%	15.3%	44.2%
Less than 10,000	15.2	13.8	15.7
10,000 to 49,999	9.9	9.7	10.5
50,000 to 99,999	4.0	3.2	4.6
Larger city	38.4	58.0	25.0
Number	(302)	(124)	(172)

TABLE 2.8.   AGE GROUPS
(MILWAUKEE AFDC
RECIPIENTS)

Age	Milwaukee
Under 30	36.3%
30 to 39	39.7
40 and over	23.4

substitute). Over half of the respondents said that their mothers had worked while they were growing up, usually as semiskilled or unskilled workers, or as service workers. Their mothers usually had no more than grade school educations.[11]

Concerning conditions in their homes while they were growing up, the AFDC recipients in Milwaukee were most likely to report that their homes were not crowded, that they had enough to eat all or most of the time, and that there was money for special treats. Their parents or other adults in the home got along very well or fairly well, according to the recollections of our respondents.

Still, about one-third of the women said that their parents had received some type of public or private assistance during the years they were growing up. Such aid was usually of brief duration. As one would expect, women who had grown up in large urban areas were more likely to come from families which had received assistance than were women from farms or smaller towns.

The respondents had completed a median of two years of high school. The median number of school years completed by all persons in Milwaukee County aged twenty-five and older is eleven, suggesting that compared to the general adult population, Milwaukee AFDC recipients are not greatly disadvantaged.

In age, the Milwaukee respondents are very like the general female adult population of the county (Table 2.8). The median age of the recipients is 32. The average number of children per AFDC family is 3.4. Perhaps it is more useful in describing AFDC families to indicate that 74 percent of the respondents have three or more children. One-fifth of these have seven or more children.

Can we make any statements about the life patterns of AFDC recipients? So far we have established that most are from intact homes, did not receive welfare aid as children, and have been married. Since most women

---

[11] Respondents' recall about parents' educational achievements is open to question. Many said they did not know about the years of schooling completed by their parents. The figures presented in this chapter are based on respondents who gave grade or school levels as replies.

enter public dependency as a result of a marital crisis, or at least crises stemming from marital complications, we need to look at a few more variables associated with marital experience (Table 2.9). For women who have been married, the broad outlines of their history are fairly clear. They have married once, at about age nineteen; they have three or four children living with them at present, after many years of marriage. And there is not much difference between blacks and whites. The husbands of these women completed a median of two years of high school, just as their wives did. Semiskilled and unskilled workers were the largest occupational group, followed by skilled workers and clerical and kindred workers, in that order. But only 71 percent worked regularly.

The above means that of the 302 Milwaukee respondents only 56 percent had had husbands who provided a regular income. Moreover, given the earnings figures that are available, we can make no presumption about the adequacy of the income. Very likely, even for women who were married to a regularly employed man, economic insecurity was a constant threat. And 44 percent of our sample were either never married or married to someone who did not work regularly.

The real differences between the two largest racial groups exist not among women who have been married, but among those who have never married. Though only one of every five AFDC recipients in Milwaukee County had not been married, among black women the percentage is three times higher. Correspondingly, black women are more likely to have had illegitimate children. Illegitimacy statistics are always open to question, in that their reliability cannot be ascertained without intensive investigation. About 48 percent of our Milwaukee respondents said that they had borne at least one illegitimate child, not necessarily while on the AFDC program.

How long do AFDC recipients stay on the program? Contrary to stereotypes, very few women spend year after year on public welfare rolls, and for most of the women we interviewed, AFDC was a new experience. One-third of the Milwaukee respondents had had previous experience with

TABLE 2.9.   ASPECTS OF MARRIAGE, BY RACE[a]
(MILWAUKEE AFDC RECIPIENTS)

	White	Black
Age when first married	19.6	18.9
Years with recent husband	10.1	9.4
Percent married only once	74.3	80.0
Number of children	3.4	3.9
Number	(113)	(125)

[a] Table includes only women who have been married. Figures represent means.

AFDC. The percentage of white women who were "repeaters" was higher than that for black women. White recipients whose parents had received welfare assistance were almost twice as likely to have had previous AFDC experience as those whose parents had not been aided. Among blacks, the percentage of women with previous AFDC experience was not related to whether their parents had received assistance.

Forty-nine percent had been in the program two years or less, and an additional 25 percent reported five years or less as AFDC recipients. The mean time on the program for the whole group was 45.8 months, or about three years and nine months. Means are given in Table 2.10 for the major racial groups, divided between unmarried and those with some marital experience. Since our respondents had to have six months' experience with the program to be eligible for the sample, we would expect to have a mean higher than the real mean for all AFDC recipients in Milwaukee County at any given time. There are, after all, many short-term cases who do not stay in the program six months. Formerly the state regulations prohibited the opening of the case unless the recipient would be in the program at least three months. This requirement has now been dropped, and it is questionable to what extent it was ever enforced. In any event, it is possible that the mean for Milwaukee County is considerably lower than the mean for our respondents.

Even with the background information presented above and the knowledge that AFDC budgets provide for what, at best, could be called extremely modest living conditions, we know very little about the lives of our respondents. Many policy questions in welfare require more specific information about the way in which women relate to others outside their households and the larger society. Here, we will consider briefly the extent to which AFDC recipients are isolated.

Most Milwaukee AFDC recipients lived in central city Census tracts, and of those, 57 percent lived in tracts specifically designated as poverty tracts. Just over 12 percent lived in public housing. Asked how often they were able to leave the house for social trips (excluding the doctor, the

TABLE 2.10.   AVERAGE TIME ON AFDC, BY RACE AND
MARITAL STATUS[a] (MILWAUKEE AFDC RECIPIENTS)

	White		Black	
	Unmarried	*Married*	*Unmarried*	*Married*
Number of months	32.8	35.6	56.6	51.0
Number	(11)	(112)	(47)	(125)

[a] "Married" means respondent had been married at some time.

grocery store, and other errands), over 50 percent of our respondents said never or once in an average week. But including errands, 94.4 percent left the house once a week.

But the AFDC recipients do not seem to be social isolates. Seemingly, other AFDC clients are not a source of companionship for most women: half said they knew no one else who was in the program. On the other hand, 77.5 percent said they had at least one relative in the community or nearby, and many women mentioned several relatives. One woman in seven said she saw a relative every day, and 35.4 percent saw relatives at least once a week. Half the Milwaukee respondents said that the people they thought of as good friends were their neighbors. However, only half of the women not married at present said that they had any social life involving men.

AFDC recipients are not withdrawn from the community. Among our respondents, 56 percent said they were active in a labor union, social club, fraternal organization, or poverty group, attended some church activity other than services, or went to PTA regularly. More women attended social clubs or groups than any other kind, with War on Poverty groups mentioned next most often. Many more go to church services fairly regularly or to PTA for parents' programs.

Given the concern with participation in voluntary groups by different social classes, it is particularly interesting that 23 percent of the women were active in some group or organization not affiliated with their church.[12] Since the respondents in this survey were primarily female heads of families, one might expect they would have less time and fewer prospects for participation than most lower class families. Yet this participation rate of 23 percent is roughly the same as the rate for blue-collar workers.[13]

---

[12] The question asked was: "Within the last three years, have you participated in, or belonged to, any organization of these types: (a) a labor union; (b) a political group—like a political party, or the NAACP or CORE, or any other group concerned with political problems; (c) any of the groups connected to the national 'War on Poverty' like a neighborhood task group or a Head Start mothers' group or any other groups or meetings associated with 'War on Poverty'; (d) a social group or sports group like a card club, a birthday club, a bowling team, or any other informal group that meets fairly regularly; (e) a social group like 'Parents Without Partners' that has parties and does other things together; (f) as a leader for some young people's group like the Cub Scouts, the Girl Scouts, or the 4-H Club; (g) any other groups or organizations?" If the respondent replied in the affirmative, she was asked, "Do you still participate?"

[13] C. R. Wright and H. H. Hyman, *Voluntary Association Membership of American Adults: Evidence from National Sample Surveys,* 23 AM. SOCIOL. REV. (1968) 284. The types of groups in which women are active are discussed in L. Freeman, Voluntary Group Participation, Integration, and the Lower Class: A Reevaluation, 1968 (unpublished Master's thesis, Department of Sociology, University of Wisconsin).

Looking at friendships and participation together, one finds that only 6 percent of the women have no friends or relatives and no outside activity. Although our measures of social isolation are crude, the evidence suggests that the AFDC mother pictured as alone and inactive is indeed the exception. It is, however, much more likely that an AFDC mother will have her social life with friends or relatives than that she will be in an organization, even including PTA's and church groups. We do not mean to exaggerate the extent of the involvement of AFDC women with primary or secondary groups. Having a relative nearby may carry no implications for communication, or for the content of communication. Friends and relatives may not serve to help in reducing problems or handling despair, though very likely in most instances they do. Likewise, the fact of attending PTA or belonging to a labor union may only marginally relieve feelings of estrangement or alienation. Reasoning from objective circumstance to subjective reaction is always chance ridden, but we do infer that for most women, there is at least some human interaction aside from children and grocers.

For Milwaukee County recipients, many of the stereotypes about AFDC clients fade into myths. Intergenerational poverty is the exception, not the rule; AFDC repeaters make up only a small percentage of the caseload. Most women on welfare have many years of state residency and marital experience behind them. Still, as heads of families usually containing several children, they have rather slender resources with which to meet the problems of an urban, industrialized economy.

Outside Milwaukee County, the Wisconsin AFDC population we interviewed assumes a somewhat more homogeneous aspect and almost wholly refutes the popular stereotype.

In all the other five counties, 90 percent of the respondents were white. There were a few blacks in Dane and Walworth Counties, a few American Indians in Sauk and Brown, and a few Mexicans in Walworth. As Table 2.11 indicates, all these women have spent many years in Wisconsin.

Half of the women in the three rural counties said they had been raised on farms, and just under one-third of those in Dane and Brown Counties so replied. Even now, the typical AFDC recipient in Walworth

TABLE 2.11. RESIDENCY INFORMATION (FIVE COUNTIES)

	Dane	Brown	Walworth	Sauk	Dodge
Percent who have lived entire life in Wisconsin	71.5%	72.1%	51.3%	84.2%	77.4%
Average years in Wisconsin of those who have not lived in Wisconsin all their lives	16.4	21.7	17.9	25.0	20.3

County lives in a community of fewer than 5,000 inhabitants. Sauk County women are fairly well divided, in that equal numbers live in towns under 2,500 and in towns between 5,000 and 10,000. Over half the Dodge County women live in a city having 10,000 residents, though a large number of them make their homes in towns with fewer than 2,500 residents. One of the many problems of welfare administration in Wisconsin counties is the fact that women are dispersed in small towns throughout the county. To develop services specific to them is all the more difficult because of their decentralized patterns of residence. On the other hand, it may be that as residents of small communities, welfare recipients are so well imbedded in networks of relationships that they do not require specially fostered programs or arrangements. At any rate, as Table 2.12 points out, many women are living in quasi-rural conditions: either they live in quite small towns, or they live in medium to small towns primarily oriented toward an agrarian market and population. In Dane and Brown Counties, almost all AFDC recipients live in the large cities of the counties, Madison and Green Bay.

The percentages saying that they had been raised by both parents were quite high, ranging from 74 percent in Dane to 88 percent in Sauk. Usually their fathers had been farmers or held semiskilled jobs. Almost every father worked regularly. Usually he had a very modest education; the percentages reporting no more than grade school completed by their fathers were between 64 and 90 percent. Most mothers of AFDC recipients did not work, which is not surprising in view of their rural or small-town background. Mothers seem to have had more formal education than fathers. For both mothers and fathers, the counties rank in the same way: Dane County parents are best educated, Sauk County parents the least educated.

Like the Milwaukee respondents, the women in the other five counties said that their homes had not been crowded while they were growing up and that they had enough to eat all or most of the time. They recalled that often or at least sometimes there was money for special treats. Still,

TABLE 2.12.   SIZE OF COMMUNITY OF RESIDENCE
(THREE RURAL COUNTIES)

	Walworth	*Sauk*	*Dodge*
Farms	8.75%	12.2%	—
Cities under 4,999	73.75	47.4	38.7%
5,000–9,999	17.50	40.4	8.1
10,000 and over	—	—	53.2
Number	(80)	(57)	(62)

TABLE 2.13. EDUCATION (AFDC RECIPIENTS
AND GENERAL ADULT POPULATION) AND MEDIAN AGE
(AFDC RECIPIENTS) (FIVE COUNTIES)

Schooling and Age	Dane	Brown	Walworth	Sauk	Dodge
Median school years completed					
AFDC recipients	11	10	10	10	9
All adults 25 and over[a]	12	11	11	9	9
Median age, AFDC recipients	31	36	35	39	39

[a] General Social and Economic Characteristics, U.S. CENSUS OF POPULATION, 1960, WISCONSIN. Final Report PC (1)–51c, at 250–55.

between 20 and 30 percent said that their parents had received some kind of welfare aid at the time the respondents were growing up; the period of assistance was usually a year or less.

The median number of school years completed varied from county to county, with women residing in more urbanized counties having some advantage. Some of the variation in education may be attributable to the age of the clients; that is, younger women tend to have completed more years of school than older women. In Table 2.13 the median schooling for AFDC recipients is compared with the median schooling for all persons aged twenty-five years and over in the five counties.

Not only had most women been married, as is shown in Table 2.14,

TABLE 2.14. MARITAL STATUS IN FIVE COUNTIES

Marital Status	Dane	Brown	Walworth	Sauk	Dodge	Total
Married	15.6%	14.0%	20.0%	19.3%	29.0%	18.3%
Divorced	57.0	62.8	46.2	50.9	50.0	54.5
Separated	9.5	18.6	17.4	7.0	1.6	11.2
Deserted	2.8	1.2	5.0	1.8	11.3	3.9
Widowed	4.5	2.3	5.0	10.5	8.1	5.4
Unmarried	10.6	1.2	6.3	10.5	0	6.7
Number	(179)	(86)	(80)	(57)	(62)	(464)
Age when first married (median)[a]	19	19	18	19	19	19
Years married[a]	9.5	11.2	11.4	14.2	13.4	11.2
Number of children[a]	3.4	3.3	3.6	2.8	3.4	3.4
Percent married only once[a]	74	84	77	84	82	79
Number	(160)	(76)	(75)	(51)	(62)	(434)

[a] Applies only to those who have been married.

TABLE 2.15. PERCENT HAVING AN ILLEGITIMATE
CHILD (FIVE COUNTIES)

	Dane	Brown	Walworth	Sauk	Dodge
Percent	31	22	24	26	21

but they had been married a number of years. They usually married in their late teens and had several children. The very high proportion of recipients, who gave "divorced" as their reason for eligibility is noteworthy. Not surprisingly, the percentages of those who said they had borne illegitimate children were lower than the 48 percent for Milwaukee (Table 2.15).

The former husbands of our respondents were usually employed in semiskilled jobs, or, in two of the rural counties, as farmers. A considerable number of women in Dane, Brown, and Walworth Counties had been married to skilled workers. Apparently, about two-thirds of the husbands had worked regularly.

The median years of education for husbands shown in Table 2.16 vary little in response to urban-rural dimensions. As was true of their parents, wives are better educated (in Brown, Walworth, and Sauk Counties) than husbands (cf. Table 2.13).

Most women are now on AFDC for the first time, though between 18 and 25 percent have had some previous AFDC experience. It is hard to know how to evaluate the fact that a county has women reporting several previous experiences with the program. Does this mean that women have been encouraged to leave the program prematurely, only to return when they were not able to be independent? Or does one agency make it easy for women to have their cases reopened, so that they move in and out of the program with greater ease? For most cases these questions are probably academic—the women are on AFDC for the first time and will not return to the program when they leave it.

Most recipients in these five counties have had several years of married life and have held jobs. But their possibilities and plans for moving out of a condition of dependency vary greatly. Thus the length of time they

TABLE 2.16. EDUCATION OF RESPONDENTS'
HUSBANDS (FIVE COUNTIES)

	Dane	Brown	Walworth	Sauk	Dodge
Median school years completed by husbands of respondents	11	8	9	8	10

have spent on the program varies. For Sauk and Dodge recipients, experiences have been considerably longer. One would expect that as time in the program increases, women become less likely to foresee an end to need for aid (except in those cases where child maturation or departure is involved) because options of employment and marriage decrease as women grow older. But expectations do not seem to be related to time in the program (see Table 2.17). About half the women in each county expect to be independent one day. Very likely they are making their assessment of the possibility of independence in terms of their own skills, aid or pressure from the county welfare agency, and opportunities for employment; possibly they are assessing their prospects for marriage or reconciliation.

How often do welfare clients get out of the house for social purposes? Regardless of county, about 60 percent say once a week or less often. Half of the women without husbands say they date, with slightly lower percentages in rural areas, but then, the women in our rural sample are older.

Most women have among their friends only one other AFDC family. Many say they know of no one else on AFDC. Given the number of women on AFDC and the fact that, in three counties, they are living in several different towns, this is not surprising. In Dane County, however, 18 percent said they knew eight or more AFDC families, which is suggestive of the potential for, or existence of, organization.

Relatives are near at hand for over 80 percent, and visiting or telephoning them is a daily business for about one-third of the women. The women in these counties also say they know many other people in their communities—a product of years of continuous residence in small and stable towns.

About one-fourth of the women in each county spoke of participation in some organization or group, with Dane County women reporting the

TABLE 2.17. MONTHS ON AFDC AND EXPECTATIONS
OF NO LONGER NEEDING AID (FIVE COUNTIES)

"How many months have you been in the AFDC program this time?" "Do you see some time in the future when you think assistance from AFDC or other welfare programs will no longer be necessary for you?"

	Dane	Brown	Walworth	Sauk	Dodge
Months	41.5	38.5	36.1	62.2	51.4
Yes on "no aid in future"	63%	41%	58%	56%	50%

highest percentage (27 percent). Of course, there is a greater density of organizations in Dane County. The most popular organizations among AFDC recipients are social clubs and sports groups. In Dane County programs growing out of the War on Poverty had involved several women, too. Women were more likely to be involved in social groups, with relatively few reporting activities in such groups as political parties or labor unions. Only about half the women with children in school have been to a PTA meeting in three years, but over 70 percent did go to a program at the school in order to meet teachers during the same time. Approximately a quarter of the women reported taking part in some church activity other than services.

It is difficult to appraise the impact of frequent church attendance, but it does seem to be a feature in the lives of many women. The percentages reporting church attendance weekly or a few times a month are: Dane 46, Brown 58, Walworth 40, and Dodge 55. Lutheran and Roman Catholic were the religious preferences named most often.

In trying to piece together a picture of the social lives of women in the five counties, we found that women in Walworth County were the least likely to participate in activities and to go regularly to church services. In the other counties, most women were involved either in an organization or a church. Depending upon the implications attached to membership, it seems that most of our respondents were active in their communities. Since we earlier found that they usually had friends and relatives in their communities, the overall picture that emerges is one of involvement with society, not isolation. As compared to the Milwaukee AFDC population, the women in these five counties appear to be much more integrated.

We have looked briefly at the characteristics of AFDC recipients in six counties. It should be clear that stereotypes of black AFDC mothers who are new to Wisconsin, represent a second generation of public welfare dependents, and have had little or no normal family experience are quite inaccurate. Perhaps it is more accurate to consider the typical AFDC respondent as a woman not too different from the other mothers in her community except for her lack of a husband and her low level of income, although in Milwaukee she is more likely to be black.

PART TWO

Administration of
the AFDC Program

Chapter 3

INTAKE, DETERMINATION OF ELIGIBILITY, AND THE MEANS TEST

In September 1968 Wilbur J. Cohen, Secretary of Health, Education, and Welfare, made the following statement about the administration of eligibility in public assistance:

> It is an unnecessarily destructive process when the determination of eligibility involves the most detailed examination of one's needs and expenditures and indeed frequently seems to search into the intimate details of one's way of life. We could do a great deal toward protecting the dignity and self-respect of assistance recipients by moving from detailed budgeting to broad categories of allowances and to simplified determinations of income and resources.[1]

This criticism about the administration of the application process and particularly the means test in public assistance is not atypical, except perhaps in its restraint. For decades it has been the received learning that eligibility determinations in public assistance are vindictively administered, that inquiries extend unnecessarily into private areas of life, and that welfare applicants suffer deeply from this humiliating experience.[2] Yet one can search the literature in vain for systematic information on what the

---

[1] Statement of the Honorable Wilbur J. Cohen, Secretary of Health, Education, and Welfare, for the President's Commission on Income Maintenance Programs, September 13, 1968, at 10.

[2] For a classic statement on the alleged evils of the means test, see J. tenBroek and R. B. Wilson, *Public Assistance and Social Insurance—A Normative Evaluation,* 1 U.C.L.A. L. REV. 237, 264–67 (1954). For the historical functions of the means test, see, e.g., J. tenBroek, California's Dual System of Family Law: Its Origin, Development, and Present Status, 16 STAN. L. REV. (Nos. 2, 4) (1964) and 17 STAN. L. REV. (No. 4) (1965); M. Rosenheim, Vagrancy Concepts in Welfare Law, in LAW OF THE POOR (J. tenBroek ed. 1966) at 187.

President Nixon in his welfare message referred to the administration of intake as "costly investigations so bitterly resented as 'welfare snooping.'" President's message on welfare reform in committee on Ways and Means, President's Proposals for Welfare Reform and Social Security Amendments 1969, at 93, 98.

intake process and the means test consist of, what is being administered, and how welfare applicants think and feel about the experience.

In this chapter we will first describe the intake process and eligibility determination as set forth in state laws and administrative regulations. From this we will try to determine more precisely what is meant by the means test. Then we will turn to the recipients themselves.

STATE POLICY

State policy is set forth in the statutes and the State Department Manual in the form of administrative regulations. Some of the regulations are binding on the county departments of welfare and others are hortatory.[3]

---

[3] The Wisconsin statutes provide that the State Department of Health and Social Services "shall adopt rules and regulations, not in conflict with law, for the efficient administration of . . . aid to dependent children. . . ." WIS. STAT. ch. 49.50 (2) (1965). The Manual is issued pursuant to this statute. Whether or not a State Department regulation is binding on a county is a complex question. Certain areas of administration are to be decided at the state level and these regulations are binding. For example, the State Department has the authority to set statewide budgets, and state regulations covering the computation of the budget must be obeyed. Other areas are within the discretion of the county departments and state regulations here serve only as guides. For example, the statute says that, "The county agency may require the mother to do such remunerative work as in its judgement she can do without detriment to her health or the neglect of her children or her home. . . ." WIS. STAT. ch. 49.19 (6) (1965). State regulations set forth guidelines for the counties, but so long as the counties do not abuse their discretion they are not required to follow the state regulations. The enforceability of regulations also depends, to a large extent, on whether the substantive area has been quantified. For example, even though the State Department has the authority to set the budget rates for rents (and therefore its regulations governing the rent grant are binding), it decided to peg rents to prevailing rents in the localities. The State Department could set the rents for each county and these regulations would be binding. Instead, the State Department said that the counties are to set "reasonable" rents. Legally, this is a binding regulation. Practically, discretion has been delegated to the counties, and unless an abuse of discretion is shown, enforcement becomes problematic.

The above are just some obvious examples. There are many degrees of enforceability, which is true of many aspects of the legal system. See, generally, L. Friedman, *Legal Rules and the Process of Social Change,* 19 STAN. L. REV. 786 (1967); J. Handler, *The Role of Legal Research and Legal Education in Social Welfare,* 20 STAN. L. REV. 669, 678–79 (1968). In practice, however, or at least for the purpose of this paper, this problem is not very important and indeed for most of the regulations, a surface reading will indicate whether the regulations are intended to be binding or not.

The regulations covering the intake process are divided between "administrative methods" (procedures) and substance—what the caseworker has to find out in order to determine eligibility.[4] The "administrative methods" regulations urge the county departments of welfare to make the intake process as painless and as smooth as possible. The opportunity to apply for public assistance shall be "freely and easily accessible to everyone"; therefore "it is important that the county agency office be conveniently located" (preferably on the first floor), well marked, and with adequate waiting rooms and other amenities. Privacy, says the State Department of Public Welfare, is important; the client is entitled to it, but also it is "conducive to good client-worker relationships." The initial contact is thought to be very important for subsequent client attitudes, and the counties are asked to be careful in the selection of their receptionists and intake personnel. Whenever possible, a caseworker has the responsibility for taking the initial application. She has a duty to give clear explanations of the procedures, services, and functions of the agency. Applicants are not to be discouraged from signing the aid applications even if ineligibility is apparent. Signing of the application should take place at the first interview and should not be held up pending a home visit. (The home visit is made as soon as possible after the application has been initiated.)

The *substantive* areas of eligibility determination are: (1) the basis of the children's dependency; (2) residence; (3) the suitability of the parent or custodian; (4) employability of the mother; (5) financial resources; and (6) financial responsibility of relatives.

Deprivation of Parental Support

The statute defines a "dependent child" as one who has been deprived of parental support by the death, the continued absence from the home, or the physical or mental incapacity of a parent, or by the parent's unemployment. This study did not include dependency caused by unemployment or (with minor exceptions) incapacity.

The AFDC statute uses the criminal definition of abandonment:

> Any person who, without just cause, deserts or willfully neglects or refuses to provide for the support and maintenance of his wife or child under 18 years (legitimate or born out of wedlock) in desti-

---

[4] Unless otherwise indicated, all quotations from the regulations are from the State Department of Health and Social Services Manual, Sections II and III, Revised 2–1–68. Statutory references and quotations, unless otherwise indicated are to the Wisconsin AFDC statute, Wis. Stat. ch. 49.19 (1965, *as revised*).

tute or necessitous circumstances shall be fined not more than
$500, or imprisoned not more than 2 years, or both.[5]

The wife must charge the father with abandonment as a condition of
eligibility. Moreover, the charge must be criminal; a civil action for support does not satisfy this eligibility requirement. On the other hand, eligibility may be recognized if there is a court order for support which is
unenforceable or if support from the father is insufficient to meet the needs
of the family. At the time of this study abandonment or nonsupport had
to have occurred at least three months prior to the granting of aid; the
three-month requirement has since been eliminated.

Eligibility based on divorce or legal separation requires an actual
court judgment. In addition, the mother "must use all the provisions of the
law to compel her husband to adequately support the child for whom aid
is sought." A nonsupport warrant is not required if it can be shown that
the husband is unable to give support.

A wife may be eligible for AFDC if her husband has been sentenced
to jail for at least three months (this time period has also been dropped).
The wife may still be eligible if her husband is on parole if the condition
of parole (or probation) is the "principal factor" limiting the husband's
ability to support the family.

AFDC is available for unmarried mothers as long as the alleged father is not a member of the household and other eligibility requirements
are met. The mother is required to name the alleged father of the child
if she has this knowledge; this is an absolute condition of eligibility.

Residence

At the time of the study, the basic residency requirement was one
year.[6] If the child for whom aid is sought is less than one year old, the
parent or relative with whom it is living must have resided in the state
for one year just preceding the birth of the child. The mother of an un-
born child must have resided in the state for one year immediately preceding the application. If a resident leaves the state but returns within a
year, the residency requirement is still satisfied. However, since the time
of the study, all this has been changed. The residency test now is whether
the applicant intends to make Wisconsin her home.

---

[5] WIS. STAT. ch. 52.05 (1) (1965).

[6] Since the time of this study, deviational residency tests have been declared
unconstitutional. *Shapiro* v. *Thompson*, 394 U.S. 618 (1969). See M. K. Rosenheim, *Shapiro* v. *Thompson: "The Beggars Are Coming to Town,"* 1969
SUPREME COURT REV. 303.

Suitability of the Parent or Custodian

The statute requires that the person having the custody of a child must be a "fit and proper person to have such custody." However, AFDC cannot be denied on this ground unless there has been a court determination of lack of fitness. If there is evidence of child neglect, the agency has a statutory duty to file a petition in juvenile court or to refer the case to a "proper child protection agency."

Employability of the Mother

Under the statute, a county agency can "require the mother to do such remunerative work as in its judgment she can do without detriment to her health or the neglect of her children or her home." The state regulations, in an attempt to guide the county caseworkers, include an extended discussion of the employment problems of AFDC mothers. In no event should a mother work if the children will be neglected or poorly cared for. Beyond this, there has to be a "careful evaluation" of the "total situation." As part of eligibility determination, "the work potential of all employable family members is discussed and evaluated. Older children [too] may need job counseling."

Financial Resources

With some exceptions, the extent of need is the difference between public assistance standards and the resources actually available to the applicant. "In evaluating resources, it is necessary to consider all income which the client is receiving, resources which could be made available to him without undue hardship or loss, and goods and services he receives or can receive without cost to him." And to implement these standards, "the agency shall assist the client in developing potential resources which can be utilized for his support. After consideration of all the available resources, a plan shall be worked out between the agency and the applicant in order that the resources may be fully utilized."

There are many specific regulations on how to calculate the value and interest in real and personal property. Home ownership is permissible provided the cost of maintenance does not exceed the rental which the family would otherwise have to pay for living quarters. Recipients may have personal property (e.g., clothing, household appliances, personal belongings) of "reasonable value in actual use." Liquid assets, including the cash value of life insurance, may not exceed $500 per family. Automobiles may not be kept unless they are essential, and then the wholesale value may not exceed $500.

There is special emphasis on support from the absent parent. In evaluating potential resources, the regulations provide for including court-ordered support that can in fact be enforced. Related to the determination of need is the federal statutory requirement that in cases of desertion or abandonment, notice be given to law enforcement officials (hereafter referred to as NOLEO).[7] State law also requires that law enforcement officials be notified of any parent who neglects to support a child or who fails to comply with a court order concerning support payments.[8] Thus, in the case of unwed mothers, referral is to be made to the district attorney, who decides whether "appropriate" legal action should be taken to establish paternity or provide support for the child. The agency is supposed to explain to applicants the legal obligation of parents to support their children and to "help parents recognize the available resources of law enforcement officials and courts, and the responsibility for cooperating with these officials." The explanation is to be made prior to the granting of assistance so that clients who object to NOLEO procedures can withdraw their applications.

Responsible Relatives

Under state law, parents, spouses, and children are legally responsible for the support of a dependent person. However, the position of the state department is that as part of social services for the client, "any relative, whatever the degree of relationship, is a potential resource to public assistance clients." "Resource" is broader than financial contributions; it includes various kinds of family services, help, and support. The regulations go on:

> To determine ability to support in whole or in part, and interest in helping, information is secured from the client and/or the responsible relative when necessary. . . .

> The social worker shall secure from the client information concerning the relative's financial situation; his financial status, if known; any contribution or service he is presently giving; feelings and attitudes of client toward relative and relative toward client; the frequency and nature of the contacts between them; and any feelings about the required investigation of resources and collateral contacts.

---

[7] 42 U.S.C. 602 (*see* 402 (a)).
[8] WIS. STAT. 49.19 (4) (f).

Much stress is laid in the regulations on the importance of contacting absent fathers for purposes extending beyond obtaining support. The caseworker is to try to find out the reasons for the father's absence, what contributions to his children he can make other than financial support, and whether he may be in need of casework services. Moreover, the caseworker is to make an effort to have him recognize the importance of his role in the family.

Although unwed mothers also come under the responsible relatives provisions, the Manual, attempting to recognize the delicacy of their situation, provides that parents need not be contacted directly "if collateral sources determine that there is inability to support. However, if there is unwillingness by the unmarried mother to have her parents informed of her condition, and it is impossible to determine accurately their financial situation without informing them of the request for assistance, no aid can be granted under the AFDC program."

Finally, the regulations contain elaborate formulas for calculating how much responsible relatives should contribute, including contribution tables, allowances, and exemptions.

The laws and regulations governing the intake process and the means test thus delegate extremely wide powers of inquiry to the intake workers. Almost everything about the welfare client can be the official concern of the agency. In determining need, not only are all resources to be considered, but the agency is authorized to work out plans in order that "resources may be fully utilized." The agency may inquire into the value and actual use of personal property, and it has influence on the extent of law enforcement efforts against absent fathers. In administering the responsible relatives provisions, official authority extends not only to the possibility of support but also to the investigation of social relationships between the applicant and her relatives. Under the "fit and proper" rule, the agency has the authority to inquire into all matters that bear on the fitness of the parents and the suitability of the home. Concerning employment, there is authority to counsel the AFDC mother and her children into working even if they are reluctant to do so.

The extensive powers authorized at intake are part of the social service approach that was grafted onto the AFDC program by the 1966 and 1962 amendments to the Social Security Act. Services are to start at intake through what the State Department calls the *social study*—the process of "acquiring and organizing information pertinent to the client as a person, his situation and his needs." The development of the study, which is supposed to continue throughout the welfare experience, is according to the Manual, the primary tool for the provision of direct casework services.

The extensive substantive power to inquire is combined with an enormous amount of discretion in the hands of the caseworker. Some intake and means test rules are narrow and fixed; with rules of this type there is little or no discretion. For example, an unwed mother must name the father of the child if she has this knowledge. This is absolute. But such rules are few, and generally it is up to the caseworker to decide within very broad limits how much and in what manner she wants to question and investigate finances,[9] responsible relatives, the suitability of the home, employability, and the more intimate aspects of the applicant's life. It is the existence of this power—both its substantive scope and its discretionary double-edged character—that causes so much concern in the literature about welfare administration, and in particular in discussions of the administration of the means test.[10]

WHAT IS THE MEANS TEST?

The means test is a condition of eligibility. But when we speak of the means test, do we intend to include some or all of the conditions of eligibility? For example, proposals to reform intake stress a simplified method for determining an applicant's income and resources. But are income and resources to be the sole condition of eligibility or are other conditions still to apply—for example, employability or "fit and proper" requirements? The extent to which gatekeeping conditions apply, as part of a means test, depends upon the purposes of the AFDC program, and these purposes have never been clearly specified.

At the very least, the means test must include inquiries about resources and needs. Resources include current available income (which requires a definition) and can encompass liquid assets (in many different forms), assets that can be liquified fairly easily, and the potential support of fathers and relatives. If the purpose of the aid program is to give assistance only when the mother is unable to obtain adequate support from the father, then his potential resources and her efforts to obtain these resources become part of the means test. If she fails to satisfy the requirements, she has an unused resource and may be judged ineligible.

Resources can also include the earning potential of the members of

---

[9] The caseworker is required to investigate and verify some types of financial information—for example, bank accounts, employment, etc. But generally it is up to the caseworker or the agency to decide whether to accept the client's word as to her financial situation.

[10] In addition to the authorities cited *supra* note 2, see J. F. Handler and M. K. Rosenheim, *Privacy in Welfare: Public Assistance and Juvenile Justice,* 31 LAW & CONTEMP. PROB. (No. 2) (1966); C. Reich, *Individual Rights and Social Welfare: The Emerging Legal Issues,* 74 YALE L.J. 1245 (1965).

the family, that is, anticipated earnings. If the purpose of the aid program is to give money to unemployables, then capacity to work becomes part of the means test in that it is part of the applicant's resources. The test of employability can range from the mother's free choice of whether she wants to work or not to requiring a mother to take a job suited to her skills with a reasonably satisfactory day-care plan, or requiring a retraining course, and so forth. Any or all of these can become part of the means test in the sense that failure to fulfil the requirement may result in a determination of ineligibility.

Defining the criteria of need is also complex. Since benefit levels are related to family size, one must define the family. The matter becomes increasingly complex once it is decided that the aid program is going to support certain types of expenditures but not others—for example, education costs but not high rents.

Finally, although the means test functions as a gatekeeper, its application is not restricted to the intake stage. Its administration extends from the time of application until the recipient leaves the program. At any time, resources and needs can change and eligibility can be lost.

In sum, one cannot tell what the means test is from an inspection of the Wisconsin laws and regulations. The purposes of the AFDC program are not clear and many of the regulations are too loosely drawn. One cannot tell the actual relationship between areas of investigation and eligibility.

The difficulty of talking about the means test is increased when one looks at it from the client's point of view. If it is analytically impossible to extract the content of the means test from the laws and regulations, how can a client ever be sure that an area of inquiry will not somehow be related to eligibility?

For purposes of discussion, then, the definition of the means test has to be somewhat arbitrary. Since a great deal of attention is focused on the intake process, it is reasonable to call the means test the determination of eligibility at intake. We can also reasonably assume that at its core the means test includes the client's income and resources; it is unlikely that some form of income and resources test for public assistance will be abandoned in the near future.

In this study we have chosen to examine other intake items. Although some or all of them can now be considered part of the means test, it is often proposed that these items should not be determinants of eligibility. The six items tested, in addition to (1) the client's financial resources and property, were: (2) the "responsible relatives" provisions; (3) the use of law enforcement officials; (4) employment; (5) marriage plans; and (6) child care. To what extent were the six areas subjects of inquiry and what was the impact on the clients?

WHAT IS ASKED AT INTAKE?

The respondents were asked whether, at the time of their first interview, the caseworker asked them "a lot of questions" concerning the six items. Table 3.1 tabulates, by county, the percentages of AFDC respondents who reported caseworker activity per item.

What accounts for the responses in Table 3.1? Undoubtedly, some welfare clients forgot what was discussed at the first interview. It is not unreasonable to imagine welfare applicants so preoccupied with income maintenance that discussions about other areas simply did not register. But we found that reported inquiry was not related to length of time on the program. In fact, in some counties, for a few of the items (child care, marriage plans) AFDC mothers who had been in the program longer tended to report more inquiries than those who had been in the program for a shorter time.

Our first principal conclusion is that, at least at intake, the primary focus of the means test is on the income-maintenance aspects of the program—financial resources and responsible relatives. The stress is on basic financial eligibility rather than on NOLEO and the more elusive and potentially more sensitive social service aspects of AFDC. We will discuss the reasons for this in the concluding sections of this chapter.

For the most part, inquiries were not related to obvious client characteristics. Although one would expect fewer employment inquiries to be made of older women than of younger, there was little relationship between age and employment questions. In five of the six counties there was no relationship between the age of the applicant and inquiries about child care; in the sixth county (Dane) we found that younger women reported fewer discussions about child care than did older women. We expected to find inquiries about marriage plans related to marital status—that unmarrieds would report the most inquiries, followed by the divorced, separated, deserted, and married, in that order. The hypothesis was supported in Milwaukee, but not in the other five counties. On the other hand, for all counties, discussions about marriage plans were related to age, as expected—more younger than older women reported such inquiries.

There was no difference in the administration of NOLEO among divorced, separated, and unmarried applicants, whereas married applicants reported fewer inquiries than the other groups. This is reasonable, since NOLEO is less applicable for this group. Also, it is interesting to note that unmarried mothers do not report more NOLEO pressure than other women.

Was administration of intake related to race? In Milwaukee County (the only county where there were sufficient blacks to make comparisons), inquiry about financial resources and employment was not related to race.

TABLE 3.1. INTAKE: THE MEANS TEST ACTIVITY

"*At the time of your first interview with the welfare department (for the most recent AFDC experience), did the caseworker ask you a lot of questions about. . . .*"

Item	Total possible respondents	Total percent	Percent responding "yes"[a]					
			Milwaukee	Dane	Brown	Walworth	Sauk	Dodge
1. Your financial resources and property	736	84.0	85.6	81.4	94.9	85.3	86.5	78.9
2. Financial support by parents or relatives	744	45.5	65.5	68.0	65.4	71.1	59.6	66.7
3. NOLEO	609	39.1	53.6	41.0	31.4	54.4	43.6	20.8
4. Possibility of a job for either you or your children	735	43.8	44.1	39.1	54.2	45.3	42.6	40.4
5. Possible marriage plans	728	66.5	47.3	37.8	31.9	23.4	36.4	36.4
6. The care you give to your children	737	45.1	48.7	39.3	47.6	54.4	63.5	41.7

[a] For some respondents, not all the items listed were applicable to their situation. Therefore, the total percentages listed in cols. 2–8 are based on the number of respondents for whom the item is relevant. For example, the questions about financial resources and property were relevant to 736 out of the 766 in the sample. And of that 736, 84.0% felt they were asked "a lot of questions" about that item.

Race appeared to be related to inquiry for the four other items. More black than white applicants reported inquiries concerning NOLEO, possible marriage plans, and child care; and the reverse was true concerning responsible relatives. However, the relationships were either weak (e.g., responsible relatives) or attributable to client characteristics other than race. For example, more blacks than whites reported inquiries about possible marriage plans, but black applicants were generally younger than white applicants and this is related to the different responses. Similarly, more whites than blacks said that they were married, and NOLEO was used less for marrieds than the other groups of applicants.

Our second general conclusion is that the administration of the six intake items was not rationally related to client characteristics. Rather, administration appeared to be highly discretionary, particularly with regard to the more service-oriented items. Areas of caseworker activity were the result of either county welfare department policy or individual caseworker initiative. For example, the Brown County caseworkers seemed to stress detailed inquiry into financial resources more than those in other counties. Dodge County caseworkers usually did not apply NOLEO. There was more concern with marriage plans in Milwaukee than in Walworth, but then Milwaukee had more unmarrieds than Walworth.

REACTIONS OF CLIENTS TO INTAKE

One can posit three different client reactions to the intake process. Means test administration invades a welfare applicant's sense of privacy; the applicants feel this, and resent it. The opposite would be that the social and psychological events requiring people to apply for assistance so humiliate them and produce such anxiety that welfare applicants lose or repress feelings of privacy and outrage. Personal disasters, such as the breakup of one's marriage or the birth of an illegitimate child, and the failure of attempts to go it alone, combined with extreme economic insecurity, produce a very frightened and dependent person. A third position would be one in which applicants feel an invasion of privacy but not a sense of outrage; they think their personal rights are being invaded but that they have no right to complain—invasion is the price one has to pay when going on welfare.[11]

---

[11] The literature that deals with the means test describes various reactions of welfare applicants. See authorities cited *supra* note 2. For two empirical studies, see S. Briar, *Welfare from Below: Recipients' Views of the Public Welfare System,* in LAW OF THE POOR (J. tenBroek ed. 1966) at 46; H. Yahr and R. Pomeroy with L. Podell, Studies in Public Welfare: Effects of Eligibility

TABLE 3.2. RESPONDENTS' ATTITUDES TOWARD CASEWORKER QUESTIONS AT INTAKE

"To what degree were you bothered or annoyed by questions on . . ."

	Financial Resources	Relatives' Support	NOLEO	Job (Self, Children)	Child Care	Marriage Plans
Percent of all respondents reporting a lot of questions by the caseworker	84.0%	66.5%	45.1%	43.8%	47.5%	39.1%
Degree bothered by questions[a]						
Very much	11.1	18.7	23.4	11.6	8.7	17.1
Moderately	7.8	11.5	9.5	6.1	7.0	6.8
Only slightly	11.8	10.8	11.7	10.3	9.3	8.6
Not at all	69.3	59.0	55.4	71.9	75.1	67.5
Number reporting questions at intake	612	471	325	310	345	234

"Do you feel that any of the questions . . . were about personal matters that should not concern the agency?"

	Financial Resources	Relatives' Support	NOLEO	Job (Self, Children)	Child Care	Marriage Plans
Percent answering yes[a]	21.7% (609)	35.1% (476)	[b]	9.1% (309)	22.0% (345)	32.6% (233)

[a] Percentages are calculated on the numbers who were questioned.
[b] The survey instrument did not include NOLEO.

The respondents who reported being questioned on the various intake items were asked whether they were "bothered or annoyed" by the questions, and whether they thought that any of the questions "were about personal matters that should not concern the agency." In each of the intake areas, then, we sought to find out whether and to what extent two types of client reactions had been felt—a sense of invasion of privacy as well as a sense of outrage.

But to what extent did applicants object at all to the administration of intake? Comparing the responses across the six intake items (Table 3.2), negative attitudes were highest for NOLEO and responsible relatives and lowest for financial resources, employment, and child care. On the three least bothersome items—financial resources, employment, and child care—the questions concern the affairs of the applicant only. With re-

Investigation on Welfare Clients, Center for the Study of Urban Problems, Bernard M. Baruch College, The City University of New York (mimeo., n.d.).

sponsible relatives and NOLEO, the inquiry extends to other people, which may cause embarrassment or even painful and dangerous experiences. Moreover, there is the element of legal coercion involved.[12] Attitudes concerning inquiries about possible marriage plans fell in between. The marriage question touches on what may be embarrassing relations with others (for example, the applicant may fear agency contact with a boyfriend), but it lacks the compulsion aspects of NOLEO and responsible relatives.

On the "core" item of the means test—questions about the applicant's financial resources and property—about 80 percent of the respondents did not sense an invasion of privacy and were either not bothered or "only slightly" bothered. In Dane County these proportions rose to 90 percent.

Negative attitudes ran considerably higher concerning responsible relatives. In all counties between 10 and 15 percent more respondents reacted negatively to this part of the means test, as compared to inquiries about financial resources.

Almost half of the respondents said that they were required to go to the district attorney's office to do something about obtaining child support payments from the father of the child. What they did at the office is tabulated in Table 3.3.

Although our numbers are very small, the clients who had to file a paternity suit had the highest proportion who were "very bothered." Signing a warrant or a complaint, etc., or going to court, on the other hand, seemed to have the opposite effect; most said that they were not bothered at all.

There was some indication that negative attitudes about NOLEO might have been related to county administration. Brown and Dodge Counties used NOLEO considerably less often than the other counties, and when they did use it, there was less negative reaction. Walworth showed a high use of NOLEO but a particularly high incidence of negative attitudes, perhaps due to the practices of the local district attorneys' offices.

Employment is the one area where feelings of privacy and annoyance with the questions diverge. Although comparable proportions of the respondents in each of the six counties felt bothered or annoyed by these questions, very few thought that employment possibilities were a personal matter that should not concern the agency. Most of the respondents had worked before applying for AFDC and, as we shall see in Chapter 6, most would prefer to work rather than to continue on the program. Questions about job possibilities were not perceived as a privacy issue.

---

[12] Discussions about child care could also lead to legal compulsion if the welfare agency thinks that there is neglect, but, in comparison with eligibility conditions such as obtaining support from relatives and the father, fear of legal compulsion would probably be both rare and remote.

TABLE 3.3. WHAT RESPONDENTS DID IN DISTRICT ATTORNEY'S OFFICE IN REGARD TO NOLEO[a]

Action	Total	Milwaukee	Dane	Brown	Walworth	Sauk	Dodge
Sign warrant, complaint abandonment papers, name father	51.2%	59.7%	22.5%	48.1%	67.4%	50.0%	58.3%
Swear out paternity suit	5.7	5.0	14.1	3.7	0	0	0
Lie detector test	3.0	0	12.7	0	0	4.2	3.0
Go to court	11.3	11.9	7.0	3.7	16.3	16.7	16.7
Fill out forms (unspecified)	9.8	6.3	18.3	3.7	16.3	8.3	0
Answer questions (unspecified)	17.9	18.2	28.2	7.4	7.0	25.5	0
Other	17.6	3.8	19.7	51.9	27.9	41.7	25.0
Number that went to district attorney's office in each county	336	156	71	27	43	24	12

[a] Percentages equal more than 100 because some respondents listed more than one thing they were required to do at the office.

Overall, questions about child care produced less negative feeling than any of the other items. Although this area lies at the very core of the family, child care is a normal part of conversations between women, and this may account for the lack of negative attitudes.

CONCLUSIONS

According to our respondents (but keeping in mind the limitations of generalizing from this particular sample), most of the intake process is devoted to the more central means test items—financial resources and relatives' support. For those who are eligible the rest of the interview is probably spent on calculating the budget rather than inquiring about employment, child care, social life, and marriage plans.

These findings are consistent with other characteristics of AFDC administration which we touched upon briefly in the Introduction and concerning which we go into detail in subsequent chapters. The one thing that has to be done at intake for those who are legally eligible is to compute need and the level of benefit. This is what the applicants are most interested in and it is often a difficult and complicated matter. In view of pressure of business, the short time available to process the application, and the lack of involvement on the part of the caseworkers, why not do only that which has to be done and which is the most important part of the program anyway? Even for caseworkers who care, more sensitive and elusive matters can be taken up later during the home visits.

The concentration on client resources explains, in part, the overall lack of negative feelings on the part of the clients to the intake process. When sensitive issues were raised, about one out of three applicants said that they were upset. If these areas had been raised more often during intake, the responses of the recipients to the whole process would have been quite different.

But what explains the general lack of bother as to inquiries concerning resources? Were the clients telling the truth? Were they afraid of reprisals from the welfare department? In the Introduction we discussed some of the reasons why we are inclined to think that the responses were accurate. Furthermore, when clients had been asked questions at intake that they did not like, they were apparently willing to say so, and there is no reason to think that they would fear reprisals for some negative responses and not others. The response to intake was fairly uniform throughout the entire sample. If there was fear of reprisal, one would think that it would be somehow related to different client characteristics as well as differences in welfare agencies. But responses were not related to either variable; generally speaking the results in Milwaukee County, with its mostly urbanized ghetto welfare population, did not differ much from the results in the middle-sized and rural counties. In addition, as pointed out in the Introduction, these responses to intake were similar to the findings of the New York study.[13]

The responses, it seems to us, also fit with what else we know about welfare recipients. When people apply for welfare, they have come from an adult life of insecurity and, just prior to welfare, a social and economic calamity. In Professor Briar's terms, when applicants apply for welfare, they are "on the edge of disaster." In his study of recipients in California Briar found that applicants come not as rights-bearing citizens claiming

---

[13] It was also pointed out in the Introduction that the New York authors thought that the pressure of caseloads and the stress on financial matters probably prevented inquiry into areas that would upset clients, and that this may have accounted for lack of negative feelings toward eligibility investigations.

benefits to which they are entitled, but as suppliants. As one of his recipients said, "You are going to them for money . . . *they* are supporting you."[14] Briar's respondents were passive and grateful. In this frame of reference the responses to intake ring true, even if we would prefer applicants to be rights-bearing citizens.

Finally, the respondents displayed a discriminating attitude. They objected least to inquiries about their own resources and employment. The applicants were less accepting of inquiries that went beyond this range, such as support from relatives and other personal matters.

The interpretation of these data depends on one's values. The percentages alone do not tell us whether the administration of intake and the means test is good or bad or whether policies and programs ought to be changed or not. Questions about noneconomic matters (e.g., child care and marriage)—the potentially prying, intrusive kind—were asked of fewer than half the respondents. The same is true for employment and the NOLEO requirement. Some would argue that not much prying goes on. For others, subjecting even one welfare applicant to this sort of thing is bad enough. Similar issues are raised concerning the findings about negative attitudes. The means test may still be considered undesirable even if its administration does not upset most welfare recipients.

If one of our policy reform goals is to make the welfare system less painful to applicants, then these data point to the possibility of a decent intake process. Most of the negative attitudes that we found could probably be reduced considerably by the elimination of NOLEO and the relative support provisions; this is where the real stress occurs at intake. The irreducible minimum of any future means test would involve a fairly routine, not-very-probing inquiry into the applicant's income and resources, such as the self-declaration system.[15] Contrary to popular belief, inquiry here

---

[14] Briar, *supra* note 11.

[15] On July 1, 1969, "the declaration method in determination of eligibility for financial and medical assistance" for AFDC applicants (as well as other public assistance categories) was supposed to be made mandatory on the states. Memorandum, Department of Health, Education, and Welfare, Social and Rehabilitation Service, Assistance Payments Administration, October 30, 1968. However, the date has now been postponed. The self-declaration method (as it is called in Wisconsin) requires the client to fill out a form containing basic eligibility questions which in general the agency is to accept at face value. "Additional substantiation or verification is to be sought . . . when the statements of the applicant or recipient are incomplete, unclear, or inconsistent, or where other circumstances in the particular case would indicate to a prudent person that further inquiry should be made." *Id.* Some of the purposes of this reform are: (a) to reduce the intake questions to what is essential for eligibility, according to state and federal law; (b) to rationalize and streamline welfare administration; and (c) to preserve the applicant's dignity and self-respect

appears not to be a significant source of irritation. Using the same general approach, the elimination of inquiries concerning the family and the home, which are now eligibility conditions or quasi-conditions, would also improve matters with applicants. Clients are not upset with questions about employment, perhaps for reasons peculiar to Wisconsin, to be explored in Chapter 6.

The crucial question will be the quality of administration. The Wisconsin data show that intake procedures with a broad substantive reach need not necessarily be very obnoxious to recipients when officials have too much to do, or are not interested in matters other than income and resources. On the other hand, even a simplified means test restricted to income and resources can be vindictively administered by hostile, suspicious officials.

---

by trusting her to give honest answers and sparing her the indignities and shame of investigations.

The declaration system is already in operation in varying degrees in several parts of the country, including about 31 counties in Wisconsin, on an experimental basis. The Wisconsin form, which can be filled out at home or at the agency, with or without agency or professional help, is six pages long and covers the basic items such as age, residence, marital status, reason for dependency (e.g., divorced), assets, and resources of those for whom assistance is sought and some special needs (e.g., whether laundry is done at home). The agency is to accept the applicant's statements concerning age, residence, assets, resources, relationship to a child, and absence of a parent, "without further verification, unless there is serious doubt of the reliability of the information based on information available to the agency." Wisconsin State Department of Health and Social Services, memo.

At the present time it is difficult to assess what would be the impact of this reform on the responses to the kinds of questions raised in this paper. There is great variety in the application of the declaration system. In Wisconsin, even under a declaration system, the laws pertaining to NOLEO, responsible relatives, the suitability of the home, and employability are still on the books. It is unclear how questions concerning these matters are to be handled. One effect of the reform may be merely to *postpone* inquiries concerning these matters until after initial eligibility has been determined. This seems to be the case with responsible relatives. The State Department instructions read: "Since primary emphasis will be placed on using relatives as a social resource, ability of responsible relatives to support will be explored during the social study. Contact with responsible relatives as a financial resource will only be pursued when information from the applicant recipient indicates the appropriateness and desirability of this course of action." *Ibid.* The amount of administrative discretion in implementing this provision should be apparent. Stricter guidelines have been set up concerning investigations, but again, one cannot predict the impact. We lack information on the incidence and type of investigations that now occur, and the regulations do have loopholes.

Chapter 4

THE BUDGET

Income maintenance is the core of the AFDC program. Beyond all else, the most basic need of the welfare client is economic. How and to what extent this need is handled bears on practically every policy issue of the program. And for this reason, some of the harshest criticisms of public assistance concern the administration of AFDC budgets.

The following are some of the major criticisms:

1. The computation of the basic budgets is very complicated and is subject to frequent changes. Caseworkers themselves frequently fail to figure the budgets correctly; they also fail to explain the reasons for the budget, as well as the changes, to the clients. The result is that the system appears to the clients mysterious, discretionary, and arbitrary.

2. The usual approach of AFDC is to set basic budgets at minimum levels of subsistence and then provide a program of extra allowances for special needs or exceptional circumstances. In some states, such as Wisconsin, the special grants provisions are quite liberal, at least as they appear on the books. Nevertheless, it is claimed that the success of these programs is largely nullified because caseworkers do not advise clients on what is available or they discourage clients from asking for extra monies. Furthermore, the system itself requires the client to ask, justify, and in fact beg for items that are really necessities, the things that other people in our affluent society enjoy without question. The result of this system is the humiliation and degradation of welfare clients.

3. A basic principle established by federal law was that AFDC assistance be in the form of a money payment and that the client have freedom of choice in spending it. One of the purposes of this requirement was to remove the stigma thought to be attached to assistance in kind. It is claimed, however, that in fact there is extensive caseworker supervision over how clients spend the money payment because budgets are calculated at very low levels, are changed often, and special needs have to be justified. Thus the caseworker does in fact review how the money is spent.

4. Budget administration of this character gives the caseworker extensive discretionary control over the welfare client and places the client in a very dependent, powerless, and resentful position vis-à-vis the case

worker. It is in fact a coercive relationship which is further complicated by the rehabilitative or social service component of AFDC. This social service component gives the caseworker extensive authority to inquire into and attempt to change the noneconomic aspects of the AFDC family. It is claimed, however, that a social service relationship cannot be built on what is already a coercive relationship, and that the result is a further invasion of the privacy of welfare clients. This is one reason why it is argued that social services must be separated from income maintenance.

These are some of the more serious charges made against the administration of AFDC budgets. First we will examine the Wisconsin state policies and then we will turn to the clients themselves.

STATE POLICY

The budget is based on the difference between the client's resources and her needs. Need is calculated on statewide standards of living established by the State Department.[1] Because both needs and resources fluctuate with changing circumstances, budget and eligibility are always subject to review.

The budget for the AFDC family is separated into three parts: (1) combined allowance, (2) shelter, and (3) special need items.

The combined allowance covers food, clothing, personal expenses, fuel, utilities, regular school expenses, and household supplies. It is reduced when fuel and/or utilities is included in the rent or other shelter cost. The allowance is a statewide standard. At the time of this study the monthly allowance for AFDC was as given in Table 4.1.

Modifications of the combined allowance can be made for such things as special education costs, or for clothing or for personal expense adjustments such as those caused by the hospitalization of a family member.[2]

The shelter allowance includes rent and expenses related to property ownership (e.g., taxes, mortgage payments, property insurance, minor up-

---

[1] The data in state policy are from the regulations of the State Department of Health and Social Services Manual, Chap. III, *Need Determination*. Unless otherwise indicated, all quotations in this Chapter are from Chap. III.

[2] If clothing and personal adjustments have to be made, the rates per month are:

	Clothing	Personal
Adult (not in an institution)	$7	$5
Child aged 13–20	9	3
6–12	8	2
0–5	5	2

TABLE 4.1. COMBINED MONTHLY ALLOWANCES
FOR AFDC FAMILIES[a]

Number of persons in assistance group	Combined allowances			
	Family[b]	If fuel is provided	If all utilities are provided[b]	If both fuel and utilities are provided[b]
1	$ 63	$ 51	$ 55	$ 43
2	99	87	91	79
3	126	114	118	109
4	149	137	141	129
5	187	171	177	161
6	217	201	207	191
7	248	232	238	222
8	275	259	265	249
9	304	288	294	278
10	329	313	319	303

11 and over add $30 per additional person to the appropriate allowance for 10 persons

[a] Effective July 1, 1967.
[b] To the above allowance add $8 for each child aged 13 through 20; deduct $9 for each child aged 5 and younger.

keep and repairs). Home ownership is allowed if the cost does not exceed "a fair rental for modest housing according to community standards." This rule is a guideline since "absolute compliance will not always be possible." The homeowning family is to be allowed $4.00 per month for minor upkeep and repairs. The rental allowance is for the actual rent that must be paid, but "the cost shall not exceed a fair rental for modest housing according to community standards." Counties can set rent maximums, subject to state review, if they are "realistic." They can also budget less than the actual rent if the rent is considered "excessive," but in this event the agencies have to budget "at least the amount of rental of modest housing."

Special need items are for "unusual needs which are not common to all recipients but are requirements to meet special circumstances of some." According to state policy, these items "are as vital to some clients as the basic need items. Careful consideration of the circumstances of each client determines which special items are needed." There are twenty-three special need items applicable to AFDC families. Some items are to bring families up to minimum standards of living—clothing, furniture, appliances, major repairs. Others are for essentials that are special or unusual because of the particular circumstances of the families—money for laundry, errands, snow shoveling, and housekeeping services will be available for recipients who cannot perform these functions because of ill health. School fees, including transportation, will be paid by the agency. Although regular expenses for normal school supplies (pencils, paper, ink, notebooks, etc.) are included in the combined allowance, special need grants can be made for book and locker rentals, towel service, laboratory and shop fees, activity fees, materials and supplies for industrial arts, home economics, art instruction and "other similar classes." Adults may also get, as a special need, the cost of tuition, books, supplies, or "other miscellaneous needs."

If the parent has sufficient earnings, the cost of child care is deducted from the earnings. If the parent is not working and is in a training course "likely to lead to employment," or if child care is necessary because of the parent's physical or mental incapacity, the cost of care can be budgeted.

During the period of this study the average grant per AFDC family in the six counties, together with comparisons of the family's "poverty line," was shown in Table 4.2. The grant per family does not necessarily reflect the family's total income.[3] About 20 percent of the respondents say that they work. Children also work. Later in this chapter we will describe in detail the various ways in which welfare recipients can keep some or all of their earnings without reductions in their welfare grants. Then there is unreported income. At the present time we lack hard data on how much total income AFDC families in fact have.[4] But we are probably safe in assuming that many families do not reach, much less exceed, their poverty lines, and even these levels are not affluence.

The Wisconsin AFDC system is liberal in comparison with those of many other states. There is no maximum grant per family regardless of need; thus 100 percent of need is always budgeted.[5] In addition, average grants per family are comparatively high. As far as the Wisconsin AFDC families are concerned, the program combines regular support at fairly low levels (at least as compared to poverty line standards) with a system of flexibly administered grants to take care of exceptional needs. This combination, it is argued, places very dependent people in the hands of

---

[3] In addition to money payments, AFDC recipients are automatically eligible for Medicaid, which covers, without cost to the recipients, medical, dental, hospital, and drug costs.

[4] In an independent study Joseph Heffernan has found that 83.6 percent of the total income of AFDC recipients comes from their grant. However, half of the women had no income other than their grant. J. Heffernan, Adequate Grants and Work Incentives in Public Assistance, Children's Allowances, and Negative Tax Programs (Institute for Research on Poverty, University of Wisconsin, unpublished paper, 1969).

[5] This was true at the time of the study. In 1970 the Legislature provided that AFDC grants should not exceed 120 percent of the national average AFDC grant. This may result in granting only about 85 percent of need.

TABLE 4.2. AFDC GRANTS AND POVERTY GUIDELINES

County	Respondent's average grant	Average family size (mothers and children)	Average grant per family of all AFDC recipients (July 1967)	Average family size
Milwaukee	$173.23	4.3	$178.37	3.9
Dane	223.09	4.0	207.07	3.8
Brown	185.92	4.6	175.13	4.1
Walworth	197.89	4.3	186.61	4.2
Sauk	151.86	3.9	146.92	3.7
Dodge	186.00	4.7	175.08	4.0

Family size	(N)	Poverty guidelines of female-headed households[a]	Respondent AFDC grants on annual basis (July 1967 × 12)	Percentage of poverty line
1	7	$1595	$1737	109
2	122	2105	1540	72
3	147	2515	1949	78
4	141	3320	2207	66
5	88	3895	2543	65
6	85	4395	2819	64
7	35	5310[b]	2917	54
8	28		3040	
More than 8	25		3502	

[a] The figures used in this column represented the poverty line as described by M. Orshansky, *The Shape of Poverty in 1966, Social Security Bulletin* (March 1968).
[b] 7 or more in family.

caseworkers having a good deal of discretionary power. It is claimed that recipients in this position are either confused or ignorant about budget computations, are afraid to ask for "extras," or are resentful and humiliated by having to ask for the amenities that are available.

ATTITUDES OF THE RECIPIENTS

The state regulations urge the county caseworkers to explain the budget to the client. While the regulations do not explicitly impose on the caseworkers the duty of disclosing to the client the availability of special grants, they do say that special grants "are as vital to some clients as the basic need items" and that "careful consideration of the circumstances of each client determines which special items are needed." In this section we will examine the clients' points of view on how these policies are carried out.

In Table 4.3 we have tabulated by county the percentages of AFDC clients who reported having discussions with their caseworkers about their budgets, and the clients' reactions to these discussions. About three-fourths of the sample reported this activity, and there was not much variation among the counties. Very few of the clients were bothered or annoyed by the discussions. Over 40 percent found the discussions "usually" or "very" helpful. Only about one-fourth found them "not at all" helpful. There was some variation among the rural counties, suggesting differences in administrative methods.

Practically all the clients (85 percent) had had their aid grants changed during the time they were in the program. There was approximately one change per year for the recipients. Thus, despite the fact that budget and eligibility are supposed to be subject to constant review, aid grants were changed infrequently. The advantage of this pattern of administration is, of course, that it gives the AFDC family a measure of stability—they know how much they can count on from month to month. On

TABLE 4.3. DISCUSSIONS ABOUT BUDGET
AND CLIENT ATTITUDES

"Does your caseworker ever discuss your budget with you?"
"To what extent does it bother you to have your caseworker discuss your budget?"
"To what extent do you find these discussions on your budget helpful?"

	Milwaukee	Dane	Brown	Walworth	Sauk	Dodge	Total
Budget is discussed	68.9%	74.9%	73.3%	77.5%	77.2%	80.6%	73.2%
Number							(766)
Bothered?[a]							
Very much	8.3%	5.2%	8.1%	3.2%	2.3%	8.0%	6.5%
Moderately	7.5	4.5	3.2	1.6	11.4	2.0	5.4
Slightly	11.7	10.4	8.1	11.3	18.2	8.0	11.1
Not at all	72.8	79.9	80.6	83.9	68.2	82.0	77.1
Number	(206)	(134)	(62)	(62)	(44)	(50)	(558)
Helpful?[a]							
Very	25.7%	18.7%	25.4%	30.6%	11.4%	28.0%	23.6%
Usually	17.5	16.4	23.8	14.5	25.0	18.0	18.2
Some	28.2	37.3	30.2	24.2	47.7	34.0	32.1
Not at all	28.6	27.6	20.6	30.6	15.9	20.0	25.7
Number	(206)	(134)	(63)	(62)	(44)	(50)	(559)

[a] Percentages based on number who reported having discussions.

the other hand, the pressure of low AFDC budgets is supposed to be relieved by the flexibility of the system: individual family needs change and budgets should change accordingly. Unless we assume that needs did not change very much over the course of a year—probably an unlikely assumption—budgets were not administered flexibly.

How did the grant changes come about? For over 80 percent of those reporting grant changes, the changes were "more or less automatic" and the client did not "have to bring special facts to the attention of the caseworker" to bring the change about. The rest of the sample participated actively in about one grant change.

Finally, more than four-fifths of those who had changes in the aid grant said that their caseworkers did tell them the reasons for the changes and that they "usually understood why the changes were made." The tabulations for the aid grant changes are in Table 4.4.

Despite the apparent low levels of support and the infrequent grant changes, almost 60 percent of the respondents said that they could "manage

TABLE 4.4.   CHANGES IN THE AID GRANT, BY COUNTY

	Milwaukee	Dane	Brown	Walworth	Sauk	Dodge	Total
Aid grant changed	83.8%	83.8%	83.7%	85.0%	91.2%	90.3%	85.0% (766)
Number of times[a]							
1	36.4	40.0	25.0	40.0	33.3	25.9	34.9
2	31.4	24.8	22.2	18.5	15.7	31.5	26.3
3	20.7	22.1	26.4	16.9	23.5	20.4	21.6
4	7.0	6.2	16.7	6.2	5.9	9.3	7.9
5	2.1	3.4	4.2	9.2	9.8	3.7	4.1
6	1.2	2.1	2.8	4.6	7.8	5.6	2.9
7	1.2	1.4	2.8	4.6	3.9	3.7	2.2
Average number[b]	1.8	1.4	2.3	2.2	2.6	2.4	2.0
Times/year	0.8	0.7	1.2	1.2	1.0	1.2	1.0
Changes "more or less automatic"[a]	84.2	82.9	73.6	88.2	82.7	85.7	83.2
Caseworker told reasons[a]	82.9	96.6	94.4	83.8	96.2	94.6	89.4
Client understood reasons[a]	87.0	95.9	94.4	82.4	90.4	96.4	90.3

[a] Percentages based on those who had grant changes.

[b] "Average" is for the last three years or since coming on the program.

pretty well" on their budgets. Perhaps the level of grant is the explanation. The Sauk County recipients are least likely to report that they can manage pretty well, and that county has the lowest average grant per family. Managing may also be related to expectations, both of clients and of caseworkers. We will explore this question more fully in later chapters but will offer some tentative hypotheses here. In Dane County the percentage saying that they can manage was considerably lower than in Brown County, yet the average grant per family in Dane County is higher than in Brown County. The explanation for the difference may lie in the *expectations* of the respondents, which are shaped by their own personalities and social characteristics, as well as the nature of county administration. The Dane County department supposedly is more professionalized and more progressive than that of Brown County. The caseworkers in Dane County are more active in stimulating clients than the Brown County department. However, in Dane County university people and activists have contact with welfare clients, and communication among welfare recipients is better developed through welfare rights activities. These may produce less willingness to say one can manage pretty well on the grant.

The special need program is conceived of as a relatively flexible response to particular needs of clients. Two-thirds of the recipients had asked their caseworker for extra money for special needs, about two requests per respondent. However, clients made only about one request per year or less, showing that although a high proportion of clients have used the special needs provision program they have used it infrequently (Table 4.5).

What do the welfare clients ask for? In Table 4.6 we have tabulated the kinds of requests, the percentage of the requests granted, and the percentage of all the respondents that had received money for these items. More than half (56.2 percent) the requests made were for essential items:

TABLE 4.5. REQUESTS FOR SPECIAL NEEDS, BY COUNTY

	Milwaukee	Dane	Brown	Walworth	Sauk	Dodge	Total
Percent asking for special needs	74.5%	81.6%	52.3%	52.5%	49.1%	54.3%	67.9%
Number of requests per respondent[a]	2.3	2.5	1.4	1.3	1.5	1.3	2.0
Number of requests per year	1.1	1.3	0.7	0.6	0.6	0.9	1.0

[a] Average for the last three years or since coming on the program.

TABLE 4.6. SPECIAL ITEMS REQUESTED
AND PERCENT GRANTED

Item	Percent of clients requesting	Percent of requests granted	Percent of all clients granted special items
Clothing	31.4	52.9	16.7
Household goods, including appliances	46.3	76.9	35.8
Day care	10.3	82.3	8.6
Telephone	23.7	55.2	13.1
Transportation	20.8	73.6	15.4
Education or employment retraining	13.2	75.2	9.9
Extra or special food, including restaurant allowance	7.5	63.8	5.0
Extra for home necessities— utilities, rent, heat, etc.	24.8	68.4	17.0
School needs	17.9	65.0	11.7
Other	6.6	35.5	1.6
Number	(766)		(766)

clothing, household goods, special food, and home necessities, as compared to requests that might be classified as rehabilitation or social service: day care, telephone, transportation, education, employment retraining, and school needs.

The percentage of requests granted seems high; overall, two-thirds of all requests for extra money to meet special needs were granted. For some items, such as day care, it may be fairly assumed that no reasonable request was denied. However, despite the special need program's good record on requests granted, few welfare clients benefited from the program because so few requests were made. With the exception of the one-third of all respondents who benefited from household goods, the proportions of welfare clients receiving extra grants were very small. Practically 90 percent of the respondents received *nothing* extra for rehabilitative or social service needs. It would not be unfair to conclude that the special grants program is a paper program only. Welfare recipients existed primarily on their basic aid grants.

In Table 4.7 we have tabulated by county the percentage of clients requesting particular items, the percentage of the requests granted, and the percentage of respondents who had their requests granted. The results would seem to indicate real differences in county administration. Taking household items as an example, almost two-thirds of the Dane County

TABLE 4.7. SPECIAL GRANT ITEMS REQUESTED
AND PERCENT GRANTED, BY COUNTY

Items	Mil-waukee	Dane	Brown	Wal-worth	Sauk	Dodge	Total
Clothing							
Clients requesting	43.0%	36.3%	16.3%	17.5%	15.8%	12.9%	31.4%
Requests granted	50.0	69.2	42.9	42.9	33.3	25.0	52.9
Percent of all							
clients	21.5	25.1	7.0	7.5	5.3	3.2	16.7
Household							
Clients requesting	49.7	62.0	27.9	28.8	35.1	43.6	46.3
Requests granted	68.7	82.0	91.7	82.6	75.0	85.2	76.9
Percent of all							
clients	34.1	50.8	25.6	23.8	26.3	37.1	35.8
Day care							
Clients requesting	14.9	11.7	8.2	1.2	3.6	4.8	10.3
Requests granted	80.0	90.5	85.7	100.0	50.0	50.0	82.3
Percent of all							
clients	11.9	10.6	7.0	1.3	1.8	1.6	8.6
Telephone							
Clients requesting	23.2	33.5	8.2	20.0	22.8	24.2	23.7
Requests granted	48.6	80.0	14.3	31.3	15.4	66.7	55.2
Percent of all							
clients	11.3	26.8	1.2	6.3	3.5	16.1	13.1
Transportation							
Clients requesting	22.2	27.4	8.1	10.1	14.0	32.2	20.8
Requests granted	76.1	83.7	71.4	62.5	50.0	55.0	73.6
Percent of all							
clients	16.9	22.9	5.8	6.3	7.0	17.7	15.4
Education; employment							
Clients requesting	14.9	20.1	9.3	5.0	3.6	9.7	13.2
Requests granted	68.9	86.1	75.0	50.0	50.0	83.3	75.2
Percent of all							
clients	10.3	17.3	7.0	2.5	1.8	8.1	9.9
Special food							
Clients requesting	9.0	9.5	9.3	1.2	5.3	3.2	7.5
Requests granted	66.7	70.6	62.5	0.0	66.7	0.0	63.8
Percent of all							
clients	6.0	6.7	5.8	0.0	3.5	0.0	5.0
Home necessities							
Clients requesting	27.5	27.4	19.8	12.6	28.0	24.2	24.8
Requests granted	65.1	83.7	64.7	70.0	62.5	46.7	68.4
Percent of all							
clients	17.9	22.9	12.8	8.8	17.5	11.3	17.0
School needs							
Clients requesting	20.5	12.3	19.8	20.1	15.8	17.8	17.9
Requests granted	67.7	63.6	64.7	81.3	44.4	45.5	65.0
Percent of all							
clients	13.9	7.8	12.8	16.3	7.0	8.5	11.7
Number	(302)	(179)	(86)	(80)	(57)	(62)	(766)

recipients have asked for the special grants, and half the recipients have received a special grant for these items. Even though the granting-of-request rate is high for the other counties, the difference in results (clients receiving money) lies in the proportions of clients making requests. Clients have to be aware of the availability of this resource and ought not to be discouraged from making the requests. For most items in Table 4.7, the rural counties and Brown County were behind Dane and Milwaukee Counties in proportions of clients making requests. A request must be based on need—a client is not likely to request a special grant for an item unless she needs it. But although we have no data on actual needs, it seems highly unlikely that the differences in clients requesting items were based on differences in actual need. Twenty-five percent of the Dane County recipients had received extra money for clothing as compared to 7 percent of the Brown County recipients; for telephones, the percentages receiving money were 26.8 in Dane compared to 1.2 in Brown; for transportation, 22.9 to 5.8, and so on. In several of the counties the proportion of recipients actually receiving money for many items was so small it may fairly be said that the availability of special grants is meaningless.

Because two-thirds of all requests were granted, it is not surprising that the welfare recipients who made requests also thought that the caseworkers were usually or always fair "in granting or refusing requests." There was some variation, however, among the counties. The Sauk County respondents were less enthusiastic about their caseworker decisions than the respondents in the other counties, and one-fourth of the respondents in Milwaukee, Sauk, and Dodge Counties thought that their caseworkers were usually or always unfair (Table 4.8).

One-third of the respondents did not ask for special grants. We have tabulated their reasons in Table 4.9. For about one-third of those who had not asked, the fault would appear to lie with local administration; the respondent either did not know about the program (12.3 percent) or

TABLE 4.8. ATTITUDES TOWARD HANDLING OF REQUESTS FOR SPECIAL GRANTS, BY COUNTY[a]

Is Caseworker Fair?	Milwaukee	Dane	Brown	Walworth	Sauk	Dodge	Total
Always fair	23.1%	45.6%	46.7%	21.4%	7.1%	29.4%	31.0%
Usually fair	48.4	46.9	37.8	64.3	67.9	44.1	49.0
Usually unfair	16.9	3.4	6.7	9.5	21.4	20.6	12.3
Always unfair	10.2	0.7	8.9	2.4	3.6	2.9	6.1
No answer	1.3	3.4	0.0	2.4	0.0	2.9	1.9
Number	(225)	(147)	(45)	(42)	(28)	(34)	(521)

[a] Percentages are of only those who made requests.

TABLE 4.9.   REASONS WHY RESPONDENTS DID NOT ASK
FOR SPECIAL GRANTS

	Percent of those not asking	Percent of entire sample
Didn't know about program	12.3%	3.8%
Had no occasion; grant is ample	35.3	10.8
Determined to get by on basic grant	27.2	8.4
Feels agency would refuse	21.3	6.5
Hostility toward AFDC program	1.7	.5
No answer	2.1	.7
Number	(235)	(766)

felt that the agency would refuse (21.3 percent). It could also be argued
—we think persuasively—that fault also lies with county administration
for at least part of the 27.2 percent who did not ask because they were
determined to get by on the basic grant. This may be a misdirected sense
of independence and one contrary to the intentions of state policy, as set
forth in the Manual. The special grants program is for needs that either
have nothing to do with personal qualities of independence (e.g., special
food, extra clothing) or are designed to *encourage* independence (e.g., employment retraining). In other words, it should be the job of the caseworkers to encourage clients to make better use of the program.

There is little indication of complete ignorance of the program on the
part of the clients; only 3.8 percent of all respondents said they failed to
ask because they did not know about the program. Also, only 6.5 percent
said they thought the agency would refuse, and fewer than 1 percent were
so hostile to the program that they did not want to ask any more of it than
they had to. On the other hand, there is evidence that the purpose of the
special grant program was never really explained or understood by the
clients. Most of the respondents did know about the program; they did
request at least once; the request was usually granted; and they thought
that the caseworker decisions were fair. Unfortunately, we did not ask the
respondents why they failed to ask for additional items. Perhaps they
thought they would be refused, or were discouraged from making more
than one or two requests.

Administration of most respondents' budgets was very static. Aid
grant changes and special requests were infrequent. A small number, however, experienced more active and direct regulation; 7.7 percent of the
respondents said that at one time or another the caseworkers had expressed disapproval of the way they spent their money (twice, on the
average). Poor budgeting, spending too much for clothing or food, buying
"extras" such as toys, treats, or bicycles for children, and buying "extras"
for oneself were some practices of which caseworkers disapproved.

TABLE 4.10. CLIENT ATTITUDES TOWARD BUDGET
DISCUSSIONS AND CASEWORKER DISAPPROVAL[a]

Attitude	Budget Discussion	Caseworker Dis-approval of Client Expenditures
Discussions helpful?		
Very	23.6%	3.4%
Usually	18.2	18.6
Somewhat	32.1	16.9
Not at all	25.7	61.0
Number	(561)	(59)
Bothered or annoyed		
Very much	6.5%	35.6%
Moderately	5.4	15.3
Slightly	1.1	15.3
Not at all	77.1	33.9
Number	(558)	(59)

[a] Percentages apply to those reporting discussions.

When regulation began to bite, as with specific caseworker disapproval, client attitudes reflected it in a much higher proportion expressing negative or hostile feelings. In Table 4.10 we compare attitudes toward general budget discussions and attitudes toward caseworker disapproval of client expenditures.

Although the group experiencing caseworker disapproval resented regulation, 31 percent felt that they had to follow their caseworker's advice "most of the time" and another 10 percent said that they had to do so "all of the time." More positive client feelings toward general budget discussions may not indicate client agreement with what the caseworker wants. They may simply indicate a lack of active caseworker regulation, or that the budget discussions were casual and indifferent.

CONCLUSIONS

Though data in this chapter do not reach all the accusations made against the administration of AFDC budgets, a pattern emerges which does qualify even if it does not refute some of the criticisms.

Lack of change in money payments and supplements is the dominant feature of the administration of AFDC budgets. Basic budgets are relatively stable, with only one grant change per year, and with clients making only one special request per year. Our evidence indicates that most clients receive the same sized check month after month. This makes for predictability but little flexibility in income maintenance. Clients do not ask for much and do not get much. Despite the low levels of budgets and the slight impact of provisions for special needs, clients generally say that they are able to manage. Even so, when asked about the bad points of the AFDC program, respondents were far more likely to complain of the inadequacy of grants than of any other feature.

The system of special grants is functioning very poorly. Although county administration is liberal in granting requests, few clients make much use of special grants. Unless one assumes that need does not exist, it would appear that there is not adequate communication about this program. Some state authorities have emphasized that the program is, after all, one of *special* needs and imply that many people would not have such needs. This seems a rather curious emphasis since clothing, housekeeping necessities, and utilities are all a part of the special needs program.

The other outstanding finding is the absence of regulation and frequent client-caseworker interaction about budgets, the opposite of what is charged. Client attitudes toward the caseworkers in the administration of budgets are generally quite positive—they do not usually report feelings of coercion. We did find that as clients made more special requests or experienced more frequent changes in their basic aid grant, they were more likely to encounter caseworker disapproval of the way they handled money. This is not surprising; if budgets become topics for discussion more often, some conflict or regulation is more likely. But it should be remembered that for most clients the level of regulative activity is very low indeed. This would suggest that part of the price for little caseworker supervision or disapproval may have been the very low level of activity, or lack of responsiveness and flexibility of the system. Under the present structural arrangements, it is indeed possible that a more flexible, responsive system for handling money disbursement would result in the very thing which is anathema to the critics of the present system: a more coercive relationship between caseworker and client.

Chapter 5

SOCIAL SERVICES AND
THE CASEWORKER RELATIONSHIP

In 1956 and 1962 the Social Security Act was amended to add a social service component to the AFDC program. Under the amendments the states were authorized to furnish "rehabilitation and other services" to AFDC families "to help maintain and strengthen family life" and to help families "to attain or retain capability for the maximum self-support and personal independence."[1] Services were to be provided by skilled workers and other specialists. The Ad Hoc Committee on Public Welfare, formed in 1961 by Abraham Ribicoff, President Kennedy's Secretary of Health, Education, and Welfare, stated:

> Financial assistance to meet people's basic needs for food, shelter, and clothing is essential, but alone is not enough. Expenditures for assistance not accompanied by rehabilitative services may actually increase dependency and eventual costs to the community. The very essence of a vital program should be full use of all rehabilitative services including, but not confined to, provision of financial assistance. The ultimate aim is to help families become self-supporting and independent by strengthening all their own resources.[2]

Pressure to do something about public assistance, and particularly about AFDC, arose in the late 1950's when it became apparent that public assistance was not going to "wither away."[3] One of the important arguments made to Congress in support of the 1935 Social Security Act was that a large public assistance program was a temporary phenomenon. As the coverage of contributory social insurance expanded and as prosperity

---

[1] 42 U.S.C. § 601, as amended, 1962.

[2] Ad Hoc Committee on Public Welfare, REPORT TO THE SECRETARY OF HEALTH, EDUCATION AND WELFARE (Washington, September, 1961), p. 13.

[3] See Gilbert Steiner, SOCIAL INSECURITY: THE POLITICS OF WELFARE (Chicago: Rand McNally & Co., 1966), ch. 2.

returned, public assistance rolls would decrease. This trend did in fact occur with the aged; the recipient rate for Old Age Assistance declined as more of the aged became eligible for old age insurance. On the other hand, AFDC and Disability rolls continued to increase, and overall, as prosperity increased, so did the public assistance rolls. A large public assistance program began to look like a permanent feature of American life.

It was in this context that the new Kennedy administration felt it had to come up with a "fresh approach," in the words of Secretary Ribicoff, a reappraisal "possibly unprecedented in its scope and depth." The reappraisal resulted in the 1962 amendments, hailed as a "landmark," a "new philosophy in welfare." Ribicoff, in testifying before Congress, said, "We have here a realistic program which will pay dividends on every dollar invested. It can move some persons off the assistance rolls entirely, enable others to attain a higher degree of self-confidence and independence, [and] encourage children to grow strong in mind and body . . . ." According to Gilbert Steiner, "the welfare professionals responsible for developing the 1962 legislative proposals were convinced that a new day had dawned."[4]

There is, of course, an age-old debate over what the poor need to improve their life chances: more money or more social services. It is claimed, for example, that if families on welfare were given more cash income, they would have the capacity and the will to accomplish the objectives of the social service programs on their own. They would have higher aspirations for themselves and their children, they would have fewer health problems and higher standards of home care, and they would lead more satisfying personal and social lives. On the other hand, it is also stoutly maintained that the problems of the poor are much more than economic and that even if family incomes were increased, many families on welfare would still need social service help. The merits of these alternatives have never been tested, but in 1956 and 1962 Congress adopted the latter alternative for the AFDC program. The amendments to the Social Security Act required a social service plan for every AFDC family[5] and, as an inducement to the states, increased to 75 percent the federal share of state rehabilitative and preventive services.

---

[4] *Ibid.* In fact, the 1962 amendments did not add much substantively to the 1956 amendments. More was done in the 1962 amendments about training and incentives to the states. Steiner argues that on balance there was not that much "new" in the 1962 changes.

[5] See J. Handler and M. Rosenheim, *Privacy in Welfare: Public Assistance and Juvenile Justice,* 31 LAW & CONTEMP. PROBLEMS (1966) 377 n. 64.

THE DEFINITION OF SOCIAL SERVICES

The State Department Manual defines social services as follows:

> Social services are those direct service activities and interactions with the client which require knowledge and skill in the area of social casework, social group, and community organization technique. These skills are applied as the individual case situation requires. The mobilization of client capacities to make productive use of himself [sic] and others is accomplished primarily through the enabling and supporting character of the relationship he shares with the social worker.[6]

The purposes of the social service program are defined in terms of the 1956 and 1962 amendments to the Social Security Act—to help families and individuals to maintain or attain self-sufficiency, independence, and dignity.

The caseworker, in a one-to-one relationship, is the principal administrator of the social service program. Through the interview method the caseworker establishes a relationship and "consciously develops for himself and the client an understanding of the client and his problems that are standing in the way of full participation in family and community life."

The need for services is established by the social study, which is supposed to be a continuous process, starting at intake and lasting until the recipient leaves the program. It consists of a "reciprocal and joint inquiry between the caseworker and the client by which the caseworker gathers information about the client and her needs. Present client behavior is to be explored in depth to determine precipitating factors and to sift and weigh these factors in relation to the client's real life situation and environmental influences." Environment is defined as "the family, religious, social, community, cultural, and economic influences in the client's life.

Social services should be related to client needs, and not all clients need social services. "For some, certification for food stamps or surplus commodities, certification for medical care and authorization of a money payment to meet a budgetary deficit is all that is needed to accomplish the goals and objectives of our program." However, when certain "defined problem areas" are identified, the family is designated by the county department of welfare as a "defined service case."

For AFDC, "defined problem areas" include "unmarried parents and

---

[6] Unless otherwise indicated, all quotations from the state regulations are from the State Department of Health and Social Services Manual, Sec. III, chap. 1.

their children . . . , families disrupted by desertion or impending desertion, families with adults or older child with potential for self-support,
children in need of protection, children with serious special problems, families with serious problems in family functioning, families with problems in
money management, families disrupted by absence of parent for reasons
other than desertion, and children in foster care . . . ."

A "social service plan" is developed by the caseworker for these
"defined service cases." The plan means "the selection of the steps to
resolve the problem, or to help the client to cope with it." As a guide to
caseworkers, the Manual lists social service activities that may be appropriate for specific problem areas. For example, for unmarried mothers and
their children, social service activities include counseling and facilitating
the use of medical care, child care, training and placement, "counseling regarding environmental conditions seriously contributing to illegitimacy,"
obtaining legal counsel, and referrals to specialized agencies and community services. For families headed by deserted mothers, activities include counseling children about the loss of the parent, attempting to maintain ties in securing support, counseling the remaining parent about dual
responsibilities, and recommending the use of specialized agencies and
community resources for serious problems.

Many social service activities are of a maintenance nature; they are
designed to help families cope at existing levels. Examples include health,
child care, home and financial management. Other activities are designed
to help families to become self-sufficient and able to get off welfare. These
include making arrangements for assessing employment skills and opportunities, facilitating training or "appropriate" employment, helping to make
the best use of educational opportunities, assisting older teenagers in
evaluating their interests and potentials, working out day care arrangements, and so forth.

Designating a family as a "defined service case" has important administrative consequences. Whereas the frequency of contact between
the client and caseworker (which is usually by a home visit) is ordinarily
left to the discretion of the caseworker, for "defined service cases" there
has to be a client-caseworker contact at least every three months "except
in cases in which the achievement of service goals warrants the tapering
off of contacts." Under the 1962 Social Security Act amendments, the
federal government pays 75 percent of the administrative costs of social
services for "defined service cases," including the caseworker's salary. Thus
there is a substantial incentive for the county agencies to classify families
as "defined service cases."[7]

---

[7] Although the Manual stresses the one-to-one caseworker-client relationship as the basic social service instrument, there are other ways of accomplish-

Under the Wisconsin definitions, every aspect of AFDC administration can be considered social service. The determination of eligibility and the administration of the budget, including special grants for special needs, if done properly, may have a social service or rehabilitative value. Indeed, the State Department takes this position. The administration of the "responsible relatives" laws, whereby certain relatives may be required to support dependents, is supposed to be part of a social service plan to build family relationships. The administration of money payments is supposed to encourage home management and client responsibility. Other AFDC activities, such as employment and retraining programs, also have (at least in theory) this dual aspect.

For the purposes of this study, we have included under social services the following topics: child care, health, home care, social life, and participation in special community programs such as Head Start, Neighborhood Youth Corps, Project Off, "Parents without Partners," etc. We have also included the client-caseworker relationship, because of the caseworker's central importance in the administration of social services.

The Wisconsin Manual considers employment as part of social services. However, since the employment of welfare recipients has policy implications that extend beyond social services administration, we are treating it separately in the next chapter.

SOCIAL SERVICE AREAS

Children

High proportions of clients reported having discussions with their caseworkers about their children.[8] In two counties (Dane and Brown) almost 90 percent reported such discussions; and the proportion for all respondents was 80.7 percent. The topics that were discussed are presented in Table 5.1. Of those who had these discussions, the median number of topics discussed was two per respondent.

The distribution in Table 5.1 indicates that caseworkers tend to avoid topics which (a) might lead to complaints and requests and (b) would result in the caseworker finding it difficult to make delivery or be of help. Given the low levels of financial support and the obvious relevance of the topic, one would expect that a high proportion of clients would report discussing how children were clothed and fed. Yet only one-third of the

---

ing social service objectives. Caseworkers are instructed to use, where appropriate, group services ("helping clients cope better with problems through a group experience") and community and other social service resources.

[8] See Questionnaire, Appendix.

TABLE 5.1.   TOPICS RELATING TO CHILDREN
DISCUSSED BY CASEWORKERS

Topics	Reporting topics discussed[a] Number	Percent
General upbringing; nothing in particular	469	75.9
Health	463	74.9
How children are clothed and fed	212	34.3
Specific school problems	364	58.9
General plans for future education/employment	205	33.2
Employment—about present job	111	18.0
Employment—whether children should take a part-time job	92	14.9
Other	58	9.4
Number	(618)	

[a] Percentage of only those respondents who reported discussing children with caseworker.

respondents reported discussions about these matters. Even though lack of sufficient money for clothing and proper food are a persistent worry among the respondents, caseworkers seem to avoid discussing these matters, which would inevitably lead to requests for more money. According to the clients, the caseworkers tend to stay away from the issues of employment for children. Of those respondents with children twelve years or older, only 35 percent reported discussions of employment possibilities.

Conversely, proportions reporting discussions about general upbringing (nothing in particular), health, and school problems are high. Discussing general upbringing and school problems may be no more than mere conversation or advice and guidance, with no direct costs or other real burdens on the agency. School problems for the most part are handled by the school authorities. Health, on the other hand, is a tangible item calling for delivery that costs money. We will discuss the mechanics of the health care program for AFDC shortly, but point out here that there are two reasons for high caseworker activity in this area. First, there is impressionistic evidence that there is a real commitment to health care by the agencies and most of the caseworkers. Second, the Medicaid program makes it easy for the caseworkers to deliver in this area even though it is costly to the counties and the state.

Slightly more than half of the respondents reported that discussions about children occur on every caseworker visit. Attitudes toward these discussions are presented in Table 5.2. The responses indicate that a substantial proportion of clients (a) find the caseworker discussions at

TABLE 5.2. CLIENT ATTITUDES
TOWARD CASEWORKER DISCUS-
SIONS ABOUT CHILDREN[a]

*"Do you find the discussions about chil-
dren helpful?"*

Very	23.5%
Usually	24.9
Somewhat	30.2
Not at all	20.9
Number	(615)

*"Do you feel you have to follow advice that
your caseworker offers concerning your
children?"*

All of the time	9.4%
Most of the time	31.2
Not very often	23.8
Not at all	31.4
Number	(592)

*"To what extent does it bother you to have
your caseworker discuss your children?"*

Very much	4.5%
Moderately	4.0
Slightly	8.7
Not at all	82.2
Number	(615)

[a] Percentages of those reporting discussions.

least somewhat helpful, (b) feel some compulsion about following the
caseworker's advice, but (c) are not bothered or upset by discussions.
Does this mean that as long as clients are helped by caseworker activity,
they are not bothered by it? Actually not. Clients who say they are helped
by the discussions are also more likely to report they are bothered by
them. That is, one of the consequences of meaningful caseworker activity
(i.e., clients reporting being helped) is to increase client upset.

Health

AFDC recipients are automatically eligible for participation in the
Medicaid program, which was established and financed under a separate
title of the Social Security Act. The cost of Medicaid is shared by the
federal, state, and county governments. The federal share per state is

based on per capita income and is subject to revision annually. In Wisconsin it was set at 56.58 percent in 1967 and has not changed. The state contributes between 80 and 45 percent of the remaining cost of medical expenses, depending on the ability of the particular county to pay. During the time of this study, the state contribution to the six counties in this study was: Milwaukee, 55 percent; Dane, 50 percent; Brown, 45 percent; Walworth, 45 percent; Sauk, 50 percent; Dodge, 50 percent. Stated in other terms, for every $100 spent on clients under the Medicaid program, the six counties contributed between $19.54 and $23.88.

According to state regulations, when a person becomes eligible for AFDC she is to be given a certificate (card) which entitles her to use the Medicaid program. On her own initiative, without prior welfare agency approval, she can go to participating suppliers of medical services—doctors, dentists, hospitals, clinics. They supply the services and bill the counties at rates which have been fixed by agreement between the State Department of Health and Social Services and the state medical, dental, and hospital associations.

There are many reasons for expecting a high use of Medicaid. Health needs do not raise moral issues, a professional of great prestige determines whether the need is justified, and the costs of the need have been predetermined by the professional organizations. No money is given to the client; it is paid directly to the doctor, dentist, clinic, or hospital. To object to this program is to challenge the medical professionals on both the existence of needs and the cost of meeting them. In sum, the Medicaid program (a) gives the agency an opportunity to deliver a tangible good, as distinguished from a "talking good"; (b) does not raise the moral issues which surround most welfare issues; (c) has independent professional judgment to control the expenditures; and (d) does not involve high political costs for county welfare departments as opposed to other kinds of welfare department expenditures.

About 72 percent of the respondents reported having discussions with their caseworkers about health problems. There was some variation in the rural counties. For example, 87.7 percent of the Sauk County respondents reported having health discussions compared to 53.2 percent of the Dodge County respondents. Legally, caseworker approval is not required before using Medicaid. Why, then, was there such a high rate of caseworker discussion and why was there some variation in the counties? It has been reported that the distribution of Medicaid cards was far from automatic and that some caseworkers did not give out the cards until the clients asked for them. This practice would account for discussions and perhaps even the variations between the counties. In addition, caseworkers may be needed to facilitate the use of Medicaid—counseling clients on how to use the cards.

where to go, overcoming fears, arranging for transportation and babysitting, etc. County differences may also be related to the *availability* of medical facilities; more caseworker stimulus may be needed when medical facilities are distant or limited. Of those who had discussions, 90.9 percent reported discussions about medical needs, 77.8 percent about dental needs, and for 32.7 percent, the discussions involved mental health problems.

Client attitudes toward caseworker discussions about health are presented in Table 5.3. Generally speaking, there was no variation in the responses or attitudes between Milwaukee County and the two middle-sized counties, but there was some variation among the three rural counties. Even though Sauk had a higher proportion of respondents reporting health care discussions, a lower proportion found the discussions helpful. Again, this may be due to variations in the availability of services or the extent of actual use. The basic findings on the health discussions, however, are that

TABLE 5.3. CLIENT ATTITUDES TOWARD CASEWORKER DISCUSSIONS ABOUT HEALTH[a]

"Do you find the discussions helpful?"	
Very	43.3%
Usually	22.9
Somewhat	24.4
Not at all	8.4
Number	(547)

"Do you feel that you have to follow advice that your caseworker offers concerning health?"	
All of the time	16.0%
Most of the time	41.5
Not very often	19.3
Not at all	21.5
Number	(541)

"To what extent does it bother you to have your caseworker discuss this?"	
Very much	1.8%
Moderately	6.5
Slightly	5.8
Not at all	85.1
Number	(548)

[a] Percentages of those reporting discussions.

most clients report having the discussions, the discussions are felt to be useful, and the clients apparently are not bothered by them. Furthermore, in contrast with discussions about child care, there is no relationship between the extent to which women are helped and the extent to which they are bothered. Apparently health care is not as sensitive an area of discussion as child care.

Home Care

Caseworker discussions about the clients' care of the house occur infrequently. The response rate for all respondents was only 10.2 percent, although in Milwaukee County 18.5 percent reported having those discussions. The topics discussed were cleanliness, cooking, nutrition and diet, and general problems of home management. Although the numbers who had the discussions were small, about 45 percent said they were usually helpful or very helpful. About 27 percent said they felt they had to follow their caseworker's advice most or all of the time, and almost 70 percent were only slightly bothered or not bothered at all by these discussions.

Social Life

Eighty-two percent of the respondents did not have a husband living with them. This group was asked whether the caseworker ever discussed their social life, specifically relationships with men, dating habits, or marriage plans. Of this group, 51.3 percent said that they did have such discussions. If the respondent was divorced or deserted, she was asked about

TABLE 5.4.   SOCIAL LIFE (RELATIONS WITH MEN): TOPICS
DISCUSSED

General encouragement—get out more, talk about men, sex	18.2%[a]
General information—whether dating? marriage plans? have a boyfriend?	44.1
Specific information—about boyfriend, baby sitting, whether want to marry child's father	28.1
Specific advice given—contraception, counseling about specific marriage plans	12.1
Caseworker hostile to social life—don't go out or have fun, don't have men around the children	3.5
Encourage marriage and reconciliation	10.5
Number	(313)

[a] Percentages of those who reported discussions total more than 100 because more than one response was tabulated.

discussions concerning reconciliation. The topics discussed are presented in Table 5.4.

Contrary to allegations in some of the literature, little of the hostile, oppressive, moralistic, or prying type of regulation appears in the responses. The most common topics are the type discussed by women over a cup of coffee.

Attitudes towards social life discussions are presented in Table 5.5.

There was some relationship between the topic discussed and client attitudes. Clients tended to get more upset when discussions moved away from general talk to specific information, and to say that discussions were helpful when they were encouraged to get out more.

Table 5.6 summarizes client attitudes toward discussions of children, health, home care, and social life. The contrast between responses to discussions about health and to those in the other three areas indicates a discriminating attitude on the part of the clients. When caseworkers have

TABLE 5.5. CLIENT ATTITUDES TOWARD CASEWORKER DISCUSSIONS ABOUT SOCIAL LIFE[a]

"Do you find the discussions helpful?"

Very	10.4%
Usually	10.8
Some	25.3
Not at all	53.5
Number	(316)

"Do you feel that you have to follow your caseworker's advice?"

All of the time	6.4%
Most of the time	19.9
Not very often	19.2
Not at all	54.5
Number	(312)

"To what extent does it bother you to have your caseworker discuss this?"

Very much	15.2%
Moderately	7.0
Slightly	14.9
Not at all	63.0
Number	(316)

[a] Percentages of those reporting discussions.

TABLE 5.6. CLIENT ATTITUDES TOWARD CASEWORKER DISCUSSIONS ABOUT CHILDREN, HEALTH, HOME CARE, AND SOCIAL LIFE[a]

	Children	Health	Home care	Social life
Helpful?				
Very; usually	48.4%	66.2%	44.9%	21.2%
	(615)[b]	(547)	(77)	(316)
Have to follow advice?				
All; most of time	40.6	57.5	27.0	16.3
	(592)	(541)	(75)	(312)
Bothered or annoyed?				
Very; moderately	8.5	8.3	26.9	22.2
	(615)	(548)	(75)	(316)

[a] Percentages of those reporting discussions.
[b] Number of responses.

something tangible to give that the clients want, the clients find social service helpful; they feel that they have to follow the caseworker's advice but say that this does not bother or annoy them. When caseworker services consist of just general talk and advice (including the nonhealth discussions about children), there is less feeling of being helped, less willingness to follow advice, and more feeling of bother and annoyance. And when discussions touched sensitive areas such as home care or specific aspects of social life, negative attitudes increased sharply. For these two areas, there was much less willingness to follow advice, and about one out of four recipients who experienced these discussions was very or at least moderately bothered or annoyed.

Special Programs

Do the caseworkers try to interest the AFDC mothers in special community programs for either themselves or their children? Nearly half of the respondents (49.1 percent) said that their caseworkers had discussions with them about special programs.[9]

Only about one-third of the respondents had participated in a special program, and three-fourths of these had discussed the programs with their

[9] See Questionnaire, Appendix. The question asked was: "has your caseworker ever talked to you about, or tried to interest you in, special programs offered for you or your children by the welfare department or some other community agency—job training, Head Start, special schooling, etc.?"

TABLE 5.7. SPECIAL PROGRAMS THAT AFDC RECIPIENTS
REPORTING CASEWORKER DISCUSSIONS PARTICIPATED IN

Adult programs	
Vocational educational or job training	65.9%[a]
Other education programs	6.6
Social (or self) improvement programs (not vocational or formal schooling)—e.g., Family Living program	28.6
Social groups—"Parents without Partners"	3.3
Other community group or action groups—e.g., Mothers Club at Head Start	11.0
Number	(91)
Children's programs	
Head Start	67.7%[b]
Other OEO programs—Neighborhood Youth Corps, Job Corps	14.5
Other education	16.1
Community groups—e.g., YMCA, Big Brothers	8.1
Summer camp	8.1
Other	1.6
Number	(124)

[a] Percentages equal more than 100 because some families participated in more than one program.

[b] Percentages are based on number of families who have children participating, rather than the number of children per program.

caseworkers. Of those who did participate, very few entered into more than one program. Since three-fourths of all participants did report discussions, it is reasonable to assume that caseworkers were instrumental in getting clients to participate. The programs respondents discussed and participated in are presented in Table 5.7.[10]

It is interesting to note that a high proportion of those respondents participating are in work-oriented or self-improvement programs. For the children, most of the participation was in OEO poverty programs; very few participated in community programs that were not strictly defined for the poor. This raises a question about orientation of caseworker discussions of programs—to what extent do they encourage clients to participate in programs or activities involving other social classes?

The three rural counties had the lower participation rates, with the numbers participating in these counties quite small. There was, however,

[10] There were 193 respondents reporting participation in War on Poverty programs. Of those, 75 percent reported caseworker discussions.

an interesting difference in the proportions participating in the other three counties. In Dane, the progressive middle-sized county, 46 percent of the respondents had participated in a special program; in Milwaukee and Brown Counties the percentages were 39 and 34 respectively. Caseworker activity, at least as measured by respondents' reporting caseworker discussions, was about the same for these three counties. However, if we look at the proportion of clients who participated as compared to the proportion who had discussions, we find that 65.7 percent of the Dane County respondents who had caseworker discussions also participated in special programs. In Brown and Milwaukee Counties this was true for only about 48 percent of the responents. Apparently, caseworker discussions about special programs are more effective in Dane County than in the other two. Differences in participation may also be due to the quantity and quality of services available, or to the accessability of alternative sources of information. Although Brown and Dane Counties are both middle sized, Dane has far more programs, and has the University of Wisconsin with its School of Social Work. Differences might also be due to commitments on the part of the county social workers. Dane County social workers are reputed to be much more oriented toward special programs than are the Brown County social workers. Finally, differences in participation might be due to the characteristics of the clients themselves.

Just under one-fifth (18.8 percent) of the respondents said they asked the caseworker about a special program for either themselves or their children before the caseworker mentioned it. In Dane and Milwaukee Counties about 22 percent did this; in Brown County, only 14 percent. What the clients asked about is presented in Table 5.8, and caseworkers' responses in Table 5.9.

Clients' requests are apparently received favorably by the caseworkers.

TABLE 5.8. SPECIAL PROGRAMS THAT AFDC MOTHERS ASKED CASEWORKERS ABOUT

Vocational for adult (typing; job training, business course; practical nursing; refresher course; nurse's aide; vocational school course; beauty school; Project Off)	37.8%[a]
Other schooling for adult (finish high school; education courses at home; child guidance; health; nutrition)	7.7
School for children (Head Start; nursery; summer school)	30.8
Special programs for children (YMCA; camp; scouts)	20.3
Special programs for adults (Family Living)	2.1
Other	1.4
Number	(143)

[a] Percentages of those initiating inquiries.

TABLE 5.9.   CASEWORKER RESPONSE TO CLIENT REQUESTS
ABOUT SPECIAL PROGRAMS[a]

Caseworker discouraged client or refused request	16.2%
Caseworker took no action	5.6
Caseworker gave support—information; told client to go ahead with idea	30.2
Caseworker helped to arrange program or apparently helped (client participating with agency approval and money)	48.0
Number	(142)

[a] Percentages of those initiating inquiries.

In about 80 percent of the cases the workers took some positive action for the clients.

In summarizing client participation in special programs, we note that the programs clients request and participate in are clearly not frivolous. With adults, the programs are primarily either for education or employment; with children, it is primarily education. However, only about one-third of the respondents have ever participated in any program, and very few have participated in more than one. When caseworkers raise this issue, participation increases markedly. Of those who had caseworker discussions, 62.2 percent have participated in a program, which is almost twice the rate for the entire group. Since clients tend to participate when programs are suggested, it would seem that the low level of participation is partly the result of the caseworkers' failure to bring programs to the attention of the clients.

Only a very small group (6.5 percent) said the caseworker suggested that either they or their children participate in programs that they did not want. The programs the caseworkers suggested and clients resisted are shown in Table 5.10.

TABLE 5.10.   PROGRAMS CASEWORKERS SUGGESTED THAT
CLIENTS RESISTED

War on Poverty programs for children	15.2%[a]
Adult vocational school	37.0
Social groups for adults (Parents without Partners)	19.6
Community groups for children	6.5
Medical or mental health for groups for children	15.2
Other	8.7
Number	(46)

[a] Percentages of those reporting unwanted programs suggested by caseworkers. Percentages equal more than 100 since more than one suggested program was reported per respondent.

No one actually participated in a program she did not want, despite the caseworker's suggestion. If the clients were not interested or thought the program was not suited to their or their children's needs, they did not participate.

Special Problems

About one-third of the respondents (31.9 percent) said they or their children had problems or continuing difficulties other than money problems. They were asked whether they had spoken to their caseworkers about these problems and if so, whether their caseworker had been able to help them in any way (Table 5.11).

Health and children's behavior account for almost all the noneconomic problems reported, and a large proportion of respondents talked to their caseworker about these problems. The percentage helped by the caseworker follows previous patterns of helpfulness responses; caseworkers are able to do less for children's behavior problems than they are for health problems.

Comparing results among the six counties, practically the same proportions of respondents discussed noneconomic problems with their caseworker in Milwaukee, Dane, and Brown Counties (again, we note the lack of difference between the large urban center and the middle-sized communities). There was little difference in caseworker helpfulness between Milwaukee and Dane Counties, but lower proportions in Brown County said the caseworker helped.

TABLE 5.11. NONECONOMIC PROBLEMS OF AFDC FAMILIES:
CASEWORKER HELP

Nature of problem	Respondents reporting problem	Talked to caseworker	Caseworker helped to solve problem
Respondent's health	21.0%[a]	78%	74%
Children's health	29.1	83	64
Children are slow in school	7.0	88	80
Children have behavior problem	37.7	75	40
Lack of transportation; communication	4.1	60	17
Problem related to husband	10.7	81	48
Number	(265)		

[a] Percentages equal more than 100 since some respondents listed more than one problem.

In Milwaukee County, when we compared the responses of black recipients with white recipients, we found the following:

(a) *Children:* For most of the topics, the reported frequency of caseworker discussions was about the same, with one exception—how children were clothed and fed. Here, blacks were twice as likely as whites to report caseworker discussions.

(b) *Health:* There was no difference in frequency of discussions.

(c) *Home care:* Twice as many blacks as whites mentioned discussions.

(d) *Social life:* No difference. In two areas, then, there seemed to be different treatment of blacks and whites. It must be kept in mind, however, that the number of respondents who reported discussions in these two areas is rather small. For example, about eighty blacks reported discussions about how children are clothed and fed and only forty reported discussions about home care.

Blacks had more favorable attitudes toward discussions about children than whites. On the other hand, blacks were more upset by discussing health matters, although they did find the discussions helpful. The reason for this may lie in the experiences that blacks encounter when using medical facilities.

There were too few recipients reporting discussions about home care to detect differences in attitudes. Finally, more whites than blacks felt that they had to follow their caseworker's advice regarding social life.

We found no differences in the response rates concerning special programs. Equal proportions of blacks and whites reported caseworker discussions about special programs, and there were no differences in rates of participation or in the kinds of programs.

Although black and white recipients did not differ in mentioning non-economic problems, blacks were much less likely than whites to turn to their caseworkers for help with these problems.

THE CASEWORKER RELATIONSHIP

We have seen what problems AFDC clients discuss with caseworkers and what their attitudes are toward these discussions. We now turn to more general questions concerning the extent, nature, and quality of the relationship between clients and caseworkers. First, we will look at the kinds of client-caseworker contact, and then at the attitudes or reactions that clients have to the caseworkers—in particular, how much the clients trust the caseworkers, think that they have good reasons for decisions, or make efforts to stay on good terms with them.

TABLE 5.12. FREQUENCY AND DURATION OF VISITS

"How often do you see your caseworker and how long does your caseworker usually stay when he or she comes to your home?"

	Milwaukee	Dane	Brown	Walworth	Sauk	Dodge	Total
More than once/month	7.0%	3.9%	2.3%	6.3%	5.3%	1.6%	5.1%
Once/month or two	40.7	19.0	26.7	27.5	29.8	30.6	31.1
Once/three months	30.5	71.5	57.0	30.0	33.3	29.0	43.1
Few times per year	13.9	4.5	11.6	23.8	28.1	35.5	15.3
Less	6.3	0.6	2.3	8.8	3.5	3.2	4.3
No answer	1.7	0.6	0.0	3.8	0.0	0.0	1.2
Number	(302)	(179)	(86)	(80)	(57)	(62)	(766)
Mean minutes per visit	33	48	34	40	39	44	39

Almost 80 percent of the respondents had had more than one case-worker since coming on the program. In all six counties, the longer the respondents stayed on the program, the more caseworkers they had experience with. The average number of caseworkers per respondent was 2.49.[11] For Milwaukee, Dane, and Brown Counties the average length of time spent with the present caseworker, at the time of the interview, was slightly less than ten months. There was great variety among the three rural counties: Walworth, seven months; Sauk, twenty-two months; Dodge, eighteen months. For all respondents, the average length of time with the present caseworker was eleven months. The frequency and duration of caseworker visits are shown in Table 5.12.

It was pointed out that under the 1962 amendments to the Social Security Act, county departments of welfare have a strong incentive to classify AFDC families as "defined service cases" and thus qualify for the 75 percent federal reimbursement. A "defined service case" requires case-worker contact (usually by a home visit) generally no less than once every three months. Officials at the Wisconsin state level report that the federal incentive has not only taken effect, but that some county departments tend to treat the minimum contact requirement as a maximum. It would appear from Table 5.12 that there is something to these fears. In Dane County, for example, almost all of the families are "defined service cases" and most

---

[11] Average number of caseworkers per respondent on the program one year or less was 1.97; from one to two years, 2.53; from two to three years, 2.84; over three years, 2.83.

of them are visited with the minimum qualifying frequency of only once every three months. Interestingly, the respondents in Milwaukee report more frequent visits than those in the other counties.

The majority of respondents (86.2 percent) felt that the caseworkers visited them often enough, regardless of whether the caseworkers visited once a month or more often, once every other month, once every three months, or only a few times per year. The average time spent visiting is slightly less than forty minutes.

Is the caseworker someone the respondents like, trust, talk to, and discuss problems with? Practically 80 percent expressed positive feelings toward their caseworker: 53.8 percent said that their caseworker is someone they very much like, can trust, talk to, and discuss problems with; 23.9 percent said fairly so; and about 20 percent said not really or not at all. Milwaukee had the highest proportion (26 percent) expressing negative feelings. The proportions in Brown and Dane were roughly the same—about 15 percent. Attitudes toward the caseworker did not vary with the number of visits; that is, regardless of the frequency of visits, the same proportions of clients had positive feelings, a pattern true in all counties.

As a measure of client-caseworker interaction other than the home visit, respondents were asked a series of questions about their own initiative in trying to contact the caseworker. Eighty-five percent had tried to contact their caseworker at a time other than the regular visit. The average number of efforts was four, and only 12.9 percent said they were unsuccessful. The respondents' reasons for calling their caseworkers are presented in Table 5.13.

TABLE 5.13.   PROBLEMS FOR WHICH CLIENTS
CALLED CASEWORKERS

	Percent of those making calls	Percent of all calls	Number
Health	33.4%[a]	18.9%	(217)
Children	16.3	9.2	(105)
Husband (situations involved)	10.4	5.9	(67)
Social service need	26.7	16.9	(194)
Finances—purchases, repairs, bills	45.1	26.6	(293)
Checks, grants	23.9	13.6	(156)
To report moving	10.7	6.1	(70)
Other	6.7	3.7	(43)
Number	(652)		(1145)

[a] Percentages of those making calls. Percentages equal more than 100 because several respondents listed more than one thing that they contacted their caseworker about.

Nearly 70 percent of the respondents attempting calls had made financial requests. Health problems included questions about changing doctors, Medicaid cards, and hospitals. Problems concerning children (other than health) varied; school, employment, children moving in and out of the home were among those mentioned. "Husband" problems usually involved visiting privileges, nonsupport, and protection from threats. Under social service needs clients mentioned requests for transportation, baby-sitters, nursery school, children's camps, Project Off, special shoes, employment and personal problems, and the seeking of general advice.

Even though requests for financial aid predominate, 53.4 percent of the respondents making calls did seek out the caseworker for a family or social service need, other than health. Although money may be involved in these requests too (e.g., payments for baby-sitter), many did not involve money and were probably not of a crisis nature (e.g., nursery school, employment problems).

Although a very high proportion of AFDC recipients did call their caseworkers on several occasions, one must not get the impression that there is intensive contact between clients and caseworkers. The number of contacts initiated by the respondents was only 1.64 per year. Dane County respondents called the caseworkers the most, but the average was only 2 calls per year. Moreover, the number of calls to caseworkers did not increase with time on the program; it decreased. Women in the program two years did not make more calls than women who had been in the program for only one year. We are not sure what this means. One possibility is that women who call their caseworker have more independent, assertive personalities and leave the program early. Another possibility is that women new to the program are more nervous, insecure, have more problems and therefore make more calls, and by the second year may become more accustomed to the system and to their status. A third possibility is that calls may be nonproductive or there may be sanctions for calling. In any event the rate of calls to caseworkers does decrease over time on the program.

What is the relationship between attitudes toward the caseworker and calls to the caseworker? Regardless of the amount of trust in the caseworker, about the same percentage of respondents made no calls (12–17) and about the same percentage (20) made a large number of calls (about seven calls).[12]

---

[12] On the other hand, there was a relationship between trust of caseworker and success in contacting the caseworker; that is, the less trust the respondent said that she felt in the caseworker, the less likely she was to say that she was usually able to reach her. Again, it is difficult to interpret this relationship. Lack of trust could result in lack of persistence in attempting to reach the caseworker. Lack of trust may have been induced by the casework-

TABLE 5.14. EFFORT MADE TO STAY ON GOOD TERMS
WITH CASEWORKER

"How often do you make special effort to stay on good terms with your caseworker?"

	Milwaukee	Dane	Brown	Walworth	Sauk	Dodge	Total
Always	65.6%	82.7%	82.6%	76.3%	78.9%	90.3%	75.6%
Usually	11.9	7.8	7.0	8.8	21.1	3.2	10.1
Once in a while	6.3	1.1	1.2	1.2	0	1.6	3.1
Never	14.6	8.4	5.8	12.5	0	3.2	9.9
No answer	1.7	0	3.5	1.2	0	1.6	1.3
Number	(302)	(179)	(86)	(80)	(57)	(62)	(766)

TABLE 5.15. CASEWORKER HAS GOOD REASON
FOR WHAT SHE DOES

"To what extent do you feel your caseworker has a good reason for what he or she does?"

	Milwaukee	Dane	Brown	Walworth	Sauk	Dodge	Total
Always	43.0%	64.8%	77.9%	50.0%	47.4%	54.8%	54.0%
Usually	31.1	28.5	11.6	36.3	47.4	35.5	30.4
Not very often	13.9	3.4	5.8	6.3	1.8	4.8	8.1
Never	8.9	1.1	1.2	5.0	3.5	1.6	4.8
No answer	3.0	2.2	3.5	2.5	0	3.2	2.6
Number	(302)	(179)	(86)	(80)	(57)	(62)	(766)

High proportions of respondents said they make "a special effort to stay on good terms" with their caseworker (Table 5.14). There was some variation among the counties; Milwaukee County respondents made the least effort.

There was a relationship between the amount of trust the respondent had in her caseworker and the frequency with which the respondent reported making a special effort to stay on good terms with the caseworker; that is, the less trust, the less effort to stay on good terms.

Do the respondents think that their caseworkers have good reasons for what they do? Again, an overwhelming majority say yes, but the proportions expressing positive attitudes are somewhat lower in Milwaukee than in the other counties (Table 5.15).

er's not being accessible when the recipient needed her. Or the client may believe that a caseworker is generally not accessible and therefore does not really trust her.

There were high correlations (from .43 to .56) in all counties between the amount of trust a respondent had for a caseworker and the
extent to which she thought the caseworker had good reason for her actions. Further, when clients felt their caseworker had good reasons for
what she did, they were also more inclined to make special efforts to stay on
good terms with her. The same relationship applied to the specific social
service areas of caseworker discussions (children, health, home care, social
life): the more a client trusted a caseworker, the more likely a client was to
feel that she had to follow her advice in one of the specific social service
areas.

Despite the very strong, positive attitudes that most respondents had
toward caseworkers, their expectations of what their caseworkers could do
for them were not very high (Table 5.16). Expectations of caseworkers
were related to the respondents' continuing noneconomic problems and
their problems of managing budgets. The more difficulty a woman reported, the higher her expectation from her caseworker. But problems or
no problems, most clients did not think the caseworker could aid them.

Some recipients were bothered or annoyed by caseworker discussions
in specific areas. These negative experiences seemed to shape their general
attitudes toward caseworkers, in that women who were bothered by discus-

TABLE 5.16.   CLIENTS' EXPECTATIONS
FROM CASEWORKERS

*"Do you think that there are things that your caseworker—
possibly if he had more time or freedom to act—could do to
help you that he isn't doing now?"*

Yes	22.5%	
Not sure	15.5	
No	62.0	
Number	(766)	

(If yes) "What is it you think he could do?"

Help respondent get more money (unspecified)	11.0%
Grant special requests more often	25.0
Help with financial problems (e.g., help with the budget)	7.6
Help respondent with other things (e.g., employment)	13.4
Spend more time with the family	23.8
Help children do things	7.0
Number	(172)

sions reported less trust of caseworkers, were less inclined to think case-workers had good reasons for their actions, and had lower expectations. On the other hand, their behavior toward the caseworkers—calling them be-tween visits, turning to them with problems, making requests for changes in basic grants, complaining about decisions—was not consistently predictable on the basis of the amount of bother mentioned. Evidently, program use is about the same for those who are bothered and for those who are not, but evaluations differ.

In Milwaukee County the responses of the black recipients concerning the caseworker relationship were quite similar to the white responses. Black and white women reported the same frequency of caseworker visits. Black respondents made the same number of calls to the caseworker and were just as successful in contacting the caseworker as white respondents. But there was some difference in general attitudes toward the caseworker; white respondents were more likely to trust the caseworker, think she usually had a good reason for decisions she made, and in turn make special efforts to stay on good terms with her. However, these differences in atti-tudes were small and far less striking than the overall similarity of re-sponses, regardless of race.

CONCLUSIONS AND IMPLICATIONS

Level of Social Service Activity

We opened this chapter with a description of the goals of the 1956 and 1962 amendments to the Social Security Act and the definition of social services by the Wisconsin State Department of Health and Social Services. To what extent are the legislative goals of the Social Security amendments or the aims described in the Wisconsin Manual being ful-filled? How widespread and successful are the preventive and rehabilitative services which are designed "to help maintain and strengthen family life" and "to attain or retain capability for the maximum self-support and personal independence"? These questions cannot be answered because there are no set definitions of such things as strengthened family life, capa-bility for maximum self-support, and personal independence, and there are no standards by which one can tell whether these qualities exist or not. There are no methods by which one can measure the impact of various social services on the AFDC clients. Is discussing children once every three months often enough? Perhaps it is in particular cases—but by whose standards? The question of whether or not the administration of social services is accomplishing legislative goals cannot be answered until we know how to measure the goals and the precise impact of the various service activities on the clients.

Within the confines of the data, we have described the level of activity in the field. We think that this evidence strongly indicates a very low level of social service activity and that a "new day" has certainly not "dawned" in the AFDC program. For the vast majority of AFDC families, social service means a caseworker's visit a little more than once every three months for a little less than forty minutes per visit, with an occasional client's call to her caseworker. Qualitatively, the dominant characteristic of the service is one of minimum intervention.

Three types of social service activities can be distinguished: (a) provision for tangible, specific things that clients want; (b) general counseling, advice, and guidance; and (c) specific advice or guidance disapproving or approving of specific client behavior. The significant social service activity providing tangible results was implementing the use of health facilities; caseworkers were active in this area and clients reacted very positively. We pointed out that because of the Medicaid program, social services in the health area were cost free to the caseworkers. But aside from health services, caseworkers tended to avoid areas which might lead to specific requests that would cost the agencies or would be hard to accomplish. This finding parallels the findings concerning the administration of AFDC budgets, where very few clients made more than occasional requests for money grants to meet unusual needs. Either they were not advised about the availability of the grants or were discouraged from making requests. In sum, with the exception of health, the caseworkers had very little of a tangible, specific nature to offer clients.

Most of the caseworker contact was devoted to general counseling, advice, and guidance. But here too, areas of activity must be distinguished. There was a definite tendency to stay away from sensitive issues—such as home care and specific aspects of social life—and to concentrate more on children and health. Even within the subject of children, caseworkers stayed away from areas on which delivery would be difficult (e.g., clothing, food, employment) and concentrated on discussions of general upbringing, school problems, and behavior problems. When social life was discussed, general matters rather than specifics were usually raised. The half-hour visit, then, was devoted to talking about general topics that are of interest to single women with families—children, school, and social life in general.

There was very little specific advice, particularly of a negative, disapproving kind. Few clients reported caseworker disapproval in any of the social service areas. There was some effort on the part of caseworkers to encourage clients to use resources in the community, but overall, participation rates were low.

TABLE 5.17. CONSTRAINT OR
ANNOYANCE BY CASEWORKER
DISCUSSIONS[a]

Clients who felt that they had to follow the caseworker's advice "all" or "most of" the time	
For four areas	0.8%
For three areas	5.1
For two areas	18.2
For one area	31.6
Never felt constrained	43.9
Number	(766)

Clients who felt "very" or "moderately bothered or annoyed" by caseworker discussions	
For four areas	0.5%
For three areas	0.8
For two areas	3.4
For one area	15.3
Never felt bothered or annoyed	80.0
Number	(766)

[a] Percentage of AFDC Respondents who felt constrained or upset by caseworker discussions in specific social services areas.

The absence of meaningful caseworker contact, either positive or negative, is reflected in client attitudes toward caseworker discussions in the four specific social service areas. In Table 5.17 we have summarized client feelings of constraint (coercion) and bother or annoyance with the caseworker discussions of children, health, social life, and special problems.

On the whole, clients felt little constraint, and even less bother. Most of the feelings of constraint arose from social services dealing with the use of health facilities, including children's health matters. Most of the feelings of bother and annoyance arose from discussions about home care and specific aspects of social life. These were sensitive issues, and it will be recalled that rates of upset for these areas were high. Overall rates of bother and annoyance were low not because clients acquiesced, but because for most clients, the caseworkers stayed away from these areas.

What emerges from the data is that, in the main, social service activity is little more than a relatively infrequent, pleasant chat. It is somewhat supportive. It is rarely threatening but also not too meaningful in the sense of either helping poor people get things they need or in changing their lives. And it seems to bear little resemblance to the legislative goals of the

Social Security Act amendments or to the descriptions in the Wisconsin State Department Manual.

Client Attitudes and the Structure of Dependency

On the whole, clients expressed very positive attitudes toward their caseworkers, but this finding is grounded in the existing level of caseworker activity. Although the clients liked the home visit, they had low expectations about what their caseworkers could do and they did not express any desire to increase caseworker contact. For them, caseworkers were visiting about often enough.

In fact, there is evidence that the level of positive attitudes probably existed because the caseworkers were not doing their official job. The Wisconsin Manual tells the caseworkers to establish a "relationship," to "explore precipitating factors and to sift and weigh these factors in relation to the client's reality situation and environmental influences" which include "the family, religious, social, community, cultural, and economic influences in the client's life." Yet for the most part, this was precisely the activity that caseworkers avoided, and when the caseworkers did discuss these matters, the clients' negative feelings rose sharply.

These AFDC recipients much preferred discussions of tangible items over mere advice and guidance and became upset when the caseworkers started to talk about home care and specific aspects of social life. Similarly, in the administration of the budget, clients reacted negatively to caseworker supervision of expenditures. *In short, positive attitudes toward the caseworker that are reported in this study existed for a program in which there was a sharp disjuncture between what was going on in practice and what was called for in federal and state policy or in social work theory. The findings of this study cannot be used to support the view that clients would welcome an expanded program of caseworker involvement in their personal lives.* Despite the fact that many AFDC families are "defined service cases," very little of the type of caseworker activity called for in official policy went on, and when it did occur, clients reacted negatively.

Client attitudes toward the caseworker varied with what the caseworker did. We refer again to the three types of activities: (a) delivery of tangible items, (b) general advice, and (c) specific advice. When the caseworkers were able to (a) deliver something that the clients wanted, the clients felt the discussions were most helpful; they said they had to follow advice, and were not bothered. With (b) general advice, there was less feeling of helpfulness or constraint (coercion). And with (c) specific advice, clients felt free to disregard the caseworker. Constraint or coercion, then, arise primarily when caseworkers can deliver things that clients want (see discussions of medical services, pp. 110, 113–14 *supra*). In the delivery of specific items we find a high degree of dependency.

Highly dependent, if not coercive, relationships arise in many welfare programs that are strictly voluntary by law. In programs of this kind, where there are no legal requirements that clients must see caseworkers, clients are still subject to manipulation because they badly need what the social worker has to give. Prominent examples are programs where social workers visit lonely old people and hospital patients. There is no legal compulsion; there is no requirement that the clients must see the social worker. But the service is highly valued, and social workers often report an ingratiating, embarrassing type of dependency.[13] This study of the Wisconsin AFDC program suports the converse: if the service is not valued, it will be rejected. Dependency arose here when the caseworkers were doing something that the clients valued. On more general topics, there was less feeling of constraint, and when the caseworkers suggested something specific that the clients did not want to do, no client said that she had to follow the caseworker's advice. In none of these situations would it seem that the *legal* requirements of the AFDC program have much significance in providing coercive elements in the caseworker relationship.

Legal compulsion has received attention in those situations where welfare administration has been punitive, moralistic, and harsh. Of course clients object (or should object) to this kind of manipulation. But what we are emphasizing is that dependency and manipulation also arise out of the discretionary distribution of *benefits*.[14] And when clients receive these benefits they do not object; they like their benefactors, and they like to please their benefactors. This attitude may be deplored, but we do not think that dependency of this nature is a peculiar characteristic of welfare clients. It exists in all social classes. In sum, we would argue that dependency is more a product of the structure of social relationships than legal requirements; it exists when there is discretionary authority over benefits that others need, and it has very important consequences for the future organization and structure of publicly administered social services.

---

[13] Anyone familiar with social work knows the power that can be exercised over dependent applicants and clients. For a discussion of coercive relationships arising in the activities of Children's Departments in London, see J. F. Handler, *The Coercive Officer,* NEW SOCIETY, 3 October 1968, No. 314 (London, England) (Reprint 19, Institute for Research on Poverty, University of Wisconsin).

[14] This point, of course, has been well expressed by others, e.g., K. C. Davis, DISCRETIONARY JUSTICE (1969); C. A. Reich, *The New Property,* 73 YALE L.J. 733 (1964).

The Organization and Structure of Social Services: Reform and Dependency

The nature or inevitability of dependency has led to efforts to reduce welfare officials' discretion over the distribution of benefits. One prominent proposal is to separate income maintenance in AFDC from the administration of social services and routinize the distribution of money payments. The Task Force Report, SERVICES FOR PEOPLE,[15] for example, favors the federal government's assuming direct responsibility for administering money payments for public assistance, through a highly routinized system, with the states and local governments assuming responsibility for the administration of social services. The REPORT suggests that social services be voluntary for the clients. The assumption is that caseworker discretionary authority over the budget gives them the power to coerce clients into accepting social services that they may not need or want, and this new approach is intended to eliminate that situation. In addition, under the present AFDC program, welfare recipients are legally required to accept caseworker visits as a condition of receiving the money grant; the proposed reform would eliminate this legal requirement. Clients would then be free to accept or reject social services: there would be no legal compulsion, and with the elimination of caseworker discretion over the budget, there would be no economic compulsion. Although the REPORT does not deal with the administration of social services, it is also argued that since social workers would be free from administering money payments (including investigations), they could spend more time and effort in administering social services.

In states where discretion is exercised over budgets, routinizing money payments would reduce dependency by curtailing the discretionary authority of welfare officials in this area. But if routinization is taken seriously, one of the costs would be the loss of individualized treatment through the use of special grants for special needs. In Wisconsin, at least, the special grant program is not very effective, and some reformers would be willing to pay this price on behalf of the welfare clients. In New York City welfare groups hotly protested this reform (routinization), and it seems to us their position was well taken. As long as basic grant levels are low, there must be provision for emergencies and other unusual losses. Furthermore, many rehabilitative programs require money—for example, education and retraining costs. Two questions, then, must be answered: Which agency—the money payment agency or the social service agency—is going to administer

---

[15] Report of the Task Force on Organization of Social Services, SERVICES FOR PEOPLE, Department of Health, Education, and Welfare, October 15, 1968.

the special grant program, and under what criteria? Routinization of money payments, if it is to accomplish its objective of reducing discretion, must *objectify* the criteria under which special grants are to be distributed. This gives clients entitlements or rights to the grants and concomitantly reduces official discretion. Yet it is one thing to specify objective criteria in the books (as is already the case for many special grants). It is quite another matter to insure that welfare officials will communicate these rights to the clients, that the clients will understand what they are entitled to and will demand what is due them rather than rely on the good will of the case-worker.[16] In certain parts of the country (e.g., New York City), much of this has been accomplished through the use of effective welfare client organizations, but it is no easy task.

Furthermore, there is the danger that expanded "improved" state and local government social service programs will increase client dependency and coercion. If social service administration does what the clients really want—which is increasing delivery of specific, tangible items, possibly including special money grants—then dependency as shown in this study will increase. This will be true regardless of whether or not social services are voluntary. Poor people who need things will be free to reject social services in a formal sense only. Experience with many legally voluntary programs amply demonstrates the development of highly dependent and coercive relationships. Problems of reducing discretion and dependency due to specific social services may be even more difficult to solve than those stemming from special money grants. In addition, if social services administration takes the federal and state policy seriously, there will be a significant increase in official intervention and control of the lives of clients, which we feel is not likely to be resisted. The extent to which welfare clients will be able to reject this interference will depend upon a number of things; one of the most important will be how much discretionary authority the social workers have over the distribution of tangible things that clients want. In Wisconsin the AFDC clients were able to resist caseworker interventions they did not like, but coercive elements were low because: (a) administration of the budget was already highly routinized; (b) there were few things that the caseworkers could give that the clients wanted; and (c) the case-workers did not insist on behavioral changes for these things (i.e., health services). In short, there was not much coercion in Wisconsin because not much discretionary power was exercised.

Another issue that is not discussed is how the present home visiting

---

[16] The enforcement of rights is an extremely difficult task. See J. F. Handler, *Justice for the Welfare Recipient: Fair Hearings in AFDC—The Wisconsin Experience,* 43 Soc. Services Rev. 12 (March 1969).

practice is to be administered if income maintenance is separated from social services. Granting that clients who participate in social service programs will be dependent and may be manipulated, it is argued that clients still should have the choice of participation. It is bad enough that they become dependent on welfare officials by necessity; they should not be required to do so by law. We agree with this position but do have a question about how client choice should be implemented. Specifically, should there be no caseworker visits (or other contact) unless the client requests the service, or should there be caseworker visits unless the client says that she does not want them?

Most of the appeal lies with the first alternative. If clients really feel that they need what social services has to offer, they will ask for it; otherwise, let them be. In our view this is a very close question. Requiring client initiative may exacerbate the already difficult problem of failing to distribute social services among the very poor. A great deal of concern, if not effort, is centered on how to make known the availability of services and how to encourage the poor to make better use of them. It is entirely possible that the caseworkers in the AFDC program (at least as described in this paper) contribute somewhat to the solution of some of these problems. For example, we pointed out that AFDC recipients automatically qualify for Medicaid and do not need caseworker approval for health services. We found that most recipients do talk to their caseworkers about health problems and report the caseworker discussions helpful. We do not know why they discuss health problems with their caseworker, that is, what psychological mechanisms are operating, and we have no data on the extent to which they would have used Medicaid without caseworker support. Furthermore, it is entirely possible that some respondents had to talk to their caseworker because Medicaid cards were not distributed to them. But it is commonly said (although some small studies indicate otherwise) that poor people do not make adequate use of available medical facilities. The caseworkers *may* be performing a valuable function in getting clients to use the health program. In the other social service areas there are lower levels of activity, but even at these levels there are indications that the clients are getting something of value. It will be recalled that practically all the clients who said they had problems other than money problems did seek out their caseworkers and were helped by them. Although not that many clients participate in special community programs, we think that the caseworkers were probably instrumental in getting these clients to participate.

Would welfare clients make less use of services if they had to call a caseworker in order to raise their problems and needs rather than have them discussed in the course of the routine house visit? Answers here are speculative, but it seems reasonable to assume that hesitant, dependent people would be more likely to raise problems and requests with a person (a) whom they see somewhat regularly, (b) whose duty is to help them, (c) who apparently has access to services and resources, and (d) whom the clients like and trust, than if there were no home visits and the clients had to take the initiative. Requiring a client to request help from an unknown official "downtown" requires her to magnify her problem and may increase her fears and insecurities about being refused and rebuffed.

One cannot push this argument too far. It could very well be that if caseworkers were not available, welfare recipients would seek other, perhaps even more efficient, sources of help. But the impressionistic evidence points the other way—that the very poor lack knowledge about and access to community resources and social services. Requiring welfare clients to take the initiative may have the effect of cutting off a reasonably valuable service that most clients, in their words, seem to like.

This is not to argue that welfare recipients should not have the right to say they do not want social security, even the home visits. Some writers on welfare reform have posited that clients will feel they have to accept social services as an implied condition to their grant, whether services are formally voluntary or not. We are quite skeptical of the coercion argument: clients know how to refuse to do things that they do not want to do. On the basis of these data, most clients would want the service (at least at its present level). A client hesitant to sign a form saying that she did not want any home visits would not suffer very much (and in fact, might very well find that she enjoyed the caseworker contact). Nevertheless, there will be some who want to be left alone, and these people should have the option of refusing social services.

In sum, much of the hoped-for benefits of separating social services from income maintenance may not in fact reduce government discretionary power over welfare recipients. Furthermore, depending on how special grants and the home visits are handled, they may even cost welfare clients some of the benefits they know and enjoy under the existing program, at least as described in this study. It seems to us that if significant progress is to be made on the deep-seated problems of client dependency and the control of official discretion, far more radical change is needed. One such change is the growth of effective welfare client groups. It is claimed, for example, that when such groups are effective, as they seem to be in New York City, significant changes in dependency relationships have occurred, including more effective use by clients of what the welfare program has to offer. Another radical change could be local community social service centers run by the clients themselves rather than, or in addition to, state and local government agencies. These, as well as other far-reaching proposals, raise many difficult issues that are beyond the scope of this book.

Chapter 6

EMPLOYMENT:
WELFARE, WIN, AND FAP

One of the most critical areas of AFDC policy is employment—should women receiving welfare be encouraged or forced to accept work or training? Although increasingly elaborate programs for work and training have been devised, their effects have been slight. Change is limited partly by the work potential and experience of the AFDC clients, partly by the amount of caseworker and agency discretion in the work programs. Reviewing the experience of past and present work programs suggests that stress on employment is likely to have modest success. Nevertheless, work and training programs continue to be held out as the solutions to the welfare crisis.

The AFDC program has had a special relationship to the issue of work. It is often assumed that when the programs were first started at the beginning of this century, husbandless mothers were not considered part of the labor force. We saw in Chapter 1 that this was not quite true. Aid was only available to husbandless mothers who were "deserving," which in that day almost always meant widows. Questions of morality were raised about the other categories of husbandless mothers, and public relief was not available for the "unfit." They had to work, and if they could not support themselves and their children, and if other sources of income or help were not available, then the children went to public institutions or to foster homes.

By the end of World War II there was more willingness to accept the idea that a working mother could benefit the family in both economic and noneconomic ways. This change in attitude toward the working mother coincided with two other changes in the AFDC program that we have already mentioned.

For a variety of reasons, after World War II the social characteristics of the AFDC rolls changed; the widow was replaced by the divorced, separated, deserted and unmarried, and in the large urban centers, blacks replaced whites (see chap. 2). Then there was the enormous growth in the AFDC rolls, despite periods of full employment, especially during the 1950's.

In the previous chapter it was pointed out that the first response to this "crisis in welfare" was the 1962 Social Security amendments which were sold to Congress primarily on the ground that welfare rolls would decrease as families became self-supporting through social services programs. Provisions were made to encourage states to institute programs of job counseling, education, and retraining. In addition, there was a liberalization of the treatment of earned income. In 1962 AFDC mothers were *encouraged* to work.

In 1967 there was another shift in public policy. The AFDC program was under heavy attack in Congress. The rolls, and costs to the federal government, had been rising steadily despite the 1962 amendments. Large industrial states of the North, which had high benefit programs, were demanding higher federally imposed standards to prevent what they claimed was an influx of poverty-stricken families from the rural southern states. It was also claimed that the administration of the program was lax; that many were on the program who should not be, that the program encouraged immorality (particularly desertion and illegitimacy), and that the treatment of earned income discouraged people from working.

Congress, in an angry mood, enacted the 1967 amendments, which were designed to do four things: (1) As of July 1969, a ceiling was to be put on the proportion of children under eighteen who might receive AFDC. (2) A new work incentive program (called WIN), to increase the employment of AFDC recipients, was to be established under the joint responsibility of the Departments of Labor and of Health, Education, and Welfare. (3) Local welfare departments would be required to provide day-care centers for the children of mothers who were training or working. (4) The treatment of earned income was again to be liberalized. There was a decided shift in emphasis from the 1962 Congress. Whereas earlier federal policy toward work had been permissive and designed to fit rehabilitative goals, the 1967 amendments were bluntly described otherwise in the House Committee on Ways and Means Report: "The Committee is recommending the enactment of a series of amendments to carry out its firm intent of reducing the AFDC rolls by restoring more families to employment and self-reliance, thus reducing the Federal financial involvement in the program."[1]

In the most recent developments since the 1967 amendments, the Nixon Administration has entered the field with the "workfare proposals" in the proposed Family Assistance Plan. Despite the liberal features of FAP, it was supported primarily on the basis that it would strengthen work incentives and requirements. Although the name WIN is to be dropped, the

---

[1] H.R. REP. No. 544, 90th Cong., 1st Sess. 96 (1967) (Report of the House Ways and Means Comm. on H.R. 12080).

Family Assistance Act actually maintains many of its features, strengthens others, and corrects what Congress felt were loopholes in the WIN work requirements. The proposed Family Assistance Act, then, represents still another phase of the centuries-old attempt to reduce welfare costs by getting recipients to seek work instead of welfare through incentives, or if that fails, coercion.

At the conclusion of this chapter we will discuss the WIN program and the work requirements of FAP. We will see that under WIN and FAP the issues of work and welfare are still being resolved at the local level. The WIN program asked an *existing* welfare bureaucracy with an *existing* clientele to respond to a new work program. FAP proposes some changes in this relationship. Accordingly, the work experience of the recipients and state and local administrative practices will be examined first and then discussed in light of the recent changes and proposals.

STATE POLICY ON EMPLOYMENT OF AFDC RECIPIENTS

Even though many of the state regulations are binding on the county departments, this is not the case with employment. Here the legislature has specifically said that discretionary authority lies with the counties and not with the state government.[2] The State Department regulations are guidelines only.

State policy starts with the initial assumption that "most individuals prefer to be independent and self-supporting." Accordingly, "the work potential of all employable family members is [to be] discussed and evaluated" by the caseworkers. Whether or not a mother should work requires a "thorough exploration and careful evaluation." The Manual recognizes that mothers may lack skills, or have no previous work experience, or may be fearful of trying to work, or that it may be uneconomical for them to work. Planning for employment requires consideration of the needs of both the mother and the children. If the mother can be employed without detriment to the children but resists employment, counseling and encouragement are based on the reasons for her resistance. But "situations shall not be condoned which may result in children being neglected or poorly cared for while the mother works,"[3] and above all, the county departments must consider the ability of the mother to cope with dual responsibilities.

----

[2] The statute reads: "The county agency may require the mother to do such remunerative work as in its judgment she can do without detriment to her health or the neglect of her children or her home." Wis. Stat. 49.19 (6).

[3] The Manual directs that the following factors are to be considered in each case: "(1) The effect of disability, death or absence of the father on

For some who have been defeated and deflated by what life has dealt them and the taxing task of motherhood and homemaking, pushing them into outside employment which they are ill-prepared to take, the result may be the breakdown of the one-parent family. The mother might be overwhelmed by all her responsibilities and the children become neglected, delinquent, or disturbed—social ills the Aid to Families with Dependent Children program is designed to treat or prevent.[4]

The costs of work, including child care, education, and training, can be budgeted. There are state rules governing the treatment of earned income, and these rules are binding on the counties. The basic rule before the 1967 amendments was that all nonwelfare income, from whatever source, reduced the welfare grant on a dollar-for-dollar basis; that is, there was a 100 percent tax rate. With earned income, however, the counties disregarded the earnings of AFDC children up to $50 per month per child with a family maximum of $150 per month. Although there was no earning exemption for adult members of the family, an automatic $40 per month was exempted for work-related expenses (additional expenses could be deducted, however). There was no earning exemption for adult members of the family as such. This was the basic rule, but there were a number of exceptions. Earnings or any other income of an AFDC family could be set aside for specific identifiable needs of children (e.g., education costs). "Inconsequential income"—defined as irregular and sporadic—could be disregarded, and the earnings of children under twelve were automatically considered "inconsequential." Then there were special provisions concerning payments under the Economic Opportunity Act and under the Elementary and Secondary School Act of 1965. The first $85 and one-half of the remainder of earnings under these laws were to be disregarded. These were the rules governing earned income in 1967, when our study was made.

Next we turn from the state guidelines and rules about employment in 1967 to the experiences of welfare clients. Our concern is identifying whether patterns of administration existed. The extent to which WIN or

---

family relationships and responsibilities. (2) The prior role of the deceased or absent father in the support and care of the children. (3) How the mother functioned in relation to her children prior to the difficulties which brought about need for assistance. (4) The employment experience and training of the mother and her age, education, aptitudes, and motivation for a specific type of training for employment, or employment, (5) The general health of the mother and her physical and mental capacity. (6) The emotional and social needs of the mother and her children. (7) The availability of suitable care for the children during the work, and/or training hours of the mother."

[4] Unless otherwise indicated, the quotations in this section of the text are from Wisconsin State Department of Health and Social Service, Division of Family Services, County Manual, Sec. III, Service to Clients.

FAP can succeed is, after all, closely related to the nature of previous administration.

EMPLOYMENT EXPERIENCE OF THE RECIPIENTS

Work Experience before Coming on the AFDC Program

Practically all of the recipients surveyed had some experience in the labor market. Since leaving school, over 90 percent had held at least one job, and most listed two or three. Almost three-fourths of the jobs listed were either (1) semi- or unskilled work (but not service) or (2) semi- or unskilled service. Fewer than 5 percent of the jobs were skilled service (beautician, cook, etc.) (Table 6.1). The total number of years worked per respondent is shown in Table 6.2.

The past work experience of the respondents is not promising. Practically all had worked, but at low-level jobs, and a significant proportion had spent a very short time in the labor market. Almost half of the respondents (45.1 percent) had either never worked or worked for not

TABLE 6.1. TYPES OF JOBS HELD SINCE LEAVING SCHOOL

Type of Job	Percentage
1. Clerical and kindred workers with trained skill, seniority position, or considerable apprenticeship (professional, technical, managers, bookkeepers, proprietors)	4.6%
2. Clerical and kindred workers with low skill (switchboard, filing, typing, unspecified clerical)	8.8
3. Sales	7.7
4. Skilled workers	1.0
5. Semiskilled or unskilled workers not in service (machine operator, drill press, coil winder, packer, sewing machine operator, inspection, assembly)	30.1
6. Skilled service (masseuse, beautician, bartender, cook)	4.6
7. Semiskilled service (waitress, food service)	21.4
8. Other service (cleaning, ironing, babysitting)	21.8
Number	(1563)

TABLE 6.2. NUMBER OF YEARS
OF EMPLOYMENT

Never worked	9.4%
Less than one year	22.4
One year	13.3
Two years	11.6
Three years or more	43.3
Number	(766)

TABLE 6.3. TYPES OF JOBS HELD
SINCE LEAVING SCHOOL, BY RACE
(MILWAUKEE COUNTY)

Type of Job[a]	Black	White
Clerical, sales, skilled work	15%	31%
Semi- and unskilled work	26	32
Semiskilled service	18	22
Other service	41	14
Number	(261)	(263)

[a] See Table 6.1 for definitions of job categories.

longer than one year. These women, then, had little work experience, probably little orientation toward work, and not much prospect for employment.

Did race make any difference to past work experience? In Milwaukee County there was no difference in length of time in the labor market. However, there were differences in kinds of jobs that the recipients held (Table 6.3).

AFDC Mothers Presently Working

More than one-fifth (22.3 percent) of the respondents were working at the time of the interview. Again, most of the respondents were either in semi- or unskilled work (22.9 percent), or in semiskilled service (14.7 percent) or other service (37.6 percent). Average weekly earnings varied somewhat among the counties. In Table 6.4 we have tabulated the percent working, types of jobs, and average weekly earnings for the three urban counties and for the total number of employed respondents.

Of the three urban counties, Brown has the highest proportion of mothers working; all but four of these women were in service work, and more than half of all the workers were doing cleaning, ironing, and baby-

TABLE 6.4. PERCENT NOW WORKING, TYPES OF JOBS,
AND AVERAGE WEEKLY EARNINGS

Status	Milwaukee	Dane	Brown	Entire Sample
Now working	19.5%	20.1%	26.7%	22.3%
Number	(59)	(36)	(23)	(171)
Type of job[a]				
Clerical, skilled	1.7	6.3	4.3	4.1
Clerical, low skilled	5.2	18.8	4.3	5.9
Sales	8.6	9.4	4.3	6.5
Semi- or unskilled workers	27.6	6.3	4.3	22.9
Skilled service	8.6	6.3	13.0	8.2
Semiskilled service	13.8	25.0	13.0	14.7
Other service	36.2	40.6	56.5	37.6
Average weekly earnings	$46.08	$32.55	$26.55	$37.05

[a] See Table 6.1 for definitions of job categories.

sitting. These same occupations (cleaning, ironing, babysitting) are listed for 40.6 percent of the Dane County working mothers; an additional 25 percent are waitresses or in food service. In Milwaukee County a little more than one-fourth are in semi- or unskilled factory work. Among Milwaukee blacks, however, service work such as ironing and babysitting was most common, whereas the largest number of white women were in semi- or unskilled factory work.

We do not know whether or not these mothers were working at the time that they entered the AFDC program. Nevertheless, practically all (90.6 percent) said that they got their job without any help from the caseworker.

The data for the mothers presently working suggest that unless there is some sort of intervention by the welfare department and/or the WIN program, AFDC mothers who enter the labor market will most likely work at semi- or unskilled, semiskilled service, or other service jobs.

Mothers Working While on the AFDC Program but Not Working at Time of Interview

Twenty-five percent of the respondents, unemployed at the time of the interview, had worked while on the AFDC program. As expected, they had held the same types of jobs as those presently working. In the three urban counties more than half of those who had worked recently were either in food service or cleaned, babysat, or took in ironing. In Milwaukee and Brown Counties another fourth to one-third had semi- or unskilled factory jobs. In Milwaukee County whites were more likely to have worked while

TABLE 6.5. REASONS GIVEN FOR STOPPING WORK

Respondent was terminated (i.e., seasonal work, place closed; lacked skills)	16.3%
Respondent needed at home; could not afford babysitting	30.1
Respondent became ill; pregnant	30.6
Respondent just said that she quit	13.8
Someone at home became ill	3.6
Respondent began training program	3.6
Other	2.0
Number	(191)

on the program than blacks. The average weekly wage for this group, at the time that they stopped working, was $39.22.

The reasons why these respondents stopped working are shown in Table 6.5. We might reasonably expect low motivation to keep working, given the character of the work, the low wages, and the high costs of work for these women. However, it is worth noting that only 30.1 percent said that stopping work was connected with lack of satisfactory day-care arrangements.

Mothers Who Have Not Worked Since Coming on the Program but Who Tried To Find Work

Almost half of the respondents (47.2 percent) had not worked since coming on the AFDC program. Eighteen percent of this group, however, had tried to find work. There were differences between Milwaukee and the other two urban counties—25 percent of the Milwaukee AFDC recipients who had not worked said that they tried to find work, as compared to only 9.6 percent in Dane County and 5 percent in Brown County. Just as many blacks as whites sought work in Milwaukee. The reasons these sixty-five women gave for not being able to get jobs are listed in Table 6.6.

TABLE 6.6. REASONS GIVEN FOR NOT BEING
ABLE TO GET A JOB DESPITE EFFORTS

Needed at home	10.9%
Unable to get babysitting	15.6
Unable to qualify for job	21.9
Job unsuitable (e.g., not enough money)	7.8
Never heard after applying	31.3
Still looking	10.9
Other	1.6
Number	(65)

TABLE 6.7.　WORK EXPERIENCE WHILE
ON PROGRAM

Now working	22.3%
Have worked while on program but not presently working	25.1
Have not worked while on program[a]	47.2
No answer	5.4
Number	(766)

[a] Of this unemployed group, 18 percent (65 women) have tried unsuccessfully to find work.

Again, it is worth noting that lack of satisfactory day-care arrangements ("needed at home," "unable to get babysitting") is not the reason most given for not getting a job. Contrary to expectations, having preschool children had no effect on whether a mother tried to find work. Women with preschool children were just as likely to have tried to find work as women with older children. In Table 6.7 we summarize the work experience of the recipients while in the AFDC program.

ATTITUDES OF AFDC RECIPIENTS TOWARD WORK AND THE TREATMENT OF EARNED INCOME

Attitudes toward Work

Respondents who were not presently working were asked whether they would like to have at least a part-time job if good babysitting or day care were available (Table 6.8). The question, of course, was hypothetical and one must treat the responses with great caution. The type of job, the

TABLE 6.8.　PERCENT WANTING A PART-TIME JOB

"If good babysitting or day care for your children were available, to what extent would you like to have at least a part-time job?"

	Mil-waukee	Dane	Brown	Wal-worth	Sauk	Dodge	Total
Very much	44.6%	33.6%	41.3%	41.0%	17.1%	19.4%	37.2%
Somewhat	16.4	19.7	17.5	19.7	22.0	19.4	16.5
Not especially	9.7	13.1	12.7	8.2	19.5	8.3	11.3
Not at all	29.2	33.6	28.6	31.1	41.5	52.8	33.1
Number	(195)	(137)	(63)	(61)	(41)	(36)	(533)

wages, and the child-care arrangements were not spelled out. Still, more than half the respondents were positive about working.

Attitudes toward work were related to past work experience. Those who had worked recently and those who had tried to find a job were more inclined to say that they would like to work, as compared to those who had done neither. In other words, the respondents who said they wanted to work, given the right opportunities, could point to their past behavior as evidence of the validity of their responses. Total years of working experience, however, was not related to work attitudes, nor did the best job held by a woman since leaving school predict how she felt about the prospect of working. Respondents who had worked in semiskilled (food) or other service (cleaning, ironing, babysitting) were just as willing to work as respondents who worked at semi- or unskilled factory jobs or in skilled service.

In addition to work experience, one would expect that social characteristics such as age, number of preschool children, and perhaps race would affect attitudes toward work. Having preschool children seems to *increase* the desire to have a job, since of those women who said they wanted a job "very much" or "somewhat" but had not tried to find one, 67.2 percent did have preschool children. It could be, then, that they did not try to find a job because arrangements could not be made for their children. Although we will discuss caseworker activity below, we can note here that caseworkers tend *not* to have discussions about employment with mothers who have preschool children. Attitudes toward work are related to age; younger mothers are more anxious to work than older mothers. Attitudes toward work are also related to race; 71 percent of the blacks want a job either "very much" or "somewhat" as compared to 50 percent of the whites in Milwaukee.

Effect of Treatment of Earned Income

Other factors may discourage AFDC mothers from working. It is assumed that the welfare treatment of earned income acts as a disincentive: Do welfare recipients know how earned income is treated, and if so, does this knowledge affect work effort and attitudes toward work?

All the respondents, including those presently working, were asked whether they understood how the welfare department treats earned income (Table 6.9).[5] Half the respondents had the general idea but either did not

---

[5] The question was: "As you understand it, how does the welfare department treat money you might make from a job you might hold—that is, do they let you keep all that you make or do they lower the amount of your aid grant and, if so, by how much; or what do they do?"

TABLE 6.9. RESPONDENTS' UNDERSTANDING
OF TREATMENT OF EARNED INCOME

Understanding	Mil-waukee	Dane	Brown	Wal-worth	Sauk	Dodge	Total
Basically correct as to dollar amounts	14.6%	52.0%	39.5%	31.3%	33.3%	35.5%	30.9%
Had process correct but dollar amounts wrong	68.2	35.8	44.2	55.0	49.1	45.2	53.3
Said there was no change in AFDC grant	5.3	3.4	3.5	1.2	1.8	3.2	3.8
Number	(302)	(179)	(86)	(80)	(57)	(62)	(766)

know the specific dollar amounts that were taxed or were vague. Since we do not know whether they thought the tax rate was higher or lower than the actual rate, we cannot determine the disincentive effects on this group.

The recipients, however, did differ in how much they knew about the treatment of earned income. Did extent of knowledge influence work effort? In comparing those recipients who were not working but tried to find work and those who did not try, we found no difference in their knowledge of the treatment of earned income. Was knowledge, then, acquired as a *consequence* of working? The results of a comparison of working and nonworking women were completely contradictory. In Brown County workers had greater knowledge than nonworkers, and in Milwaukee County the results were exactly the opposite. In Dane County there was no difference in knowledge between workers and nonworkers.

Probably the decision to seek work depends on many factors, only one of which is earned-income knowledge. This would account for no difference in knowledge between those who tried to find work and those who did not. But what accounts for the differential lack of knowledge among those who are working? Why do some know about the specifics of the policy and others not? The most plausible explanation is that the earned income policy is not uniformly enforced. We have some quantitative evidence that in Dane County AFDC respondents who work are taxed at a far lower rate than the state regulations call for and that the working Dane County mothers in fact keep a good deal of their earnings.[6] Caseworkers and State Department officials say that the policy is not en-

[6] J. Heffernan, Adequate Grants and Work Incentives in Public Assistance, Children's Allowances, and Negative Tax Programs (University of Wisconsin, Institute for Research on Poverty, 1969) (mimeo.).

forced in other counties as well. They point out that in the present administrative context there is very little of a specific, tangible nature that caseworkers can do for clients. If clients are working and the caseworker knows about it, the caseworker can exercise her discretion by treating the income as "inconsequential." This would be particularly easy in Brown County, where most of the working mothers are cleaning, ironing, and babysitting. This exercise of discretion benefits the caseworker in a number of ways. She can do something for the client which the client wants, resulting in a better relationship, and moreover, she is saved the job of recomputing the budget. This decision costs the agency money; but it is easier for the caseworker to charge the agency by ignoring clients' earned income than to ask for an increase in the client's budget. Somewhat similar considerations would lead a caseworker to encourage a client not to report earnings to the caseworker. The caseworker becomes a "good guy," in addition to saving herself some extra work.

There are also pressures on the caseworker that consciously or unconsciously prevent her from asking whether or not the client is working. As was pointed out in chapter 5, caseworkers generally visit the clients once every three months for a little more than thirty minutes per visit. This pressure of caseloads plus general professional social work orientations results in the caseworker discussing general family matters rather than specific regulation during the home visit. Clients report that caseworkers do not go over the budget, do not deal with specific social matters, and generally keep away from sensitive areas. This indicates that caseworkers avoid asking clients if they are working, especially since an affirmative reply might lead to more work for the caseworker, to incurring the wrath of the family, or to making an illegal decision.

What do welfare recipients think about the earned-income policy, and does this affect work effort or attitudes toward work? As Table 6.10

TABLE 6.10. RESPONDENTS' ATTITUDES TOWARD EARNED-INCOME POLICY

	"Do you believe that this is the best policy?"						
	Mil-waukee	*Dane*	*Brown*	*Wal-worth*	*Sauk*	*Dodge*	*Total*
Yes	30.8%	27.4%	38.4%	25.0%	28.1%	25.8%	29.6%
Not sure	10.6	16.2	15.1	16.3	26.3	24.2	15.3
No	46.4	49.7	36.0	46.2	31.6	33.9	43.9
Don't know	12.3	6.7	10.5	12.5	14.0	16.1	11.2
Number	(302)	(179)	(86)	(80)	(57)	(62)	(766)

shows, large numbers of women in all the counties disapproved of the earned-income policy. Those who approved of the policy either said that "the rule is fair" or that "the policy encourages you to do the best you can for yourself, but still helps you." Those who disapproved said that deducting the earnings hurts initiative and that a person on welfare who works ought to be able to keep all her earned income. Although the number of respondents who answered "not sure" is small, their reasons indicated that they disapproved of the policy; that is, they generally gave the same reasons as those respondents who said directly that they did not believe the department's policy was the best policy.

We expected to find that working women, who would be most aware of the official policy, would be the more likely to disapprove of the treatment of earned income. However, in Milwaukee and Brown Counties those presently working tended to favor the policy as compared to those who are not working. This again suggests that the policy was not being applied to them, and that these welfare recipients were doing what is fairly common among welfare recipients—distinguishing between themselves as "deserving" and others as "undeserving," and willing to have restrictive policies applied to the latter. Those who know more about the treatment of earned income are more likely to say that they would want to work (if good baby-sitting were available) as compared to those who know less about the treatment of earned income. Those who have no idea whatsoever about the treatment of earned income are the least inclined to work. It may be that women who work, or who want very much to work, disregard the official earned-income policy in their decisions to seek employment. If employment is a way to leave the AFDC program, to get out of the house regularly, to move away from the role of a welfare dependent, perhaps the treatment of earned income receives little weight in decisions about whether to work. On the other hand, other studies show that the poor are very likely to make decisions about working solely in economic terms: given their skill levels and work experience, they cannot and do not expect security in work, job satisfaction, etc. They are working primarily for income, not for fringe benefits. This again would lead to the conclusion that the earned-income policy does not have a disincentive effect because of the lack of enforcement.

In summarizing client attitudes toward employment, we find (a) most AFDC recipients would like to work if their children could be taken care of, especially younger women or women with recent employment; (b) most have short work histories, held low-level jobs, and were only a short time in the labor force; and (c) although most are aware of the policy on the treatment of earned income and do not approve of it, it is not clear that this affects their desire to work.

THE CASEWORKERS

Attitudes and Activities

The AFDC caseworkers in the six counties were asked a series of questions designed to tap their attitudes toward employment. Generally, there were very few differences in attitudes among the caseworkers. All agreed that discussions about employment possibilities were very important "in helping the client to independence." They felt that employment possibilities should not only be discussed with the clients but that the caseworkers should initiate the discussions.

The caseworkers' approach to employment problems was through personal services. When asked about introducing changes, most said that "vocational rehabilitation plans" in agency programs "should definitely" be increased. They were decidedly less enthusiastic about liberalizing the earned-income policies, supporting families when the father is in the home (AFDC-UP, which has subsequently been enacted), and providing a minimum income to all people below the "poverty line." These three reforms are designed to get more money to poor families but would also reduce the authority of the caseworker. Liberalizing the earned-income policy would provide a market stimulant for self-help, as distinguished from a counseling stimulant or social service. Under AFDC-UP the caseworker obviously has less of a role, with the family intact, and continued welfare support is tied very closely to employment and the state employment services rather than to caseworker discretion. Minimum-income plans are usually advanced as nondiscretionary grants and have work-incentive tax rates. Thus, although the caseworkers had a very "positive" attitude toward the importance of employment and their role in helping clients in this area, their approach is very traditional—counseling and training programs.[7]

Professional social workers view employment within a rehabilitative framework and are not in favor of an AFDC mother working simply to reduce welfare costs. They favor work if it means a more useful and satisfying life for the family and prefer retraining rather than relaxation of the earned-income policy, since the latter would merely provide an incentive for the mother to leave the home to increase earnings at low-level jobs.

---

[7] Among the three urban counties (Brown, Milwaukee, Dane), there was some variation in the responses. Brown County caseworkers attached more importance to employment discussions, and more women in Brown County worked. Milwaukee County caseworkers were more strongly in favor of vocational and rehabilitation programs, which may reflect the difficulty that Milwaukee AFDC mothers have in obtaining employment. However, these differences were quite small.

Whether or not an AFDC mother should work is considered by caseworkers to be a professional social work decision (which means in theory a decision made by the clients but with professional advice). In addition, professional social workers have always been suspicious of employment programs, and, it might be added, with good reason. This country has had a long history—which is by no means over—of menial work being imposed on welfare families for the sole reason of reducing welfare costs, without any regard to the welfare of the family itself. Therefore, it is natural for social workers to view employment as only one of several techniques available for rehabilitation (and not necessarily the most important technique, at that), and to be very uneasy about losing control of employment decisions, particularly to another government agency.

Clients' Attitudes toward Caseworkers' Activities

Welfare clients' views of caseworkers' activities present a very different picture from what the caseworkers said they were doing. Presently unemployed recipients (556 respondents) were asked whether the caseworkers "ever discussed a job for you or tried to find a job." Fewer than one-third (31.5 percent) said yes. In comparing the three urban counties, 52.4 percent of the Brown County respondents reported such discussions as compared to 29.5 percent in Milwaukee and 27.1 percent in Dane.

Are caseworker discussions related to employability (skills and experience), to work orientation (attitudes) of the clients, or to social or family characteristics? One might expect that the caseworkers, who feel employment is important to achieving independence, would discuss employment or help find employment for those clients with experience and motivation, even though clients with little work experience and low work orientation would be more in need of caseworker assistance to enter the labor market. We therefore expected to find more caseworker activity among women who were younger, had fewer preschool children, had longer work experience and higher skills, were more interested in working, and were white.

For the most part, there was no relationship between work experience and caseworkers' discussions or help in finding a job. In five out of six counties the same proportions of women reported discussions regardless of whether or not they had worked since coming on the AFDC program (or within the last three years, whichever was shorter). The one exception was Brown County, where more clients who had worked reported discussions than those who had not worked. Nor was there any relationship between the number of jobs a respondent had had since leaving school and caseworker discussions about employment. Similarly, there was no relationship between the total number of years employed prior to coming on the program and caseworker discussions. In other words, work experience does not seem to have much effect on whether a caseworker discussed work with an AFDC mother.

Caseworker discussions were related to such social characteristics bearing on employability as respondent's age and number of preschool children living in the home. Younger women were more likely to report discussions than older women, and the more preschool children she had, the less likely the respondent was to report caseworker discussions. Finally, in Milwaukee County discussions were related to race—more white respondents reported such discussions than blacks.

Attitudes toward work were related to caseworker discussions; the more a client wanted to work, the more likely she was to report discussions with her caseworker. This relationship was strongest for those who both wanted to work and who had had work experience. On the other hand, the relationship between attitudes toward work and caseworker activity did not hold for blacks. Even though more blacks wanted to work than whites, caseworkers still tended not to discuss employment with blacks.

If caseworker behavior—as reported by clients—reflects the caseworker's assessment of employability, then the most important employability factors are age, number of preschool children, and attitudes toward work. Skill and experience are apparently not considered very important, and they may not be important for the type of job that the AFDC mother is likely to get—semi- or unskilled factor, semiskilled service, or below. The differential treatment afforded black AFDC mothers seems to indicate that caseworker activity reflects, and therefore supports, the general societal pattern of discrimination in employment.

Respondents who did have employment discussions with their caseworkers were asked what happened and what their attitudes were toward their caseworker's activity. The responses are tabulated in Table 6.11.

Very little happened with over 80 percent of this particular group: the respondents were not interested or the caseworker just gave general advice and encouragement. In Milwaukee and Brown Counties something specific did happen; a small group of respondents reported that the caseworker made a special effort or that they got a job or went to school.[8] Interestingly, in Dane County—the county that is supposed to be the most progressive—only two clients reported specific help.

Most women who had these discussions said they were not bothered by them. Clients who thought they were helped were more likely to say

---

[8] It is not clear from the data whether the job or schooling was or was not the result of caseworker efforts. We are assuming that it was, since this was the answer that the respondents gave when asked what happened as a result of caseworker discussions.

TABLE 6.11.   CLIENT RESPONSES TO CASEWORKER
DISCUSSIONS ABOUT EMPLOYMENT[a]

	Counties			
Questions asked	Milwaukee	Dane	Brown	Total[b]
Caseworker discussed employment	29.5%	27.1%	52.4%	31.5%
"What happened as a result of the discussions?"				
Nothing	8.1	15.8	6.1	8.0
Respondent not interested; needed at home; medical difficulties	37.1	44.7	27.3	42.0
Caseworker just gave general encouragement	32.3	34.2	45.5	33.3
Respondent got job or schooling	12.9	2.6	15.2	9.2
Caseworker made specific effort to find job or schooling	9.6	2.6	6.0	7.4
Number	(62)	(38)	(33)	(174)
"Did you find the discussions helpful?"				
Very	27.4	7.9	21.2	17.2
Moderately	17.7	13.2	15.2	14.4
Somewhat	22.6	28.9	36.4	29.3
Not at all	32.3	50.0	27.3	39.7
"Did the discussions bother you?"				
Very much	8.1	13.2	12.1	11.5
Moderately	3.2	5.3	12.1	7.5
Somewhat	14.5	15.8	21.2	14.9
Not at all	74.2	63.2	54.5	66.1
"Did you feel that you had to follow the caseworker's advice?"				
All the time	14.5	5.3	9.1	9.8
Most of the time	22.6	10.5	39.4	27.0
Not very often	14.5	13.2	24.2	16.1
Not at all	48.4	65.8	27.3	46.0
Number	(62)	(38)	(33)	(174)

[a] Of those not employed.
[b] Entire sample, i.e., including the three rural counties.

they were not bothered by the discussions; and 80 percent of the clients who were very bothered reported not being helped at all. As with social services, when caseworkers had something tangible to give to the clients (as distinguished from general advice or conversation), clients tended to say the discussions were helpful and were more inclined to say they had to follow their caseworker's advice. Here, the number of clients who had been helped specifically by caseworker discussions about employment is too small for a refined analysis. However, we do note that in Dane County—where the least specific help was reported—significantly higher proportions of respondents said that they were not helped at all by the caseworker discussions and that they did not have to follow the caseworker's advice.

The respondents who were not presently working, and who said that the caseworkers had *not* discussed employment, were asked whether they had ever asked the caseworker to help them find a job. Only twenty-eight respondents (7.7 percent) of this group (not working and no caseworker discussions) said yes.

CONCLUSIONS: THE ECONOMICS OF WORKING AND WELFARE PRACTICES

Although most welfare recipients say they would like to work, they apparently do not use their caseworkers to discuss employment problems and on the whole, the caseworkers do not do much for the clients either. Under the rules existing at the time, it is easy to see why the caseworkers stayed away from employment; there was very little reason for an AFDC mother to work unless the rules on the treatment of earned income were ignored.

A welfare family would presumably choose work rather than welfare if its earned income exceeded the welfare grant plus the minimum work-related expense allowances. Under the earned-income rules at the time of the survey, everything over expenses was supposed to be taxed at 100 percent; therefore the full-time wage was the breakeven point. If the full-time wage were more than the welfare grant plus expenses, the family would be motivated to choose work; if it were lower, to stay on welfare.

In 1967 the basic need for a family of four, which was met at 100 percent in Wisconsin, was $218.[9] There was some variation in the expense allowance. In Dane County, in what was described as a "typical expense allowance," there was the automatic $40 exempted from income; $64 (or $16 per week) was allowed for child care, $10 for transportation (assuming public transportation), and $2 for miscellaneous items such as uniforms, hose, shoes, etc., for a total of $116 for work expenses. Added to this was the basic grant of $218, for a total of $332 per month, or $77 per week, as the breakeven level.

Where possible, estimates were made of the prevailing wage rates during 1967 for the job categories in which the AFDC mothers had worked

---

[9] The average grant per welfare recipient (for both Wisconsin and the six counties in the survey) is about $50 per month, which is very close to the basic need of a family of four.

in the six counties.[10] If we assume that AFDC mothers can work full time at a job at least commensurate with their occupational level before welfare, then only about 5 percent were definitely capable of earning wages at about the breakeven level. These included all skilled workers, skilled clerical, and skilled service workers in Dane and Milwaukee Counties. Another 9 percent could earn wages fairly close to the breakeven point. These include all low-skill clerical workers and sales workers in Dane and Milwaukee Counties. Probably some of the skilled service workers in the rural counties could come near the breakeven point, but there would certainly be some low-skill clerical and sales workers in the urban counties who would not equal the breakeven wage. Although these estimates are crude, it is still difficult to see how more than about 15 percent of the AFDC recipients are capable of self-support.

Therefore, unless a caseworker can disclose to the recipient that the earned-income policy will not be applied, there is little point in having discussions about employment with clients. Even working full time, very few recipients will be able to get off welfare.

This, then, was the situation in 1967. Despite the promises of the proponents of the social service amendments, the issues of work and welfare were at a standoff. Clients could not only hold part-time jobs, and caseworkers could not or would not help clients get work because of the

---

[10] Ronald Hurdlebrink, a graduate student in the Department of Economics, University of Wisconsin, made the wage-rate estimates from BUREAU OF LABOR STATISTICS, U.S. DEP'T. OF LABOR, AREA WAGE SURVEY OF THE MILWAUKEE, WISCONSIN METROPOLITAN AREA, BULL. 1575–67 (April 1968); id., AREA WAGE SURVEY FOR THE GREEN BAY, WISCONSIN METROPOLITAN AREA, BULL. 1530–5 (August 1966); MANPOWER ADMINISTRATION, U.S. DEP'T OF LABOR, EARNINGS MOBILITY OF MDTA TRAINEES, MANPOWER EVALUATION REP. 7 (April 1967); WISCONSIN STATE EMPLOYMENT SERVICE, SURVEY OF WAGE RATES IN SELECTED OCCUPATIONS, BULL. 3142 (December 1967). Wages reported in the above wage surveys were not reported under the same classifications used in Table 6.1 of this study, but for specific jobs. We placed as many jobs as possible in the Table 6.1 categories and then averaged the wages for all jobs in each category. All wages given were either medians or averages, and in many categories the sample was quite wide. Using the average wage probably overstates what would be available to beginning workers, even with experience. Another possible upward bias arises because most of the jobs do not differentiate between male and female wage rates, and the former are almost always higher than the latter.

No data were available for Sauk and Walworth Counties. However, the figures for Dodge County were fairly typical of 21 areas surveyed by the WSES SURVEY OF WAGE RATES, except for Dane County. Therefore it is assumed that Sauk and Walworth were the same as Dodge. We also assumed that wage rates in Dane County were the same as Milwaukee County when separate figures were not available.

clients' level of skill and because of the job market, without engaging in deliberate fraud. In the meantime, welfare rolls and costs kept rising. In that context the WIN program was enacted.

THE OPERATION OF WIN

The Program in Theory

Under the WIN program, the Department of Health, Education, and Welfare (through the state and county departments of welfare) refers welfare recipients to the Department of Labor (that is, state employment services) for work or training. Each member of an AFDC family aged sixteen or older who is not in school full time is eligible for referral, with the following exceptions: (1) recipients who are ill, incapacitated, or of "advanced age"; (2) recipients "whose remoteness from a project precludes effective participation in work or training"; and (3) recipients whose presence in the home is required because of the illness or incapacity of another member of the household. Welfare recipients may also request referrals. A recipient making such a request to the welfare agency must be referred "unless the State [welfare] agency determines that participation . . . would be inimical to the welfare of such person or the family."[11]

The WIN program has teeth. If a person who has been referred to the Department of Labor refuses without "good cause" to participate in a "work incentive program" (which can include training) or to "accept employment in which he is able to engage which is offered through the public employment offices of the State," or rejects without "good cause" a bona fide offer of employment from a private employer, then that person's needs will no longer be taken into account in determining the family AFDC grant. Aid for that person can continue for a period of sixty days, in the form of protective or vendor payments, only if that person "accepts counseling or other services (which the State [welfare] agency shall make available . . .) aimed at persuading such [person] . . . to participate in such program. . . ."[12]

Recipients referred to the state employment services are to be handled in one of three ways: (1) If at all possible, they are to be moved immedi-

[11] 42 U.S.C. §§ 602 (a) (19) (A) (iv)–(vii) (Supp. IV, 1969), *amending* 42 U.S.C. § 602 (a) (1964).

[12] 42 U.S.C. § 602 (a) (19) (F). There is a right to a fair hearing on any of these determinations. For a recent discussion of the fair provisions under the WIN program, see Comment, *Public Welfare "WIN" Program: Arm-Twisting Incentives,* 117 U. Pa. L. Rev. 1062 (1969).

ately into regular employment or on-the-job training positions under existing federal programs. In deciding the appropriate action for each referral, the state employment services are to inventory the work history of all referrals and use aptitude and skill testing if indicated. The earnings exemption (explained below) would be applicable; but if earnings are high enough, the family leaves the AFDC program. (2) The state employment service may recommend training that could include "basic education, teaching of skills in a classroom setting, employment skills, work experience, and any other training found useful." Recipients would be "assigned to the training suitable for them and for which jobs were available in the area."[13] During the training period the family would continue to receive its AFDC grant plus up to $30 a month as a training incentive, for not more than a year. (3) Special work projects would employ "those for whom jobs in the regular economy cannot be found at the time and for whom training may not be appropriate."[14] These projects will be furnished by public agencies and private nonprofit agencies organized for a public purpose. Participants are guaranteed that their total income will be at least equal to their AFDC grant plus 20 percent. If the wages do not equal that amount, then the state welfare agencies will make a supplemental assistance grant.

Congress encouraged the Department of Labor to develop jobs and placement facilities. Special efforts along these lines are required since "it seems obvious that the regular labor market channels are insufficient, and sometimes discriminate against those on welfare."[15] The program is also to provide "follow-up" services for those families who return to welfare after an unsatisfactory work experience. Authority is granted to help families relocate "in order to enable them to become permanently employable and self-supporting." However, no family is to be required to relocate.

The Senate Committee believed "that many mothers of children on AFDC would like to work and improve the economic situation of their families if they could be assured of good facilities in which to leave their children during working hours."[16] Accordingly, state welfare agencies were required to make "arrangements for adequate day care facilities." The state agencies were also encouraged to explore the possibility of using AFDC mothers to care for the children of other AFDC mothers who took jobs.

The 1967 amendments liberalized the treatment of earned income. Under the new law, all of the earnings of children up to a maximum of

---

[13] S. Rep. No. 744, 90th Cong. 1st Sess. (1967) (*U.S. Code,* 2 Cong. & Admin. News, 2985).

[14] *Id.*

[15] *Id.*

[16] *Id.* at 2992.

$150 per family are exempt as long as the child is in school full time or, if in school part time, not a full-time employee. All other employed AFDC family members can retain the first $30 of their monthly earnings plus one-third of all the rest, without reduction in their welfare benefits.

The ceiling or "freeze" on the number of children on the AFDC rolls was designed as an incentive to the states to develop the WIN program and the AFDC-UP program. The "freeze" applies to children receiving AFDC because of the *absence* of the father; it does not apply to children receiving AFDC because of the death or incapacity or unemployment of the father.

Although the Department of Labor administers the WIN program, AFDC recipients must be referred by state welfare agencies. The statute says that the agencies shall make provision for the "prompt referral" of "appropriate" persons, with three stated exceptions (noted above), which are fairly narrowly drawn.[17] In other words, a state welfare agency *cannot* refer a person who falls within any of three stated exceptions; but the state welfare agency must still decide from among those potentially eligible, who is "appropriate."

The regulations of the Department of Health, Education, and Welfare attempt to guide the state and county departments of welfare in deciding who is "appropriate" for referral.[18] First, HEW adds to the list those persons who *cannot* be referred: (1) a child attending school full time; and (2) "a person whose presence in the home is required because adequate childcare services cannot be furnished."[19] From the pool of potentially eligi-

---

[17] The Senate Committee Report listed two other exceptions, neither of which appeared in the final legislation. One was for mothers (or a person acting as a mother) who was in fact caring for one or more preschool children and whose presence in the home was necessary and in "the best interest of the children." The other was even more broadly drawn. A person need not be referred "whose participation the State welfare agency finds would not be in his best interest and would be inconsistent with the objectives of the program." However, these very broadly drawn discretionary exceptions were not included in the final bill because the House-Senate Conference Committee thought that the state welfare agencies would have this power anyway when they decided who was "appropriate." Conf. Rep. No. 1030, 90th Cong., 1st Sess. (1967) (*U.S. Code,* 2 CONG. & ADMIN. NEWS 3179, 3204).

[18] The Department of Health, Education, and Welfare Regulations on the WIN program are found at: Proposed HEW Reg. § 220.35, 34 Fed. Reg. (January 28, 1969).

[19] This latter provision could be very important and may even defeat the coercive features of the WIN program altogether. The regulations state that out-of-home child-care services must meet state and federal licensing requirements. In-home care must meet state standards which, in turn, "must be reasonably in accord with the recommended standards of related national standard setting organizations, such as the Child Welfare League of America and the National Council for Homemaker Services." But in any event, "such care must

ble referrals (i.e., those determined to be "appropriate"), the state welfare
agencies can decide who is eligible for *mandatory* referrals or *optional* referrals. The difference between the two methods of referral is that the
sanctions for refusal to participate or for quitting without good cause only
apply to those who are referred on a mandatory basis. Unemployed fathers
and children sixteen and over who are not "substantially full-time in
school, at work, or in training and for whom there are no educational
plans" must be included in the mandatory referral category. All other
AFDC recipients can be considered in the optional category if a state so
wishes. A state may decide that all others should be referred on a mandatory basis or only some of the others should be in the mandatory referral
category. For example, mothers with no preschool children could be referred on a mandatory basis, while mothers with preschool children could
be on an optional basis. But all recipients who volunteer must be referred
on an optional basis.[20]

The Wisconsin State Department of Health and Social Services has
taken the narrowest allowable position—only unemployed fathers and
children sixteen and over are to be referred on a mandatory basis. All
others are to be considered, in effect, volunteers. In other words, at least
according to the State Department, there shall be no coercion with regard
to AFDC mothers.[21] However, as will be discussed below, the extent to
which state policy superceded the authority of the county departments or
employment divisions was not settled by the WIN legislation.

Through its definition of "good cause," the Department of Labor
took the position that AFDC recipients should not be coerced into accepting employment or training.[22] Some of the reasons that constitute "good

---

be suitable for the individual child, and the parents must be involved *and agree
to the type of the care provided." Id.* (emphasis added). In other words, according to the regulations, the mother has a veto power over the referral decision. The language is clear—the mother has to agree to the type of child care
provided. No doubt, a "reasonableness" requirement will be read in—the
mother's refusal has to be "reasonable." It would seem, though, that if the day-
care services failed to meet statutory and regulatory standards, refusal to agree
could not be considered "unreasonable." In any event, despite the clear language of the HEW regulations dealing with day care, there will be a leeway
for state and local administrative discretion.

[20] Social and Rehabilitation Service, CB-11, sec. 41 (1969). U.S. Dep't
of Health, Education and Welfare, Guidelines for Work Incentive Program.

[21] Letter from Robert S. Baldwin, Chief, Administrative Services Section,
Division of Family Services, Wisconsin State Department of Health and Social
Services, August 12, 1969.

[22] The Department of Labor regulations are in MANPOWER ADMINISTRA-
TION, U.S. DEP'T OF LABOR, WORK INCENTIVE PROGRAM HANDBOOK (July 25,
1968).

cause" simply restate the legislation (e.g., incapacitation); others are fairly narrow (e.g., the job offer is below Department of Labor wage requirements); but others are quite broad—for example, "the mother's child care plan has broken down and alternative child care cannot be arranged"; "the job is not within the physical or mental capacity of the person"; or "acceptance of the assignment would be detrimental to the family life of the individual."

The effect, then, of the WIN amendments was as follows: (1) The very troublesome issues of work and welfare, which have always plagued welfare policy and administration, were not "resolved" by Congress in 1967 despite its rhetoric. These issues were once again delegated to state and local governments. (2) New weapons were given to those welfare agencies that want to reduce welfare rolls by requiring recipients to work. Most of these agencies already had discretionary power over employment and many, no doubt, reduced welfare rolls by requiring people to work even when legal power was lacking. But the WIN amendments will help these agencies when they meet resistance from clients, clients organizations (and their lawyers), and HEW. (3) The WIN program, if adequately financed by Congress and capably administered by the Department of Labor, will assist those welfare agencies that want to help welfare recipients who want to become self-supporting through work or retraining. Greater opportunities and incentives can now be made available. (4) Agencies that are indifferent to work and retraining can probably continue as before. In sum, the WIN amendments have introduced another government agency (the Department of Labor) into the work and welfare mix, but local welfare agency discretion still remains a key element in the administration of employment programs for welfare recipients. Nobody gets into a WIN program unless he goes himself or gets a referral from the department of welfare.

The Administration of WIN in Wisconsin

The WIN program in Wisconsin is administered by the Wisconsin State Employment Service.[23] Although the WIN program has been in operation for less than a full year, it is fairly obvious that many of the claims,

---

[23] Much of the data on the actual operation of the WIN program in Wisconsin was collected by Michal Fentin, a graduate student in sociology, and Ronald Hurdlebrink, a graduate student in economics, as students in Professor Handler's seminar on welfare administration at the University of Wisconsin, spring semester, 1969. In addition to documentary research, they conducted several interviews with state and local officials administering the WIN program. We gratefully acknowledge their help.

both positive and negative, made at the time of its enactment will never be realized. Despite congressional statements to the contrary, we have seen that departments of welfare still retain crucial control over employment decisions involving most AFDC families. On June 30, the "freeze" was quietly repealed by Congress. The new taxing rules on earned income— the $30 and ⅓ rule—was mandated on the states as of July 1, 1969, but many states are still not in compliance because state law has not yet been changed. It is also quite clear that WIN will not make much of a dent in welfare rolls. First, not enough positions are funded, and second, in weighting the economics of working versus staying on welfare, the new taxing rules favor staying on welfare, since the breakeven point is now higher.

In 1967, when WIN was enacted, there were approximately 1.2 million AFDC families, comprising nearly 5 million individuals. Congress authorized training for 100,000 persons in 1968, with the proposed number to be trained to be increased each year to 280,000 in 1972, or a total after five years of 860,000. The Senate Finance Committee estimated that there would be no full-time job placements during the first year of the program (1968), approximately 50,000 in 1969, with an increase to 95,000 in 1972, for a total of 290,000 full-time job placements after five years of operating. Of course, we have no reason to suppose that AFDC rolls will not continue to increase, too. In 1969, on the average, there were over 21,000 families on AFDC in Wisconsin, including 1,057 on AFDC-UP; the number of WIN slots allocated for the state was 1,786. In 1970 AFDC rolls rose to about 23,400 families and the allocated WIN slots were 2,280. AFDC-UP accounts for a little more than 5 percent of the total AFDC caseload in Wisconsin, but because AFDC-UP fathers must be referred first, they have already taken 40 percent of the WIN slots. Finally, during the first year of operation of WIN only about 70 percent of the slots were filled. We will discuss the reasons for this below, and it could be that eventually all the WIN slots will be filled. But even so, the total number of mothers on AFDC will not decrease appreciably simply because the WIN program will reach so few recipients.

It is hard to predict what effect the new tax rates will have on AFDC caseloads and welfare costs, since there is great doubt about what the effective tax rate is now on the earned income of recipients. But at least in theory, under the WIN amendments costs initially should rise. For those AFDC recipients who are working and taxed at 100 percent, more of their earnings will become "tax free" and their welfare payments will probably increase. One commentator, Leonard J. Hausman, says:

> As you raise the minimum payment in the absence of other income to be more humane, and as you reduce the "tax rates" on

earnings that are built into the program to provide financial incentives to work, you raise the level of income at which the program payments are reduced to zero. For example, in the case of an AFDC mother who now receives $2,000 per year in assistance payments, reducing the welfare tax rate from 100 percent to the zero—66⅔ percent combination of the new law results in her being allowed to get some welfare payments until her earnings reach $4,110—her new "breakeven" level of income.[24]

Using Hausman's figures, we have a breakeven of $4,287 per year for a four-person family in Wisconsin with the $30 and ⅓ rule, or just over $82 per week. At this figure, only 5 percent of the Wisconsin AFDC caseload is capable of self-support. Nor will retraining make that much difference. After analyzing wages of welfare recipients who completed MDTA training, Hausman concludes: "The WIN program can, if properly implemented, enhance the employability of recipients; but it cannot, *given their present productive powers and the amount of resources that will be invested in their rehabilitation,* bring a large proportion of them to total self-support within the near future [author's emphasis]."[25] Several Wisconsin officials dealing with the administration of WIN agree with this conclusion, particularly with regard to female-headed households. They view the WIN program as a way of getting more money to the family by reducing but not eliminating welfare payments, and as a way of giving the mother work experience to prepare her for the time when she leaves welfare.

During its first year of operation Wisconsin WIN was only able to fill about 70 percent of the allocated slots. In part this was due to delays in getting the Department of Labor guidelines, federal delays in funding, and the difficulties in hiring new staff. In some areas of the state the WIN staff cannot now handle the number of recipients that are being referred; in other areas, the welfare agencies are not able to provide enough referrals to keep the WIN staff working to capacity. One problem is arranging day care that complies with federal standards, particularly if the mother wants to leave the child with neighbors—which seems to be the preferred alternative. A more basic problem of low referrals has to do with the welfare agencies. WIN officials complain that caseworkers are not referring clients because they were unfamiliar with the WIN program, are not really in favor of employment and retraining, or were suspicious about this particular program because of its legislative history and coercive provisions. Case-

---

[24] L. J. Hausman, *The AFDC Amendments of 1967: Their Impact on the Capacity for Self-support and the Employability of AFDC Family Heads,* LABOR L.J. 496, 500 (1968).

[25] The Welfare System as a Rehabilitation and Manpower System 19 (November 1968) (mimeo.).

worker turnover and vacancies—perennial problems in public assistance—also serve to reduce referrals. Many caseworkers are simply not sufficiently familiar with their clients to recommend referral. Milwaukee is having a great deal of difficulty in making referrals just for this reason and, with forty caseworker vacancies, is having difficulty in just keeping up with its normal work. Finally, AFDC-UP fathers must be referred first; since these take up considerable caseworker time, this too cuts down on the AFDC referrals.

As a result of the dual responsibility between Labor and HEW, WIN officials say that they spend a great deal of time explaining the program to welfare departments in efforts to get better cooperation. WIN says that the program is strictly voluntary as far as women are concerned. In fact, according to local WIN administration, the woman has to make some positive effort to get in—she has to arrange for her own medical examination and child care, even though welfare pays for both.

It is really up to the local departments of welfare to determine how voluntary the program is going to be. State law still gives the county departments substantial authority over the employment conditions of welfare, and state welfare officials admit that counties can make involuntary referrals if adequate child-care arrangements are made. Although one can only speculate about what would happen if particular "work-oriented" counties took a hard line with referrals, our guess is that they would have their way. If a county agency is really serious about requiring a mother to work, she would be foolish to refuse to participate in a WIN program. If WIN rejected her because of her refusal, she would then be subject to the usual welfare agency sanctions, which no doubt would be less attractive than the WIN program.

Upon closer examination, another "new direction" in welfare policy looks pretty much like the same old one. The administration of employment services for AFDC will (a) be highly decentralized and subject to broad administrative discretion at the local level, and (b) touch very few AFDC recipients. In this respect the rehabilitative services of WIN are no different from other social service programs that have been enacted for AFDC. Nationally, funding is too low to make much difference and caseloads are too high to allow for much redirective effort by caseworkers and employment service personnel. As with social services, in various parts of the country imaginative officials will be able to help small numbers of AFDC families, while elsewhere punitive officials will exercise their new weapons. But in the main, for the millions of individuals on AFDC, there will be no employment services other than those provided by the welfare agencies.

The one part of the 1967 amendments, however, that could make a difference in the status quo is the new rules dealing with the treatment of earned income. At least on paper, they do provide a substantial incentive for AFDC mothers. Under the new rules the breakeven level is higher than under the old rules—from $77 to $82 per week—which means that even fewer AFDC recipients will probably be able to earn their way off welfare. However, there now will be strong incentives for the recipients to supplement their grants by working, and they can do this without using county welfare department caseworker services and without committing fraud.

THE WORK REQUIREMENTS OF THE FAMILY ASSISTANCE ACT

The Family Assistance Act takes the same basic approach to the work test as the WIN legislation. The incentive features are retained and Congress envisages that much of the work of employment services under the WIN program will continue. There are some changes, however. One apparently important change is that much of the discretion of welfare agencies over the referral process has been taken away. All who are eligible for FAP benefits —and this includes, of course, the female-headed house now covered by AFDC—must register with state employment service offices for "manpower services, training, and employment." There are, however, several exceptions to the mandatory referral, the principal one being mothers or other relatives who are taking care of preschool children.

If an individual who has registered has been found by the Secretary of Labor (after "reasonable notice and opportunity for hearing") to have refused without good cause to participate in "suitable manpower services, training, or employment," or to have refused suitable employment offered through the employment service or a bona fide offer of employment, then that individual loses his benefits, although his income will still be counted as part of the family income.

At this point it is very difficult to predict how the proposed work requirements will affect the welfare population now covered by the AFDC program. Once again one sees the importance of field-level administration —who is doing the administering and under what standards and controls. In the WIN program, despite the publicity and announced intentions of Congress, state and local departments retained most of the control over employment of welfare recipients. As FAP now reads, this issue is still not settled. First, it is not clear who is going to administer FAP. The bill provides that the states can contract with HEW to have HEW administer state welfare programs, or HEW can contract with the states to have them administer some or all of FAP. If the usual practice were continued, HEW would contract with the states to administer FAP through the state and local departments of welfare. This would maximize state and local discretion in administration. Moreover, the Secretary of Labor must obtain HEW's agreement

> with regard to such policies and programs which are under the usual and traditional authority of the Secretary of Health, Education, and Welfare (including basic education, institutional training, health, child care and other supportive services, new careers and job restructuring in the health, education, and welfare professions, and work-study programs). . . .[26]

Thus there is ample opportunity for welfare agencies to play a large role in the employment program, and, again, in light of the WIN experience, this eventuality is not unlikely. What will constitute good cause for refusal to participate in employment programs? How meaningful will promises be of no sanctions against voluntary registrants who decide not to participate? There are many ways to persuade welfare recipients that it is in their best interests to volunteer and participate—welfare departments have a wide range of benefits that recipients need and want—and it is very difficult to control this type of administrative discretion.[27]

The largest unknown will be the state employment service agencies. In Wisconsin, for example, at least some of the agencies seem to be committed to voluntary employment and to upgrading skills and providing opportunities rather than cutting welfare costs. In other parts of the country, no doubt, there will be employment agencies that need no further help from local welfare officials in requiring welfare recipients to take menial, dead-end jobs against their will. Reports of discriminatory practices, such as considering housework or cleaning lavatories in the courthouse "suitable" for black recipients but never for white recipients, may be a harbinger of things to come.

With our understanding of the work of welfare agencies and other public institutions that deal with poor, disenfranchised, and dependent people—police, voting registrars, schools, and juvenile courts—it should be clear that there is no way to systematically control the exercise of official discretion at the field level. Standards in statutes and regulations will be vague—for example, that work has to be "suitable"—and even if they are clear and objective, there is no way to ensure compliance. Substantive standards and procedural due process are for those who have the ability to use them, and despite the significant work of welfare client organizations,

---

[26] S. 2986, 91st Cong., 1st Sess. § 435.
[27] For an elaboration of this point see J. Handler, *Controlling Official Behavior in Welfare Administration,* 54 CALIF. L. REV. 479, 493–95 (1966).

the vast majority of welfare recipients are simply not in a position to challenge local officials. We are committing a grave injustice if we think otherwise.

We may anticipate, therefore, the same outcome from the work requirements in FAP's proposals that emerged from the WIN program. For the vast majority of those now on the AFDC program the work requirement will be a meaningless formality. Either jobs will not be available or state employment services will merely act as a clearinghouse. These agencies will become swamped with work, and their reaction will be either to "cream" (to work with only those of the highest employment potential) or to become highly routinized. Employment agencies in some parts of the country, those that have the will and the resources, will do some good for some poor people. The sad part is that additional weapons have been provided for those agencies wanting to harass and punish the mothers of a household in poverty. Former Secretary Finch's own words should give aid and comfort to those who still think that coercion is the way to make the poor work:

> The program includes a strong work requirement: those able-bodied persons who refuse a training or suitable job opportunity lose their benefits. For this reason, the program is not a guaranteed annual income. It does not guarantee benefits to persons regardless of their attitudes; its support is reserved to those who are willing to support themselves.[28]

[28] 115 Cong. Rec. S. 11,724 (daily ed. Oct. 2, 1969).

Chapter 7

STIGMA AND PRIVACY

It has always been assumed that stigma has important consequences for welfare policy. In chapter 1 we saw that in the nineteenth century official policy was to create deliberately a sense of shame and moral inferiority on the part of those who sought relief rather than work. This policy was defended both by those sympathetic to the poor and by those who wanted to save public money. They believed that the failure to earn a living was a sign of moral decay, and that indiscriminate giving of aid would hasten the downward slide to pauperism. Shame was used to discourage people from applying for public assistance and to encourage recipients to get off welfare.

The problem of stigma is one of the central rallying points of those who condemn AFDC and seek to reform it or replace it altogether. They claim that the means test degrades and humiliates recipients and that administrative practices perpetuate feelings of shame. Reform efforts at creating rights and entitlements to welfare—making "need" the sole criterion for eligibility, introducing a simplified means test based on the applicant's affidavit, standardizing and routinizing administration—are designed in part to reduce feelings of stigma. Recipients, it is urged, are no less entitled to dignity and social acceptance than the rest of the population.

Closely related to stigma is the concept of privacy. Disclosing assets and resources, revealing names of one's friends and associates, submitting to investigations and questioning, accounting for expenditures and social behavior—these are the price of receiving welfare. Loss of privacy is loss of dignity and is part of the shame of being a welfare recipient.

What is stigma and what are its consequences? Despite the importance of stigma in interpersonal relationships, not much has been written about it specifically. Most commentators seem to view it in terms of societal disapproval. For example, Erving Goffman says, "the central feature of the stigmatized individual's situation in life . . . is a question of what is often, if vaguely, called acceptance. Those who have dealings with him fail to accord him the respect and regard which the uncontaminated aspects of his

164

social identity have led them to anticipate extending, and have led him to anticipate receiving."[1]

The attitudes that society ascribes to welfare recipients are emphasized by David Matza. He enumerates five characteristics common among AFDC recipients that make them "disreputable": (1) illegitimacy, (2) absence of the father due to imprisonment, (3) absence due to desertion and separation without a court decree, (4) lack of status conferred by the man's occupation, and (5) long-term dependency. Matza claims that this disrepute demoralizes recipients; conscientious effort withers and moral standards decline.[2] This may be an aspect of Goffman's argument that the stigmatized individual responds to the denial of acceptance by "finding that some of his own attributes warrant it." The literature on delinquency and deviant behavior claims similar consequences: stigmatized individuals react in terms of their labels or ascribed characteristics.[3]

Stigma in the welfare context separates into a number of distinct questions. What characteristics does society ascribe to welfare recipients? How do the poor respond to society's attitudes? Do they know about them? Do they care? Further, distinctions have to be made between those who are discouraged from applying for welfare because of their perceptions of society's feelings and those who nevertheless still seek welfare. Aside from feeling bad, do those on welfare who feel stigma have different attitudes toward welfare than those on welfare who do not feel stigma? Do they behave differently?

Some of these issues have been dealt with at least indirectly in the preceding chapters, where we presented data on client attitudes toward the intake process, various administrative practices, and the caseworker. In this chapter we will use an independent measure of feelings of stigma. In discussing client attitudes it should be recalled that the respondents in this survey had been on the AFDC program at least six months at the time of the initial survey. Therefore the conclusions here are not applicable to those who are discouraged from applying for welfare, those whose applications are rejected, and those who have been on the program only a short time. These respondents have made at least some adjustment to their welfare status.

---

[1] E. Goffman, STIGMA (1963). See also E. M. Lemert, *Some Aspects of a General Theory of Sociopathic Behavior,* 16 RES. STUDIES STATE COLL. OF WASHINGTON 23, 28–29 (1948).

[2] D. Matza, *Poverty and Disrepute,* in CONTEMPORARY SOCIAL PROBLEMS (R. Merton & R. Nesbit eds., 1966).

[3] See generally, Gryzier, *The Concept of the "State of Delinquency" and Its Consequences for Treatment of Young Offenders,* 11 WAYNE L. REV. 627, 642–45 (1965).

First, we will define our measure of feelings of stigma and will attempt to relate these feelings of stigma to the background characteristics of the welfare clients. Then we will see if feeling stigma makes any difference in terms of the welfare experience. Do clients who feel stigma respond differently than those who do not in their attitudes toward the means test, social services, the caseworker, privacy, and the welfare experience in general? Do they use the program differently—for example, request special grants for extra needs—or take part in special programs?

WHAT IS STIGMA?

We are using as indicators of feelings of stigma two questions that were asked of the respondents:

> Some ADC mothers have said that when they are with friends or other people not on ADC, they feel embarrassed or uncomfortable about receiving welfare support. Other ADC mothers say they don't feel this way at all. How do you feel when you are with people who don't receive ADC . . . would you say you are never embarrassed or uncomfortable, sometimes embarrassed or uncomfortable, often embarrassed or uncomfortable, or always embarrassed or uncomfortable?

> In general, how do you think people in this community feel about people like yourself who are in the ADC program? Would you say they feel very understanding, fairly understanding, indifferent, fairly hostile, or very hostile?

The two questions are designed to tap what AFDC clients think are attitudes held by others. For example, a recipient may feel that the community is generally understanding, but that the people that she has to deal with (neighbors, small businessmen, etc.) are hostile. Or she may feel the reverse; she has support from people around her, but the community is hostile.

The distribution of respondents on the two indicators of stigma is shown in Table 7.1. The two indicators are strongly related; those who feel embarrassed or uncomfortable with friends also tend to perceive the community as hostile toward welfare recipients (Table 7.2).

As shown by the two indicators (embarrassment and community hostility), more than half the respondents feel at least some stigma: 52.2 percent (385) say that they are either "sometimes" or "often" embarrassed *or*

TABLE 7.1. FEELINGS OF STIGMA (TWO INDICATORS)

Frequency of being embarrassed or uncomfortable with friends or other people not on welfare

Never	50.7%
Sometimes	35.8
Often; always	13.5
Number	(748)

Characterization of community attitudes toward AFDC recipients

Understanding	49.5%
Indifferent	18.8
Hostile	12.2
Don't know	19.3
Number	(749)

that the community is "hostile" to AFDC recipients. Although the answer that the community is "indifferent" to AFDC recipients is ambiguous, in its relationship to the embarrassment responses it suggests that the respondents see "indifference" as a form of community rejection—"the community doesn't care about us." This would be a feeling of stigma under our definition. Then, 61 percent (447) of the respondents would feel at least some stigma.

Respondents were also asked, "Have you or your children had any difficulties or problems with people or businesses in the community that you think happened because you are a welfare recipient?" Fewer than 20 percent said yes, but this too was strongly related to the two indicators of feelings of stigma (Table 7.3).

TABLE 7.2. FEELINGS OF EMBARRASSMENT AND PERCEPTIONS OF COMMUNITY HOSTILITY

	Feelings of Embarrassment		
Community Attitudes	Never	Sometimes	Often; always
Understanding	55.8%	48.3%	33.0%
Indifferent	16.7	20.4	23.0
Hostile	5.4	15.5	28.0
Don't know	22.1	15.8	16.0
Number	(371)	(265)	(100)

TABLE 7.3. FEELINGS OF STIGMA (TWO INDICATORS)
AND PROBLEMS ENCOUNTERED IN THE COMMUNITY

"Have you or your children had any difficulties or problems with people or businesses in the community that you think happened because you are a welfare recipient?"

	Feelings of embarrassment with nonwelfare people			
	Never	Sometimes	Often; always	Number
Yes	11.3%	20.1%	32.0%	(124)
No	88.7	79.9	68.0	(598)
Total	100.0	100.0	100.0	
Number	(371)	(254)	(97)	(722)

	Community attitudes toward welfare recipients				
	Under-standing	Indifferent	Hostile	Don't know	Number
Yes	13.2%	23.2%	41.2%	5.9%	(123)
No	86.8	76.8	58.8	94.1	(598)
Total	100.0	100.0	100.0	100.0	
Number	(363)	(138)	(85)	(135)	(721)

WHO FEELS STIGMA?

Feelings of stigma are not related to either size or type of community in which the respondents live. For both indicators of stigma there were no differences between people who live in rural areas, towns, small cities, Green Bay (population 125,082), Madison (population 222,095), or Milwaukee (population 1,278,850).[4] In this respect the Milwaukee ghetto residents felt neither more nor less embarrassment or community hostility than the residents in towns and cities of other sizes.

In theory, years in residence could have contradictory implications for feelings of stigma. On one hand, it could be argued that long-term residents would know the community and its people better and therefore feel stigma more keenly; comparative newcomers might be unaware of community feelings. On the other hand, longer-term residents might feel that people

---

[4] Population figures for the metropolitan areas, 1960.

and the community were more understanding, while new arrivals might be supersensitive to their status as newcomers going on relief. In any event, we found no relation between the two indicators of stigma and years in residence: long-term residents responded the same way as comparative newcomers.

Respondents were asked about welfare and nonwelfare friends and relatives. One would assume that those who had more friends and relatives would feel less stigma than those who were more isolated. We found no relationship between perceptions of community hostility and (a) how many relatives and friends a welfare recipient had, (b) how many AFDC families the recipient knew in the community, or (c) how many of these AFDC families were "good friends" whom the recipient saw "fairly often." With feelings of embarrassment, there was some relationship: Respondents who had fewer relatives but who knew more AFDC families were more likely to feel embarrassed with nonwelfare people than those who had more relatives or did not know many AFDC families. By these very crude indicators, those who seemed to be more exposed—that is, had fewer relatives but more AFDC friends—tended to say they were more uncomfortable when outside their AFDC circle. But the more an AFDC recipient is embarrassed about being on the program, the more she will tend to discuss welfare problems with both friends (nonwelfare) and relatives.

Concerning other personal characteristics, blacks tended to perceive the community as more hostile than whites, but the relationship was very weak. Race made no difference in feelings of embarrassment. Younger recipients (under forty) felt more stigma on both indicators, but these relationships were also weak. There was no relationship at all between the two indicators of stigma and (a) number of children, (b) previous AFDC experience, (c) whether parents had been on welfare, or (d) employment record. Concerning employment, responses for both indicators were the same whether recipients (a) were presently working, (b) had never worked, or (c) had spent many or few years in the labor force. There was no relationship between feelings of stigma and education. High school graduates or better responded no differently than those who only finished elementary school or less. Those recipients who were presently married felt less stigma than the other recipients, but there were no differences between the divorced, the separated, the deserted, and those who had never married.

In sum, although feelings of stigma do exist among AFDC recipients, our indicators of stigma are only very weakly related or not related at all to the more obvious background characteristics of welfare recipients such as race, employment experience, education, type of community, length of residence, or friendships.

STIGMA AND ATTITUDES TOWARD WELFARE

Feelings of stigma should be related to the recipient's "adjustment" to the welfare experience. We would expect that those who feel stigmatized by being on welfare would tend to be dissatisfied with their welfare experience, would not have a very satisfactory relationship with their caseworker, and would be more upset by welfare administration practices.

The respondents were asked a series of questions concerning their attitudes toward the welfare experience in general: (a) how satisfactory their experience with the welfare agency had been "in view of what you needed"; (b) what the good and bad points of their experience had been; (c) the changes they would like to see in welfare; and (d) whether they benefited from services other than basic financial aid. In general, among these Wisconsin AFDC recipients, there were high proportions who were satisfied with the program (25.3 percent reported "very satisfied" and 59 percent reported "satisfied"). As revealed by the succeeding questions on good points, bad points, and changes, the primary reason for satisfaction was that the AFDC program gave them basic financial security (even though at a low level) and, given their economic and social predicament before welfare, this was no small matter in their lives. The major dissatisfaction was not enough money, and the major change desired was more money. There were very few complaints about the caseworkers or other forms of regulation, since the Wisconsin AFDC program is best characterized as one of minimal caseworker intervention and regulation.

However, among the respondents who felt stigma (on both indicators) there was decidedly less feeling of satisfaction than among those who did not feel stigma. The former said that they were less satisfied with their welfare experience in view of what they needed, they mentioned more bad things about welfare, and they had more changes to suggest than the latter. There were no differences between the two groups concerning the good points of welfare.

There were also differences in attitudes toward the caseworkers. The respondents who felt more stigma (on either indicator) were less inclined to say that their caseworker was someone they liked, trusted, could talk to and discuss problems with, and they were less inclined to say they made a "special effort to stay on good terms" with their caseworker than those recipients who did not feel stigma. Respondents who felt embarrassed or uncomfortable with nonwelfare people were less likely to say that the caseworker had a good reason for what she did than those who did not feel stigma on this one indicator. Here, too, there was a difference in the attitudes of the recipients; those who felt stigma were less "adjusted" than those who did not.

Lack of "adjustment" is also reflected in attitudes toward work and the treatment of earned income. AFDC recipients who were not working were asked whether they would like at least a part-time job if good baby-sitting or day care were available. Respondents who said they were embarrassed or uncomfortable with nonwelfare people were more inclined to say they would like to work than the others. Respondents who felt stigma (on both or either indicator) were more likely to disapprove of the policy for handling earned income than those who did not feel stigma.

STIGMA AND PRIVACY

We used two sets of indicators to measure feelings of privacy and their relationship to stigma. Presumably those who feel more stigma would also be more conscious of invasion of privacy. It will be recalled that for intake, budget, social services, and employment clients were asked their attitudes toward the caseworker discussions—whether they were bothered or annoyed, whether they thought the matters discussed were personal, and whether they felt they had to follow their caseworker's advice. Feelings of stigma were not related to client attitudes on these separate items. Those who felt stigma were neither more nor less upset or coerced than those who had no feelings of stigma.

The other measure of feelings of privacy dealt with unannounced visits by caseworkers. Respondents were asked whether the caseworker usually called at the home unannounced or got in touch first, whether the client felt that it was all right for the caseworker to call unannounced, and whether a welfare client had the right to refuse to let in a caseworker who called unannounced. The responses are tabulated in Table 7.4.

There were great variations in caseworker practices among counties. For example, almost 90 percent of the Dane County respondents reported that the caseworker got in touch first; this was true for only about 30 percent of the Milwaukee and Brown County respondents. Differences in caseworker practice were not related to the presence or absence of telephones; over 70 percent of all respondents had telephones. In the two rural counties, where caseworkers get in touch with fewer than 10 percent of the recipients, two-thirds of the recipients had telephones.

Client attitudes toward the unannounced visit follow fairly closely whatever their own experience had been. Sixty percent of the clients who experience unannounced visits said the practice is all right. Those who had not experienced them said it is not all right (Table 7.5).

Needless to say, the relationship in Table 7.5 is surprising. It has commonly been assumed that one of the most objectionable features of

TABLE 7.4. ATTITUDES TOWARD
UNANNOUNCED VISITS
BY CASEWORKERS

"Does your caseworker usually call at your home unannounced or does he get in touch with you first to let you know that he is coming?"

Unannounced	47.3%
Gets in touch	42.6
Both	9.1
No answer	1.1
Number	(766)

"Do you think it is all right for caseworkers to call unannounced or do you think that they should notify clients in advance?"

All right	50.3%
Should notify	49.1
No answer	0.7
Number	(766)

"Should a welfare client have the right to refuse to let in a caseworker who calls unannounced?"

Yes	27.7%
Not sure	14.1
No	57.8
No answer	0.4
Number	(766)

the welfare system was the unannounced visit. Yet according to these responses, most clients who have experienced the unannounced visit do not seem to object. The relationship, however, is consistent with the clients' experiences with and attitudes toward the caseworkers. As pointed out, caseworkers visit infrequently for a short friendly chat; they are mildly supportive and not threatening. Therefore, those who experience the unannounced visit have not been particularly hurt by it. Those who get called in advance are used to their experience and wary of the unfamiliar.

Attitudes toward the unannounced visit were related to whether the client should have the right to refuse to let in a caseworker who calls unannounced, but there was not a one-to-one relationship (Table 7.6).

As Table 7.6 indicates, of those who approve of unannounced visits, almost three-fourths also said that a welfare client has no right to refuse

TABLE 7.5.   ANNOUNCED AND UNANNOUNCED VISITS,
AND CLIENT ATTITUDES

Client Attitudes	Caseworker's Practice		
	Calls Unannounced	Gets in Touch First	Both
Unannounced visits all right	60.6%	37.1%	59.4%
Unannounced visits not all right	39.4	62.9	40.6
Number	(358)	(326)	(69)

to let in a caseworker who calls unannounced. This is a strong position, and it is held by more than one-third of the entire sample. Those who do not like the unannounced visits were evenly divided about client rights; almost half said that clients must accept this undesirable practice. Less than one-fourth of the sample say that the practice is undesirable and clients have a right to refuse entry.

Feelings of stigma are related to attitudes toward the unannounced visits. Those welfare recipients who are embarrassed or uncomfortable with nonwelfare people are more likely to say that unannounced visits were not all right and clients have the right to refuse entry. Those welfare recipients who did not feel stigma (on this indicator) were more likely to approve of the unannounced visit and say that clients did *not* have a right to refuse entry (Table 7.7).

TABLE 7.6.   ATTITUDES TOWARD
UNANNOUNCED VISIT AND RIGHT
TO REFUSE VISIT

Is it all right for a caseworker to come unannounced?	Should a welfare client have the right to refuse to let in a caseworker who comes unannounced?	
	Yes	No, should notify
Yes	12.8%	43.5%
Not sure	15.1	13.3
No	72.1	43.2
Total	100.0	100.0
Number	(384)	(375)

TABLE 7.7.   FEELINGS OF EMBARRASSMENT AND ATTITUDES
TOWARD UNANNOUNCED VISITS

	Feel embarrassed or uncomfortable with nonwelfare people		
	Never	*Sometimes*	*Often; always*
Disapprove of unannounced visit; client can refuse entry	31.8%	41.4%	50.9%
Approve of unannounced visit; client cannot refuse entry	68.2	58.6	49.1
Number	(233)	(140)	(57)

STIGMA AND WELFARE ACTIVITY

We have seen that welfare recipients do have feelings of stigma that are related to their attitudes toward welfare. Those who have feelings of stigma are less accepting of welfare practices and the caseworker and have a sense of invasion of privacy. But what are the operational consequences of stigma? Does it affect behavior, and if so, how?

One measure of behavior is the use that a welfare client makes of the welfare program. Theoretically, feelings of stigma should affect use of the program. One would expect a low use of the program by people who felt ashamed of being on welfare, who suffer feelings of social disapproval. These people would accept their basic income grant—they have no choice here—but would then withdraw and remain passive.

One difficulty in testing this hypothesis is that in general there was little use of the program among all the recipients surveyed. Comparatively few requests for special grants were made, there was little participation in special programs, and social services operated at a minimum level.

Within that level of activity, however, the data indicate quite the opposite of what was expected: recipients who feel stigma (on either indicator) seem to use the program more than those who do not feel stigma. Even though recipients who feel stigma have less positive feelings toward the caseworker, they make more use of special grants, they complain more to the caseworker, and they make a greater effort to get the caseworker to change decisions that they dislike, as compared to recipients who do not feel stigma. Recipients who feel stigma are not withdrawn or passive; as compared to the others, they seem to be far more aggressive in asserting what they think they are entitled to under the program.

On the other hand, recipients who are embarrassed or uncomfortable with nonwelfare people tend to participate less in special community programs than those who do not have these feelings.

Recipients were asked whether they had "problems or continuing difficulties other than money problems" and if so, whether they discussed these with their caseworker. Recipients who felt stigma (community hostility) were more likely to have problems but less likely to discuss them with the caseworker than those who did not feel stigma.

In four specific social service areas—child care, home care, health, and social life—the respondents were asked if the caseworker discussions were helpful. Helpfulness varied from item to item, but there were no differences in feelings of stigma. The explanation we favor is that social service activity in these areas was so low anyway that it lacked salience for the respondents. Only for health services (i.e., Medicaid) was activity high and meaningful, and use of this necessary benefit would override feelings of stigma. Medicaid was a tangible benefit that the caseworkers pushed, and apparently recipients who did not feel stigma did not hesitate to use what the caseworkers offered. Perhaps this is the difference—recipients who do not feel stigma will use what is thrust upon them but will not ask, whereas recipients who do feel stigma will request and complain if they feel that they are not getting what they are entitled to.

CONCLUSIONS

We have defined feelings of stigma in a very limited way—welfare clients' characterization of community attitudes toward welfare recipients and clients' feelings of embarrassment in the presence of nonwelfare people— for a particular class of welfare recipients—those who have been on the welfare program for at least six months. Within these limitations, a fairly consistent picture emerges. Because the Wisconsin AFDC program meets the single greatest need of the families—the provision of basic economic security (even though at a low level)—and because the administration of the program involves minimum regulation, there is a high level of satisfaction on the part of the recipients. Within this basic pattern, however, there is a decided difference between those who feel stigma and those who do not. The former are less content with their welfare experience. They are less satisfied with the program and less accepting of the caseworker. Moreover, they "do better" with the program than those who do not feel stigma. They ask for more, they complain more, they feel invasions of privacy more, and they participate in more of what is offered.

Feelings of stigma, then, do seem to make a difference in the behavior of women who are on welfare. But we have no evidence as to why some recipients feel stigma and others do not. There were no relationships between our indicators and the background characteristics of the clients.

We think the data cast doubt on the idea that particular welfare experiences produce feelings of stigma—that is, that the attitudes and practices of the agency or of individual caseworkers give recipients feelings of stigma. Clients who felt stigma were less happy with their caseworkers and the program, but they used the program more and asked the caseworker for more.

A factor not considered in this study, but which may make a difference in attitudes and feelings of stigma, is the rise and growth of welfare rights organizations. These organizations began to be formed in the middle and late 1960's (the first national convention was in 1967) and, at the present time, there are organizations in Dane and Milwaukee Counties. However, welfare rights organizations came late to Wisconsin and, at the time of the study, were virtually nonexistent.

It is difficult to assess the impact of these organizations on the kinds of problems that we have dealt with. The leaders and the activists have been aggressive in pressing for benefits, policing possible abuses, and socializing other recipients into the system. Both the Dane and Milwaukee County organizations have staged demonstrations which attracted a great deal of attention, but as with other forms of confrontation politics, calculating gains and losses from these activities is not easy.

Even more difficult is the problem of assessing the impact of welfare rights organizations on the masses of recipients. Their membership is small, as compared to the total number of recipients; but recipients who are not members, or if members, not active, may be influenced by the activists or by the publicity these organizations generate. Furthermore, there is evidence that the welfare agencies have modified their practices under pressure from the organizations. At present one can only speculate concerning most of the questions raised about client groups. Our guess is that those recipients who feel stigma, who were more upset by their welfare experience, and who ask for more are also more likely to join welfare rights organizations. Feelings of stigma (at least as measured by our indicators) seem to reflect an independent mind.

The data on stigma reveal the difficulties and paradoxes involved in reforming welfare, and more particularly in reforming welfare administration to make it more humane and more sensitive to the needs of recipients. Recipients who feel stigma are upset about being on welfare, and they should be, in view of the popular social and political attitudes toward the AFDC program. Moreover, they do something about their situation by making greater use of resources of the program. If we are correct in our guess that these are the people who are more likely to join welfare rights organizations, then they are also more likely to seek out lawyers or other people with access to power, such as community organizers, when they have complaints against welfare. They are the ones who call attention to welfare abuses and to the denial of rights and entitlements.

When the pressure is strong enough, even welfare bureaucracies change. The administrative response, however, is to satisfy the demands of those who complain rather than to treat those demands as symptomatic of more general problems experienced by all welfare recipients. There are many reasons why welfare agencies take this attitude; probably the most important is the need to keep costs down. We have seen that the agencies generally grant special requests but will not advertise the availability of special grants. Recipients who know and are willing to ask will benefit; the silent will not.

Large-scale change means not only additional money and effort, but changes in caseworkers' attitudes as well; and, as we have seen, the case-workers deliver the most when it is easiest (health care, special requests—where made) and resist change that would call for more intensified service (see chap. 2). For those who have made public assistance a career, change means a recognition that what they have had a hand in building is a failure, or at least is not working out the way they would like to believe.

The paradox, then, is that those recipients who do have independent minds and who are not adjusted to their welfare status are probably far more capable of controlling official discretion than those who do not feel stigma. This, of course, is not to argue that stigma is a desirable thing. What the data show for this group of recipients is that, unfortunately, people will act in socially desirable ways because of feelings of shame.

The more worrisome cases, we think, are the recipients who do not feel stigma. They seem to be passive, accepting, satisfied, and unable to take advantage of the few things that the AFDC program has to offer. High levels of reported satisfaction and a lack of complaints and requests are welcome to welfare agencies; they are signs that things are going well. To us, on the other hand, it is extremely unfortunate that caseworkers do not have the courtesy to telephone in advance and that such a practice is accepted by welfare recipients. Similarly it is difficult to believe that lack of requests and use of the program are really based on lack of need, as officials maintain.

Perhaps most disturbing is the failure of most reform proposals to take into account the problems of this passive group. Reformers want to separate income maintenance from social services and to make the latter strictly voluntary in the sense that services will be available only for recipients who actively seek them. Yet those who could perhaps best use services may be the least likely to ask.

The great reform drive now is to routinize the administration of income maintenance in order to cut down official discretion in the distribution of benefits and sanctions. On the whole, this will be a great improvement for both active and passive welfare recipients, but there will be significant problems in making sure that the written rules are being carried out and that a significant fraction of the welfare population somehow gets to use the special welfare and service programs that are available. Pressure from the bottom for change has been mounting steadily, and it is the "well-adjusted" recipient who is the more likely to suffer even after reforms are implemented.

Chapter 8

LEAVING WELFARE

The life of a woman dependent upon AFDC is not a pleasant one; payments are low and services are relatively few and far between, with the exception of health care. Although women do not mind their caseworkers and even find them relatively likable, they do not think they benefit much from their visits. Moreover, a large proportion of the women interviewed felt stigmatized by being on welfare. Given all this, the drive to leave AFDC should be fairly strong.

But the possibilities for exit are severely limited. Most AFDC mothers have several children, few job skills, and only brief labor-force experience. Although most have attended or completed high school, they would have difficulty supporting themselves at even the modest level of their welfare checks, and in many communities there are few full-time jobs for which they would qualify.

Aside from employment, the other logical path of exit is marriage, or remarriage. For some women this option is not realistic because of age, family size, or the availability of men willing to assume the obligations of a ready-made family.

Often, then, there is no viable alternative to remaining on AFDC. Clients have no other prospects. Twenty-five percent of the AFDC mothers interviewed said they could not foresee any time in the future when they would no longer require AFDC assistance or some kind of welfare aid.

Quite separate is the question whether women should leave welfare, whether their long-term interests and those of their children might be better served if they were to remain in the program rather than seek a job. Since social pressures on welfare recipients to find employment are very strong both in rural areas and in cities, we assume that the drive to leave welfare is equally strong in all the Wisconsin counties in this study. On the other hand, the opportunities to leave, as well as the numbers leaving, vary.

Two years after the initial survey was undertaken, 272 respondents (35 percent of the original sample) had left the program. Of this group, 73 percent were interviewed approximately two months after they left the program.[1] By the time of the interview, 34 (17 percent of those who had left welfare) had found it necessary to return.[2]

In this chapter we will describe the characteristics of those who leave welfare, including those who returned. We will be concerned with how women leave (manner of exit), what part the welfare program and the agency played in their leaving welfare, the use these people made of welfare, and their attitudes toward the caseworker and their welfare experience. We will also be concerned with whether attitudes toward the caseworker and the welfare experience change when respondents are off welfare and looking back. In the final section of the chapter we will compare the group that left welfare with the group that remained.

The percentage of women who left AFDC in two years was not evenly distributed by county. In general, the two most urban counties had the lowest incidence of leaving and the rural counties had the highest. In Milwaukee only 26.4 percent exited and in Dane County 32.9 percent left the program. Elsewhere, the figures ranged from a high of 54.6 percent for Brown County to 38.6 percent for Sauk County (Dodge, 48.4 percent; Walworth, 47.5 percent). These differences in exiting cannot be attributed to "natural" turnover of welfare rolls—that is, women with longer case histories at the time of initial interview would be more likely to leave the program. For example, Walworth women, with the shortest time in the program, exited at a high rate, as did Sauk County women with much longer case histories. Overall, the rate of return seems low (17 percent) and there was no relationship, by county, between exit rates and rates of return. Although it is possible that women may return to AFDC some time after exit, in general the pattern presented in chapter 2 is borne out. Most women are on AFDC only once; when they leave, they do not return.

---

[1] This figure is based on 199 completed interviews as of August 7, 1969. Interviews were not completed with all women leaving the program for the following reasons: twelve had died, seven refused to be interviewed, and fifty-four could not be located. The interviewer schedule is shown in the Appendix. A shorter, but comparable schedule was used for women who had returned to AFDC by the time of reinterview. Since the number returning was small, this schedule is not shown in the Appendix.

[2] Since the time lapse between program exit and interview was relatively brief, it is very likely that the rate of recidivism is considerably higher than 17 percent among those remaining in Wisconsin. Some women also return to welfare through general assistance programs, and they are not included in the 17 percent, which pertains only to AFDC.

MANNER OF EXIT

Marriage or Reconciliation

Approximately one-fifth of the respondents gave marriage or marriage plans as their principal reason for leaving the program. The economic position of these women seemed to be improved considerably. Practically all the respondents said their husbands worked regularly. Although a majority of the husbands had unskilled, semiskilled, or service jobs, one-third had skilled work. As reported by the respondents, the median "usual take-home pay" was $104 a week. About one-fourth of the respondents were also working, usually full time, with a take-home pay of $48 a week. The average household contained about five persons. Most of the husbands or husbands-to-be (69.7 percent) came without children or without obligations to support their children living in another home.

An additional group of recipients (10 percent) were also either married or planning to get married, but they did not consider this to be the reason for leaving welfare. Eighty-two percent of this group was employed. Then, a few husbands returned. The returning husbands worked at the same kind of jobs as the new husbands, as regularly, and for the same weekly take-home pay. In a few instances, a husband's recovery from illness or release from prison was given as a woman's reason for leaving welfare.

Combining all groups, over 40 percent of the women leaving AFDC returned to or created families headed by males. Clearly, the availability of men plays an important role in welfare exits. Very few respondents said the caseworker or the agency played any role in their marriage, intended marriage, or reconciliation.

Employment

About one-fourth of the respondents gave employment as the main reason for leaving welfare. The jobs they held were semi-skilled service (20.9 percent), semi- and unskilled factory or farm labor (30.2 percent), clerical and kindred work (32.6 percent), other service work (13.9 percent), and managerial or skilled labor (2.3 percent). Practically all these respondents said that they worked regularly. The average number of hours worked per week was forty-three and the median "usual weekly take-home pay" was $69. Eighty-four percent of these employed women were still single at the time of the reinterview, with an average family size of 4.3. It is difficult to see how they are supporting themselves on their earnings alone. Their take-home pay is above the average welfare grant ($50 a month per person) but still below what we estimated, in the previous chapter, to be the breakeven levels for these families (about $77 per week). It seems unlikely that these single women will be able to stay off welfare.

Fewer than one-third of these respondents said the welfare agency helped to get them jobs; they listed vocational training, War on Poverty programs, and academic training as examples of assistance. Most of the recipients discussed employment with their caseworker. About 40 percent said it was the caseworker who suggested the respondent get a job; most of these said the caseworker thought a job would be good for the respondent and her family. Only a few thought the caseworker wanted them off welfare to save the agency money. About one-third of the working respondents said their caseworkers did not care whether they got a job or not, and only a very few said the caseworkers were opposed to their working.

But very few recipients (11.6 percent) said their caseworkers did anything concrete in helping them get a job—such as finding a job for them, or recommending them for a job, or even helping arrange child care. Most of the respondents found jobs through friends or relatives or newspaper ads, or "just went in and applied"; three-fourths claimed it was easy to find a job. Just over one-half of the working women needed someone to take care of their children, and most of these (71 percent) had to pay for this service. Fewer than 15 percent said they were having trouble in making babysitting arrangements.

Practically all the respondents who gave employment as the reason for leaving welfare said they were glad that they were working and off welfare. A few said they were worried about the effects on their family. No one said she was sorry she was now working.

The respondents who were working at the time of the reinterview, but who did not say a job was their reason for leaving welfare, gave similar employment information about type of job, regularity of work, and usual take-home pay. For this group, however, the agency and the caseworker were even less important; more had to go job hunting themselves, and more said it was difficult to find a job.

Children Ineligible

Almost one-fifth (19.2 percent) gave a change in the status of their children as the reason for leaving welfare. In most of these families the children either reached age eighteen or left school, thus becoming ineligible. Usually the children still lived at home and were working. Another reason for families losing eligibility was that the children (including foster) left the home.

These three reasons for leaving welfare—marriage (or return of the husband), jobs, and changes in the status of children—account for three-fourths of all respondents who left welfare. The others left for a variety of reasons. For some (4.8 percent), other forms of outside aid became available—for example, Social Security, a veteran's pension, support from relatives. A few respondents got additional support from their husbands. About 9 percent said they did not like the program and quit, and 5 percent said the agency told them to get off. Most of this latter group said the agency dropped them because of misconduct regarding financial matters; they were accused of not reporting earned income or gifts, or of misspending welfare money. One-half said that the agency was "correct" in its accusation.

In Table 8.1 we have tabulated the main reasons given for leaving welfare. More than two-thirds of the respondents left welfare by their own efforts.

Many of those who later returned to the welfare program had voluntarily left AFDC—usually to find work, or because their husbands returned. But often new jobs did not provide adequate support, or husbands left again. That a woman takes the initiative in leaving welfare is no guarantee that she will "make it"; about one-fifth of the women failed in their efforts to break away from welfare dependency.

Most of the respondents (66.5 percent) who left notified the agency of their change in circumstances; they did not "cling" to welfare. Still, 15 percent thought they should not have had to leave the AFDC program. Agency decisions, usually based on regular income of another member of

TABLE 8.1. REASONS FOR LEAVING
WELFARE

Client-initiated	
Marriage (or planned marriage)	20.4%
Husband returned	12.0
Employment	26.9
Respondent quit	9.0
Total	68.3%
Passive exit	
Change in status of child	19.2%
New support from ex-husband	2.4
Other support became available	4.8
Respondent told to get off	4.8
Total	31.2%
No answer	0.6
Total	100.1%
Number	(165)

the family, rule infraction, or insistence that respondents work, were contested as unfair: respondents said alternative income was inadequate, that they had violated a rule that was unfair, or that they were not well enough to work. Eleven of this group (twenty-six in all) said they complained to the agency about losing AFDC support, but no one sought to invoke the right of having a fair hearing.[3]

However, for most recipients, the role played by the welfare agencies in their leaving was quite insignificant. The agencies were fairly active in getting alternative sources of support for families (e.g., Social Security, veterans' pensions), especially if alternative support could easily be arranged. Fewer than 15 percent of those who left through employment said the agency played any part in helping them find a job, and practically no one said the agency was involved in marriage or a return of the husband. All in all, only about 10 percent of those who left welfare said the agency played any positive role in the process. Or, to give the role of the agency a different emphasis, more people thought they were forced to leave welfare than thought they were helped to do so. In sum, most of the AFDC recipients left welfare under their own initiative and without any assistance from the welfare agency.

PROGRAM USE

We have seen that for most women the agencies play a small role in the exit process. What kind of support and service did agencies afford women while they were still in the program? Is there a relationship between the use a woman makes of the program and the manner in which she leaves AFDC?

Practically all the families made some use of medical aid paid for by the welfare agency. About 40 percent used medical assistance for check-ups and minor ailments, 13 percent for maternity care, and more than 33 percent had a serious medical problem (e.g., broken bone, ulcers, gall bladder surgery, etc.). When asked who usually suggested getting medical assistance, 30 percent said the welfare agency or caseworker encouraged them to do so; the rest sought service on their own initiative, using their Medicaid cards. About 70 percent also used the welfare program for dental work, mostly for check-ups, fillings, and other routine dental care. Most said they took advantage of this service "on their own," but about 21 percent said the welfare agency was active in encouraging them to get dental care.

---

[3] One respondent complained to the district attorney, but apparently nothing happened.

Twenty-six respondents (15.6 percent) said either they or a member of the family received help for mental or emotional problems that was paid for by the agency. Caseworkers were more active in this area; half said they received aid as a result of the caseworker's initiative. A small group (eleven, or 6.6 percent) said that at one time or another they had requested medical aid but the agency refused.

There was much less use of other programs or services. Only 13 percent ever had a homemaker visit for help with housekeeping, cooking, nutrition, or child care. Only 17 percent of the respondents had their children participate in special programs such as Head Start, Job Corps, Neighborhood Youth Corps, or other OEO programs. About one-fourth of the adults participated in some program either sponsored by or paid for by the welfare agency. These were predominantly vocational or education courses.

Milwaukee County made food stamps available, and surplus commodities were available in four of the other counties. (Walworth County had no food program.) Only about half of the Milwaukee County respondents had used the food-stamp program. Of those not using the program, about half said that either they did not know about the program or that they did not need the stamps. Only a very few said they were denied stamps or were too embarrassed to ask for them. Practically all who used the food stamp program said they found it "very" or "fairly" convenient, even though one-third of these users encountered problems. The problems were usually confusion about what items could be purchased with the stamps or embarrassing treatment from clerks or other customers in the store. Rates of use were higher for the surplus-food-commodities program; in one county over 90 percent of the respondents used the program, and the overall rate of use for the four counties was 76.9 percent. On the other hand, there was less satisfaction with this program than with the food-stamp program: respondents complained about the quality of the commodities or that they often did not need the commodities that were offered. Still, participation in food-stamp and commodities programs was far higher than in rehabilitative or life-changing programs—probably because the food programs are routine and nondiscretionary.

There was a relationship between program use and leaving welfare. In Milwaukee County those who used the food stamps were more likely to have made an active or client-initiated exit as compared to those who did not use the program. In the other counties those who used the surplus food commodities and medical programs or who participated in adult programs were more likely to have actively exited as compared to the others.

THE CASEWORKER RELATIONSHIP

The respondents were asked a series of questions concerning the activities of the caseworker and their attitudes toward the caseworker. In Table 8.2 we have tabulated the topics "discussed most often" with the caseworker.[4] The bulk of the discussions are general and either about finances (the greatest concern of these families) or general discussions about children or the respondents themselves. The caseworkers stay away from personal matters of a sensitive nature (e.g., house care, social life, or jobs). Only 28 percent of the respondents said that during the discussions the caseworker would try to find ways that she could help the client.

Respondents were then asked whether they could mention some things their caseworker did for them that they thought were helpful. More than one-third of the respondents (35.9 percent) said their caseworker did nothing helpful for them. The others mentioned two things, on the average. What the caseworkers did that respondents said was helpful is presented in Table 8.3.

As with the respondents who were interviewed while on the program, most of those who left welfare had positive attitudes toward their caseworkers, but within a framework of very low expectations. Just under three-fourths said their caseworker was either "very" or "moderately"

TABLE 8.2.   TOPICS DISCUSSED "MOST
OFTEN" WITH CASEWORKERS

Finances: budgeting, need for more money	34.1%
Children: school, health, general ("How are they getting along?")	43.7
General personal ("How are you getting along?")	8.4
Health	2.4
House care	1.2
Social life with men	2.4
Jobs	3.0
Other	4.8
	100.0%
Number	(248)[a]

[a] Respondents (165) listed more than one topic discussed "most often."

---

[4] The question asked was: "As you recall, what things did you and your caseworker(s) discuss *most often*? (Anything else?)"

TABLE 8.3. HELPFULNESS
OF CASEWORKERS

"Can you think of several things your caseworker(s) did for you or your family while you were on the program that you thought were helpful? Such things could be services they performed, things they arranged, or perhaps just advice they gave? Are there three or four things you could mention?"

Finances: got more money, helped with budget	21.6%
Health	9.4
Household matters: mostly a series of minor arrangements	20.0
Suggested rehabilitation programs for respondent or children	11.5
Advice on general problems (other than children)	21.6
Advice on problems with children	9.4
Help on employment problems	3.6
Other	2.9
Total	100.0%
Number	(190)[a]

[a] 107 respondents listed 190 topics; 35.9 percent said "nothing."

helpful in seeing that they got "the most good out of the ADC program," but when asked whether there were some things that the caseworker could have done that they did not do, 67.7 percent said "nothing." Asked about the frequency of caseworker visits, three-fourths said they saw the caseworkers "about often enough" (i.e., about once every three months), and fewer than 20 percent said "not often enough." Most (70.1 percent) were not bothered at all by questions the caseworker asked or information they had to give while on welfare.

This was the general picture—caseworkers came around relatively infrequently, they were mildly supportive, rarely threatening or embarrassing; they did little but the clients expected little. A sizable minority of respondents, however, did not share this general view; they were bothered by the caseworker visits, either slightly (13.8 percent), moderately (6 percent), or very much (9.6 percent). Most of these respondents complained of invasions of privacy or pressure to do things they they did not want to do—for example, getting a job or taking legal proceedings against a husband.

ATTITUDES TOWARD WELFARE

Attitudes toward the welfare experience in general centered around the financial aspects of the program; in evaluations respondents always returned to the income-maintenance aspects of AFDC. This was the most salient thing in their lives. Almost all (88.6 percent) thought that they had "always" or "usually" been treated fairly by the agency and the caseworker. About one-third of the respondents did list complaints against the welfare experience; the overwhelming majority of these complaints had to do with money matters—general complaints that the grants were too low or that respondents could not buy specific things they needed. Fewer than 10 percent of all those who left complained about caseworker practices (e.g., hostility, incompetence) or specific regulations.

When asked what were the worst things or the least beneficial things about welfare, the most often-mentioned complaint, by far, was the inadequacy of the grant. Aside from the very common complaint of too little money, about 13 percent of the respondents complained about feelings of stigma or invasions of privacy, and about 8 percent complained about the caseworkers—they were inexperienced, or rude, or not very understanding.

When asked whether their experience with the welfare agency was satisfactory in view of what they needed, over 80 percent said the experience was either satisfactory or very satisfactory, and 65 percent said they benefited either "moderately" or "greatly" from services other than basic financial aid. When asked to list the "one most beneficial" thing that welfare did for them, more than half said it provided basic economic security; it prevented the family from breaking up. Most of the others mentioned medical care, with very few mentioning caseworker services or special programs.

THOSE WHO EXIT; THOSE WHO STAY

Although we have a good idea why women leave welfare and what kinds of experiences their welfare dependency has entailed, we want to turn to the question whether women who leave welfare differ greatly from those who remain in the program. We would expect that the women with more resources—education, some labor-force experience, and youth—would be more likely to leave welfare than the relatively disadvantaged. Moreover, we want to know whether the women who make the most use, and the best use, of the resources of the welfare system are also the women who depart from it and return to "normal society."

Accordingly, we have compared the women who remain in the AFDC program with those who voluntarily made exits, or initiated exits, and did not return to the program. In instances where women who made unsuccessful attempts or passive exits are different, we will indicate as much.

In earlier chapters we have reported that in general women evaluated their welfare experiences favorably. We want to see whether the women who leave are less favorable to AFDC, whether attitudes toward the program are related to departure. A few women did say they disliked the AFDC program so much that they left it.

Women leaving the program successfully were, on the average, somewhat older—36.6 years of age as compared to 33.5 for those who stayed. Women making unsuccessful exits were about the same age as those who stayed on welfare. Marital status was not related to leaving welfare, although the women who had left had smaller families. They had an average of 2.8 children in their homes as compared to 3.4 children for women still in the program.

Race was important in deciding whether a woman could successfully leave welfare. Whereas 72.4 percent of the original sample was white, 82 percent of the successful exits were made by whites, and only 69.1 percent of those remaining in the program were white. Twenty-five percent of the original sample was black, yet only 16.9 percent of the successful exits were made by blacks, and 28.6 percent of those remaining in the program were black.

In general, those who left had better educations than those who stayed. For example, among those who had at least some high school education the rate of successful exit was twice that of those with less education.

Since many women who leave do so through employment, one would expect that women with better employment histories would be more likely to have made successful exits from AFDC. This was not the case, however. Neither job holding nor number of years of work experience relate to exit.

The factors associated with successful exit, then, are: better education, being white, and having a smaller family.

Previous experience with AFDC was not related to whether a woman would make a successful exit or not, but then relatively few AFDC recipients were repeaters. Much more important in deciding who would leave was the length of time a woman had been in the program *this time*. Successfully leaving women had been in the AFDC program 52.6 months at the time of the initial interview, whereas those who did not leave had been in the program 42.9 months. Those who had to return to the pro-

gram had been on AFDC only 28 months before attempting, unsuccessfully, to manage without welfare.

Women making successful exits seemed to make more use of their
caseworker than the women who stayed. For example, although frequency
of caseworker visits was the same for both groups, the former made more
requests for special need items, and even though the latter were more
inclined to say they had noneconomic problems, the former were more
likely to call on the caseworker for assistance when they did have these
problems. Although participation in special programs was low overall, it
was slightly greater among women who made successful exits. Another
way in which women may get more from the welfare system is by calling
the caseworker between visits. On this, the two groups did not differ.

In their evaluations of their relationships with caseworkers and their
appraisal of agency services, the women who exited successfully did not differ from those who stayed in the program. Among those who made successful exits, there were a few more complaints about decisions caseworkers had made and a few more suggestions about how the welfare system
should be changed, but these women also said they tried harder to stay
on good terms with their caseworkers. If distaste for caseworkers or rejection of the idea of welfare is important in a woman's decision to initiate
exit, she is no more explicit in her complaints and attitudes than women
who remain in the program. As we pointed out earlier, most women do
not chafe against caseworkers or the system: they accept its financial support and its inconveniences largely because the amount of active intervention in their lives is quite small.

Finally, then, do women who initiate successful exits from welfare
differ in their relations with the outside world from those who remain?
Seemingly women who leave the program have more ties: they have more
relatives and more friends. They go to church more often and are more
likely to say they have turned to church for some help. If they have had
problems in areas other than welfare, such as trouble with their landlord,
nonsupport from husbands, or difficulty with the police, they are more
likely to have turned to lawyers for assistance. It appears they are better
connected with the community, whereas the women remaining in welfare
seem more confined in their patterns of activity. The women still in the
AFDC program, for example, say they know more other families who
are in AFDC.

The picture that emerges is that women more likely to get out of
welfare programs have advantages of race and education, make somewhat
better use of the welfare system, and, moreover, have more ties to the
"outside world." They are better able, overall, to deal with society as it
is constituted.

In other words, it is what a woman brings with her to welfare, rather than what the welfare resources do for her, that shapes her possibilities of leaving and her decision to do so. For those with initial advantages, AFDC furnishes a base of minimum financial security until they are able to mobilize their own resources to leave the program. For the less advantaged, welfare is more likely to be prolonged. If it does not interfere unduly with the lives of clients, neither does it offer them prospects for achieving independence. The failure of the AFDC program to supply more than minimal financial security becomes especially clear when one compares the experience of blacks with whites. Black AFDC recipients, in the main, much more than whites, experience long-term dependency. At the time of the original interview they had been on the program considerably longer, and at the time this study was concluded fewer blacks had left. Their welfare experience was comparable, particularly their use of the program and their caseworker relationships. But, handicapped by background characteristics and little aided by the welfare system, black women had much less success in achieving independence.

Women must, then, mobilize themselves for welfare exit and not look to the agency for more than financial security and occasional (minimal) service or assistance.

PART THREE

Conclusions and Implications

Chapter 9

THE LIMITS OF REFORM

The AFDC program has both changed and stood still. Size and costs of the system have dramatically increased and background characteristics of the recipients have altered as well. In this respect AFDC today is very different from what it was in earlier decades. At the same time, efforts to change the program through legislation and administration have for the most part been notably unsuccessful. Throughout this study we have discussed various attempts to change the system. Although often described in momentous (if not ominous) terms at the time of enactment, these efforts have usually had very little or no impact on the program at the field level. In this concluding chapter we will discuss some of the reasons for this and the implications for future reform efforts.

Almost all efforts at welfare reform, whether attempting to improve caseworker services or providing supplementary or complementary programs for recipients, have been forced to depend on the response of the welfare bureaucracy and the clients. Theoretically, a reform effort could circumvent this dependence if the change were sufficiently radical. An example would be a large-scale redistribution of income through something like a children's allowance system administered automatically by an entirely separate bureaucracy. But this type of reform is unlikely and is not even being discussed seriously. The most talked-about proposals for reform call for modest shifts of income to the poor and require the meeting of many conditions in order to obtain aid. President Nixon's proposed Family Assistance Act of 1969, for example, has both a means test and a work test and provides for social services. Thus his proposal requires significant administration; moreover, although the connections between the federal program and the state programs are not spelled out, state welfare administration will continue to play a very important role. As Moynihan has suggested, we may get "important, incremental changes," but not a clean sweep.[1] Therefore, bureaucratic and client responses remain the ma-

---

[1] D. P. Moynihan, *The Crisis in Welfare,* THE PUBLIC INTEREST (Winter 1968) 6. In arguing for President Nixon's proposed Family Assistance Act of 1969, Moynihan now speaks in terms of a "radical, revolutionary change." N.Y. Times, November 16, 1969, p. 32, col. 1. Perhaps he, too, is following

jor determinants of reform in welfare. In this chapter we will draw together what we think are the major characteristics of the bureaucracy and the recipients that can be generalized from this study and then discuss implications of these characteristics for reform.

THE WELFARE BUREAUCRACY

Perhaps the single most important characteristic of the welfare bureaucracy is its decentralized structure. In about half the states, AFDC is administered by county departments of welfare and supervised by state agencies. Since this was a study of a county-administered system, we have no empirical data on the workings of a state-administered system. We can assume that the factors producing decentralization are more pronounced in the former than the latter, but, for reasons which we will discuss shortly, we think that decentralization is a major characteristic of state-administered systems, too. Four factors produce decentralization in welfare administration: (1) the jurisdictional division of authority (analogous to federalism); (2) the structure of welfare rules; (3) the nature of the work of the agency (including professional orientations); and (4) problems of supervision and control. All of these except the first apply to a state-administered as well as a county system.

In Wisconsin the county departments of welfare are no mere adjuncts of the State Department of Health and Social Services. The AFDC program started at the county level and for a century there has been a constant struggle between the counties and the state agency for control over critical features of the program. State power has increased, particularly in the last two decades, but the counties still exercise considerable authority and have considerable political power in the state legislature in regard to welfare. It will be recalled that the Wisconsin legislature was reluctant to establish a strong state agency and only did so in the late 1930's to comply with federal requirements. Since then, the legislature has refused to make major jurisdictional decisions between the counties and the State Department. Subsequent increase of state power has occurred as a result of opinions by the Attorney General, federal pressure, and various kinds of administrative practices, such as consultation, liaison work, state-run training sessions, etc. But state officials acknowledge that converting Wisconsin to a state-administered system is "out of the question" at the present time.

---

the path of earlier reform advocates, a path which he cautions against in the PUBLIC INTEREST article.

The refusal of the legislature to intervene and change the state-county power relationship is a form of legislative decisionmaking. Although it is always hazardous to comment on the meaning of legislative inactivity, this does seem to reflect the political power of county governments in the legislative halls. The other explanation is the normal tendency of legislatures to avoid fights as long as they can. Legislatures are generally reactive institutions; they will avoid dealing with a problem until the political costs of inaction outweigh the political costs of taking a stand. Although the jurisdictional conflict between the counties and the state agency is serious, of long standing, and with high stakes, so far enough compromises and adjustments have been worked out to allow the legislature to remain aloof. This tendency of the legislature to avoid intervening, which is not unique to Wisconsin, fosters decentralization.

In implementing welfare policy, county departments bring to bear their own histories, traditions, and ways of doing things. They are primarily responsive to their political governing body—the county board of supervisors—and their community. In chapter 2 the county welfare directors emphasized how important they felt these groups were. The state agency exercises countervailing pressures. From time to time it examines records and reports, and investigates particular agencies. It expends a great deal of effort in liaison and consulting work. It is called to consult on the appointment of new county welfare directors, and it sets statewide standards for personnel. The extent of state agency influence varies from county to county, but the starting point in examining administrative decentralization is to recognize that the counties and their departments of welfare are independent, separate governments with varying degrees of political power, working in a local context.

The rules in welfare push toward a decentralized administration. There are some specific statutory delegations of authority to the county departments, as exemplified by county departments having discretionary authority over AFDC employment decisions as a result of legislation. The dominant characteristic of welfare legislation, however, is its high level of abstraction. AFDC statutes usually do not define even the most basic elements of the programs—for example, what constitutes need, the level of benefits, how much responsible relatives should contribute, the moral conditions or standards of welfare parents, what social services are and to whom and how they should be applied. Some problems are really not readily susceptible to objective, clearly defined standards or it would be unwise to attempt to build them in. It would be perfectly easy for the Wisconsin legislature to say that regardless of need, there will be a fixed, maximum amount of money that any family can receive. Many states do this, and with harmful results. Vagueness and abstraction in statutes also reflect the power conflicts between state and local government and in particular the role of the legislature in avoiding troublesome issues involving intense moral conflicts. Rules which are vague constitute delegations of decision-making authority. In Wisconsin the administrative agencies have been delegated the authority to decide need, levels of benefits, moral conditions, and employment, as well as many other issues.

Within the administrative system, similar decentralization effects are often produced by the structure of the rules. For example, the Wisconsin State Department specifies in great detail the allowances for most items in the budget. However, rent allowances are treated differently; they are to be "reasonable" in light of local conditions, and thus discretion is created. But even where allowances are specified in fixed dollar amounts, the conditions that have to be met in order to qualify for the fixed allowances are not specific. Standards and criteria for the application of most welfare regulations are in fact quite vague. Vagueness appears throughout the entire rule structure, starting with the legislature and extending down through the agencies; and vagueness in rules means a decentralization of authority.

The nature of the work at the field level results in a decentralization of authority because of individual family needs and the professional response to those needs. The income-maintenance component of AFDC is to provide a fairly uniform subsistence grant with provisions for extra money for special needs, with social services tailored to individual family needs. Thus it is official administrative policy to recognize that welfare families have different problems, will make different types of demands on the agencies, and should get different treatment. The emphasis in the regulations is on flexibility at the field level. Social work training also lays great stress on individualized professional treatment. Although most public assistance caseworkers do not have professional social work training, we saw in chapter 2 that they adopt the professional position, at least at the rhetorical level. Caseworkers vary in whether they will apply particular rules (e.g., ask certain questions at intake, disclose the availability of special grants, etc.) and in the manner of application (whether they are sympathetic and understanding, or suspicious or hostile). They will talk about different things during the home visit, depending on whether they are concerned about employment or men in the house, whether they will encourage children to pursue education and training, and so forth. Not only do the problems and needs of welfare families differ; it must also be kept in mind that these problems and needs change over time, and families can be on welfare for many years. Thus a flexibly structured system is administered so as to adjust to changing circumstances.

Finally, decentralization is a result of the lack of systematic control of field-level activities. Under existing methods of supervision and control, a great many discretionary decisions made by the caseworkers are not capable of detection at the state level, and possibly even at the county supervisory level. It is claimed, and our data in chapter 4 seem to verify, that caseworkers significantly fail to disclose to clients what is available or what they are entitled to under the program. Sins of omission do not readily come to the attention of supervisors, at the county or the state level, through normal methods of supervision. Individual caseworkers report they do not bother to enforce responsible relatives laws, or require disclosure of the father from an unwed mother, or apply the rules about earned income. These, too, are not the types of things that can be readily checked. Furthermore, it was our impression after talking with state supervisors and county welfare directors and caseworkers that the top bureaucrats really did not have a precise grasp of the details of field-level operations. Distracted by other administrative concerns, such as agency morale and community relations, supervisory personnel from time to time may read case records under federal quality control procedures and monitor statistical reports indicating large differences in expenditure patterns, but they are often not aware of how administrative discretion is being exercised over a whole range of issues.

The other principal method of control relied on is the complaining client. For a long time, AFDC recipients have had the right to appeal any decision that they felt was wrong.[2] The fair hearing appeal is from the county department of welfare to the state agency, and one of its purposes is to detect weaknesses in county administration or illegality which can then be corrected by hearing officer decisions or changes in state regulations. In general, the fair hearing process, as a method of control, is almost a complete failure. The vast majority of clients are ignorant of their rights, or do not know how to exercise their rights, or do not have the resources (including access to lawyers), or are not willing to challenge the caseworker and the agency. Yet the fair hearing remedy entails risks for clients who still have to deal with the agency after the appeal, and it is our conclusion that most AFDC recipients are more interested in security and a measure of stability than in exercising their rights vis-à-vis the welfare department.

The situation is different, of course, where welfare recipients are organized and have access to capable, energetic lawyers. Under these cir-

---

[2] An empirical study of fair hearings in Wisconsin is reported in J. Handler, *Justice for the Welfare Recipient: Fair Hearings in AFDC—The Wisconsin Experience,* 43 SOCIAL SERVICE REV. 12 (1969).

cumstances, clients have had notable success in controlling official discretion by curbing welfare abuses and in obtaining legally specified benefits.[3] But, because of the recent publicity and attention that has been given to the activities of welfare rights organizations, it is easy to exaggerate their importance. Most recipients are passive, dependent, and interested in stability. Their ignorance of what they are entitled to combines with their low expectations, so that they do not perceive injustice or feel aggrieved. Needless to say, these characteristics greatly hamper the growth of welfare rights organizations. It is an open question how many clients are members of these organizations, but we would guess that the organizations involve only a very small minority of recipients. In addition to the overall weakness of client organizations, there is also considerable doubt about the effectiveness of lawyers in producing significant changes in welfare administration. Poverty lawyers complain about the frustrations and difficulties of dealing with agencies and in particular of obtaining enforcement of court decrees and fair hearing decisions. Finally, it should be recognized that the effectiveness of welfare rights organizations may make life more difficult for many recipients; the bureaucracy, if it responds at all, will respond to those who are active and make demands rather than to silent, passive, dependent recipients. At the present time, one must conclude that the control exercised by client organizations and their lawyers at best works sporadically for relatively few recipients. They still lack the power to accomplish across-the-board changes in rules or levels of benefits.

In sum, the jurisdictional structure, the structure of welfare rules, the nature of the work, and the lack of supervisory control all contribute to produce an enormous amount of discretionary authority at the field level. AFDC caseworkers have great leeway in administering the program. Therefore, one would expect great variation in the actual administration. We have studied six different welfare departments located in very different communities—a large urban county; two middle-sized, partly urban counties of quite different political, economic, and social cultures; and three rural counties that also differed markedly. Since welfare administration involves moral, political, and social conflicts, we would expect the agencies to be responsive to the communities. This was true of the welfare directors; they differed in background and attitudes toward their agency, their conception of the program, their priorities and goals. But this was not true of administration at the field level (as reported by the clients). There were some differences among the county departments. Dane County

---

[3] For one of the many descriptions of the ability of welfare rights organization to obtain benefits, see W. Gellhorn, *Poverty and Legality: The Law's Slow Awakening,* 9 WM. & MARY L. REV. 300 (1967).

seemed to be more generous with special needs than Brown County. Brown County seemed to emphasize employment more than Dane or Milwaukee Counties. But administration was uniform or similar throughout the six counties. Given the flexibility in administration and the quite different political, economic, and social environments, what accounts for this general pattern of uniformity?

The answer, we think, lies in structural factors that produce a strategy of *withdrawal*. Whereas there are structural factors that produce discretion, additional factors operate to push caseworkers to exercise their discretion by not getting involved. Four factors produce this lack of involvement or withdrawal: (1) the pressure of work; (2) lack of commitment; (3) the accepting or unquestioning attitudes and low expectations of the recipients; and (4) the paucity of benefits or resources at the disposal of the caseworkers.

One cannot emphasize too strongly the effect of sheer numbers on administration. The major elements of AFDC administration—eligibility determination, budget, and social services (including employment)—assume individualized treatment, but individual attention requires time and energy, commodities which public assistance caseworkers simply do not possess. Harsh and punitive administration as well as liberal and progressive administration requires time and effort. With large numbers of applicants, there is no time to go into detailed and complicated questions concerning the possibilities of support by relatives or the employment of the mother or even the whereabouts of the father. For most clients there is no close supervision of budget expenditures, no careful exploration of special needs (unless the client raises the issue), no investigation of earned income, no meaningful social service programs, and no real concern for moral behavior unless something happens to make the case unusual. Complaints of neighbors (especially if made to the district attorney or the police), a sudden and dramatic deterioration of family life, or an emergency will alter this pattern. But absent something unusual, the caseworker is likely to do no more than make the minimum number of home visits and fill out the prescribed forms.

Administration, harsh or liberal, also requires a commitment; the caseworker has to care enough about her job and her clients to work out a social service program, or process special needs, or look for men in the house. Public assistance caseworkers, when interviewed, adopt professional social work rhetoric but in practice seem to lack the requisite commitment demanded by individualized administration. For the most part, they are quite young, are college graduates with only modest professional training, are not members of professional social work organizations, have been with the agencies only a very short time, lack field experience elsewhere, and do not expect to be in public assistance work very long. In short, they view their jobs as way stations, and this is borne out by their very high turnover. For instance, most clients in our sample saw the same caseworker only about three times before a new one appeared. Lack of commitment or concern about the job means getting through the day as quickly and as painlessly as possible, which means lack of individualized administration.

Client attitudes and expectations about the welfare program and the caseworker fit the needs of the public assistance caseworkers. The great majority of recipients in this survey expressed positive attitudes toward the welfare program and the caseworker, but within a framework of very low expectations. Other than providing basic economic security (at a fairly low level), the program and the caseworkers did little for them. While they spoke well of their caseworkers, they were not interested in increasing caseworker visits and said they did not think there was much else the caseworker could do for them. We will discuss why we think clients reacted this way shortly, but the point to stress here is that these positive attitudes were based on what we have called a friendly chat about general topics of concern to single women running families. For the most part, the caseworkers stayed away from sensitive issues (e.g., social life, relations with men, home care) or specific issues, or issues which might have led to complaints or demands. Within this context, clients found the home visit somewhat pleasant and nonthreatening. Those who experienced the unannounced visit, for the most part, did not object.

There were exceptions to this pattern and client attitudes varied with different administrative practices. When caseworkers disapproved of conduct, clients reacted negatively. Conversely, when caseworkers had something tangible to give, clients reacted much more positively. When caseworkers helped in intangible ways (i.e., a "talking good" instead of a "tangible good"), clients acknowledged the help but they also said they were "bothered or annoyed" with the discussions; and when clients said they were bothered or annoyed with specific caseworker discussions, they were also more likely to say they were less trusting of the caseworker, had even lower expectations of what the caseworker could do, and were less inclined to think that the caseworker generally had a good reason for what she did. In other words, as long as the caseworkers avoided playing a meaningful role in the lives of the clients (whether positively or negatively), they could count on client passiveness and, even more important, overall satisfaction. Unless the caseworkers could deliver tangible goods, a more meaningful interaction ran risks.

With the exception of health care, there was very little that caseworkers could do for the clients. Some caseworkers worked hard at getting their clients grants for special needs or into special programs, but this was unusual. There are just not many extra benefits to distribute in AFDC. The usual strategy for the public assistance caseworker was, therefore, to stick to general topics and avoid raising expectations that might lead to unpleasantness, if not more work. This strategy also called for ignoring illegal or questionable practices (e.g., failure to report earned income, relations with men, particular expenditures, etc.). This was something the caseworker could do for a client that paid off well for both parties.

To sum up, looking at the welfare bureaucracy from the top down, one sees a great downward flow of delegated discretion and of considerable potential flexibility. At the field level, this discretion is principally exercised as noninvolvement, a minimum of regulation, with the result that AFDC is basically a low-level income-maintenance program, and very little else; much more routine than flexible.

THE WELFARE RECIPIENTS

The dominant pattern of administration sheds light on many responses of the recipients: why they report so few grant changes and requests, why there are few requests for special needs, why there is little use made of special programs. The superficiality of the home visit results in little feeling of coercion or bother and annoyance. The recipients are inclined to say the discussions are somewhat helpful and they like their caseworkers, but do not expect very much from them. Thus a relationship that is not very meaningful is also not very threatening. Finally, because the AFDC program provides little more than minimum support—a kind of holding operation—the use that the clients make of the program and their manner of exit depends primarily upon the resources of the clients themselves and opportunities in the community. Those who are younger, white, married, with a better education and a smaller family are more likely to achieve independence; they can mobilize their own resources, without much help from the agency, to take advantage of what the community has to offer.

But what accounts for the generally high levels of satisfaction about most aspects of the program? And why should those who have already left the program still maintain these same positive attitudes? The answer, we think, lies in a concept of relative deprivation. The attitudes of the recipients are shaped by their frame of reference—what they have experienced before welfare, what they thought they needed and received from welfare, and their expectations and aspirations.

As recalled by the respondents, their own family life declined sharply as compared to the life they had experienced while growing up. In chapter 2 most respondents said they were raised in intact families. Although their fathers' and mothers' occupations did not differ that much from the occupations of the respondents and their husbands, most of them said their parents were able to support their families without resorting to any welfare program. Although these families were clearly not affluent, the respondents painted a picture of harmony, stability, and moderate comfort. For most, living conditions were not crowded, there was always enough to eat, there was money enough for special treats, and their parents got along well.

For most of these women, adult life has been harsh. Economic insecurity was probably a constant threat for almost all respondents. Those who married did so at an early age and neither they nor their husbands had much educational or occupational skill. Only about half the respondents had husbands who provided a regular source of income (however low); the other half were never married or they were married to someone who did not support the family consistently. And then, practically every respondent was abandoned by the father of her children. Given the sizes of their families and the occupational skills, these women simply could not support themselves.

The AFDC program, in strictly economic terms, provides a *regular* source of income at a level higher than they could earn. Without doubt, this was the single most important thing in the respondents' minds. Time and again they emphasized that what they liked about the AFDC program was that it provides a steady source of income, which meant that most were thus relieved of the troublesome task of trying to obtain support from the man who abandoned his children.

The length of time between becoming eligible for AFDC and applying was relatively short, which suggests that the economic predicament of the family was quite serious. And the administration at intake, generally restricted to checking financial eligibility and calculating the budget, fit their needs as they saw them. The checks came regularly and without much variation, and the caseworkers usually did not intervene actively in client affairs, either by investigating possible misconduct or by suggesting options such as better use of special grants or participation in special programs. The attitudes of the clients in expecting little and being satisfied with what they got fit both their needs and the needs of the caseworkers. The caseworkers, for the most part, were not inclined to work hard, and, even if so inclined, could not command sufficient resources anyway. Thus clients were better off making the quite rational calculation that the system would not reward them and their concern for security and stability would be satisfied best by not becoming too involved in the system.

This is the modal pattern, but there were two other patterns that are important for policy purposes. Although most clients were quite satisfied with their welfare experience, some were not. It will be recalled that this group, the group that was not that "well adjusted" to welfare status, made better use of the welfare system than the others; they were less satisfied, less accepting, but asked for more and participated more in what resources the program had to offer. The other important pattern is the result when caseworkers can give clients tangible benefits. It will be recalled that this produced what we felt was a remarkably high degree of dependency in the clients.

IMPLICATIONS FOR REFORM

The malaise of welfare administration is staggering. Flexible administration, which is supposed to work to the advantage of the client, really works to permit regulation at whim and to increase client dependency. The bureaucracy is at present uncontrollable and therefore arbitrary and unjust. Decentralization and lack of control means that the implementation of the program will depend on the individual proclivities of the caseworkers or the welfare agencies. The Wisconsin administration appears, in the main, to be relatively benign; but this is only in the sense that the caseworkers seem not to engage in much punitive regulation. That system is unjust and arbitrary in that it fails to disclose the availability of benefits and rights to welfare recipients. We would guess the Wisconsin pattern is fairly typical throughout the country, not because other states necessarily have liberal and progressive traditions, but because public assistance administration is characterized by heavy caseloads and a high turnover of caseworkers with low commitments to their jobs. Thus the flexibility of the system and its decentralization allow it to respond in lawless ways. There is plenty of evidence that agencies in some parts of the country are very harsh and punitive. These agencies may be staffed by people who unfortunately really do care about their work or the agencies may be responding to political and social attacks on welfare or to the need for cheap labor. Furthermore, even such a system as portrayed in Wisconsin is probably dependent to a large degree on recipient cooperation. The recipients are dependent and satisfied and do not make demands, and in turn, the agencies leave the recipients alone. This can change on an individual basis— in case a family begins to cause trouble—or even on an agency basis. Because of client characteristics and the weaknesses of welfare rights organizations, in our judgment, most welfare recipients can be kept at bay by the bureaucracy.

In light of these basic characteristics of the welfare system (both the bureaucracy and the clients), we will discuss the implications of three techniques for reform: (1) The use of coercive rules with protective standards; (2) people-changing rehabilitative social service programs; and (3) the discretionary distribution of benefits. Needless to say, all three techniques are often combined in a single piece of welfare legislation.

The present welfare system contains many coercive rules that are or may be conditions for aid, with some protective standards for clients. For example, an unwed mother in Wisconsin must supply the name of the putative father if she has this knowledge. The qualification, theoretically, protects her, and she does have a right to a fair hearing if she thinks the decision against her is wrong. It is easy to see, however, how questionable this protective standard really is. Who has the burden of proof, and how can she prove that she really has no knowledge? What evidence does she have to come up with? And for all these situations, one must keep in mind the social context within which they arise: a woman who is applying for welfare has suffered a severe personal crisis, and she is faced with the critical problem of having to provide the necessities of life for her children. Her social and economic condition, and particularly her lack of psychological and economic resources, seriously qualify her ability to take advantage of protective provisions, even if they are fairly administered by the welfare agencies.

The most prominent example of a coercive rule with a protective standard and the one that is most important for current reform proposals has to do with employment. Employment requirements in various forms (as we have seen) have always been conditions for public assistance. The protective standards are variously stated: the offer of employment has to be "bona fide," there have to be "adequate day-care" arrangements for the children, the work or training must not be detrimental to the "best interests of the family," the work or training has to be "suitable," and so forth. As pointed out, the structure of these rules has the effect of delegating discretionary authority to the field level. Under the bureaucratic conditions that we have described, this discretion will mean that for most recipients the work requirements will be a minor irritant and a formality; lower-level officials will have neither the time nor the interest to bother about getting recipients work or training. For some, opportunities will be created. But for others, there will be the possibility of punitive regulation and harassment in various forms. In our present state of ignorance about field-level operations, we will only be aware of very gross practices, usually on a statewide basis. We have no way of knowing how various officials or even particular agencies will interpret and apply these vague standards.

We can also be sure, for the reasons that have been stated before, that the vast majority of recipients will not be able to protect themselves from the various types of employment decisions. In addition to being passive, dependent, and without knowledge of and access to resources, the recipients have to maintain a continuing relationship with agencies having at their disposal a wide range of sanctions, including the withholding of information and benefits.

The considerations that have been discussed with regard to administration of work requirements apply to all coercive rules with protective standards. As a practical matter, protective standards do not protect welfare recipients. Whether coercion will be applied depends upon the discretion of officials.

The data of this study should cast serious doubt on the efficacy of rehabilitative social service programs as a technique of welfare reform. It is by now commonplace to say that no real social service activity goes on in public assistance. There are various definitions of social services, but what is usually meant, at the core, are services that require fairly intensive personal interaction between the social worker and the family or particular members of the family. Social services are not necessarily restricted to psychological problems, as is commonly thought; in fact, the modern approach eschews a psychological orientation. Professional, personal interaction can be used for all sorts of problems that are designed to improve family functioning—for example, working out an employment program so that a particular job can be fitted into good day-care arrangements, or a vocational program for a teenage daughter, or help on the budget and home care matters, or facilitating the use of community resources, including health. In other words, there are a variety of problems of a practical nature for which families on welfare could use professional help. But meaningful social services require competent caseworkers, sufficiently interested, and who have the time and resources (notably lacking in public assistance), and it is idle to pretend that this situation will change greatly in the near future.

At least in light of the Wisconsin AFDC experience, we think the federal government should be most reluctant to continue financing public assistance social service programs. Since there are no real standards for evaluating social services except very crude quantitative indicators (e.g., a caseworker visit at least once every three months), it is very easy for an agency to qualify for federal aid without changing service levels. This was in fact the situation in the Wisconsin counties that we studied. According to the clients, very little service activity went on, and this was corroborated by state officials, as well as the quantitative data. There is actually little incentive for the agencies to do anything beyond the minimal federal requirements, which do not in any way insure meaningful social services.

In our view, the most serious and the most intractable problem in welfare administration arises out of the third technique: the discretionary distribution of benefits. At least from a liberal reformist perspective, the policy issues and goals involved in the first two techniques are fairly clear and are capable of considerable reform, if there is the will. Coercive conditions can be stripped out of a welfare system. Eligibility can be made dependent on a fairly simple income and resources test administered by a self-declaration system. This has been done in some parts of the country, and while all problems of intake are not solved, a great many are. We have a fairly good idea of the issues, the policy considerations, the costs, and the remedies for responsible relatives laws, men-in-the-house rules, and regulations dealing with moral behavior. Similarly, if it is considered important to encourage welfare recipients to seek work as an alternative, we can rely on adjusting the welfare grant reduction as earned income increases and creating job opportunities, rather than forcing people to work under pain of losing their benefits. Solutions for social service programs are much more complicated and not as clear cut. It would seem to us that the general approach should be as follows: If social services are considered to be important (which we think they are) and if public assistance welfare agencies are not really capable of administering them, then different agencies (public or private) should be funded that are independent of the public assistance system. Judging from our past experience, particularly with OEO legal services and Medicaid, this solution is by no means free of difficulties, but at least it may be free of the public assistance difficulties that we have described.

The issues raised by the discretionary distribution of benefits were developed at length in chapter 5 (dealing with social services and the caseworker relationship). There we argued that client dependency was created not so much by the use of coercive powers as by the power of caseworkers to give clients tangible things they wanted, and that when caseworkers exercised this power, client gratitude, satisfaction, and feelings of coercion increased considerably. Client dependency arising from this relationship will remain as long as individual treatment is needed in welfare systems. The great emphasis of reform today is to routinize welfare administration by simplifying procedures for the determination of eligibility and the level of benefits. Routinization reduces official discretion, and thus client dependency. However, unless benefits are very high (which is unlikely), there will always be many families who, for a variety of reasons, are not able to function. Failure to function will not necessarily be caused by an inadequate basic budget. A family may have unusual debts or expenses, or be incapable of handling what they receive. The present AFDC program (at least in Wisconsin), in theory, recognizes this situation and provides special needs grants which may be for emergencies or for unusual circumstances of a continuing nature (e.g., special diets). Unless we are willing to impose the social costs of hardship and deterioration on the family, some system of individualized treatment must be made available, and this raises exactly the problems of discretionary administration that we have been discussing. Progress can be made toward objectifying standards, requiring communication of information, setting up different administrative structures, and so forth, but these improvements, it must be recognized, will ultimately depend upon the quality of administration.

Dependency arising out of the distribution of benefits is also an inherent part of social services. Under our analysis, dependency will increase to the extent that social services have something worthwhile to give. For us, this is an additional reason for not strengthening the social services departments of public welfare agencies; either they will not carry out the social services programs, or if they do, the power of agencies over welfare recipients will increase.

Developments in England are an illustration of our point.[4] Until 1963 the Children's Departments of the Local Authority governments (for our purposes, roughly equivalent to county government) administered child protection programs; they would receive children "into care" when parents could no longer take care of them or when courts ordered children removed from the home because of delinquency, dependency, or neglect. In 1963 their powers were significantly extended to deal broadly with the "problem family"—families in which there were problems with the marriage, child rearing, the police, budget management, creditors, housing authorities, poor health, etc. The Children's Departments, as the Local Authority's principal social work agency, were given the power to make emergency cash grants for "unusual circumstances" and also the power to work out arrangements with other public and private agencies that figured prominently in the lives of problem families.

As a decentralized social service program, with minimal central government control, the activities of the Children's Departments varied considerably. With some variation and with some exceptions, the departments exercised highly coercive regulatory powers over their clients because of

---

[4] See generally, Report of the Committee on Local Authority and Allied Personal Social Services (The Seebohm Report), H.M.S.O., Cmnd. 3703 (1968).

their extensive discretionary powers over rewards and sanctions.[5] They had money to pay bills, including rent and utilities. Through their arrangements with other public agencies, they were often critically influential in negotiating with the police over delinquency matters (i.e., staying court proceedings while the agency "worked with the family"), in obtaining priority rehousing from the public housing authorities for certified "families at risk," in avoiding or at least delaying neglect proceedings threatened by the health and school authorities, in avoiding or at least delaying truancy proceedings threatened by the school authorities, and in obtaining more money from the Ministry of Social Security which administered the basic income-maintenance program. In many instances, people in trouble were referred to the Children's Departments by these public agencies; in others, people sought out the services of the Children's Departments on their own. In either situation the Children's Department officers became enormous wielders of power either through their own distribution of benefits or as brokers and intermediaries with other agencies. This is a vastly oversimplified picture of the operation of these Children's Departments, but it does serve to illustrate the point we have made throughout the study concerning the relationship between the discretionary distribution of benefits and dependency.

It is because of the present condition of public assistance welfare agencies (even taking account of the most optimistic predictions for reform), the lack of bureaucratic controls, and the condition of poor people that we prefer the creation and support of social service agencies outside the public assistance structure. We recognize that this may create the problem of many workers visiting the same family, complicating the communication and referral process. There will also be problems of getting services to people in the less populated areas and getting people to use services that are available, but these problems already exist under current arrangements. From our point of view, the main advantage of our proposal is that it fractionalizes discretionary power by creating options for welfare recipients. The problem of dependency and coercion will not be materially lessened by merely making social services voluntary as long as they are administered by one central government agency. We feel there is a better chance of lessening dependency by making available a diversity of offerings. This is the second main advantage of our proposal. With the breaking apart of a single structural arrangement—the public assistance welfare agencies—there is the opportunity for experimentation in the

---

[5] See J. Handler, *The Coercive Children's Officer*, NEW SOC'Y, No. 314, 3 October 1968 (London, England) (also available as Reprint 19, Institute for Research on Poverty, University of Wisconsin, Madison, Wisconsin).

organization and delivery of social services. A variety of approaches have been developed in law and medicine which may be applicable to social services: for example, neighborhood and community centers (with or without community control), offices staffed by professionals fully supported by the government (e.g., OEO legal aid offices), private organizations under government contract, and private practitioners paid by the government on a case-by-case basis. It seems obvious that a great variety of structures will be needed to meet the many different kinds of problems of delivering effective services.

The title of this book is the "deserving" poor. The mockery, of course, is that the class that is the subject of this study—husbandless mothers and their children—has never been considered deserving. The administrative characteristics of welfare programs for those considered the deserving poor are routinized money payments, clear entitlements, absence of regulatory conditions, and the assumption that recipients are free to take advantage of other services offered by the community. Stated in other terms, welfare programs for the deserving poor are characterized by the absence of discretionary official controls. The Aid to Families with Dependent Children program is the opposite. Our effort has been to show how this discretion is exercised, the lack of control of this discretion, and its effects on welfare recipients. Our suggestions for reform are not panaceas. Poverty and dependency will not be eliminated by reforming administrative structures. But what we have shown, we think, is that the usual methods of reform will not serve the interests of this dependent population. Reforming administration by coercive rules with protective standards, public assistance social service programs, and the discretionary distribution of benefits underestimate the power of the bureaucracy to resist change and overestimate the power of the recipients to protect themselves from the lawless exercise of official discretion. The poor of this study bear many burdens in our society, and will continue to do so as long as they remain in poverty; but one of the burdens that could be lightened is the cost of being subject to so much discretionary power. We have reduced this burden for the deserving poor. Husbandless mothers and their children in poverty deserve no less.

Appendix

COMPARISON OF RESPONDENTS AND THOSE WHO REFUSED INTERVIEWS
ON SELECTED CHARACTERISTICS MILWAUKEE, DANE, AND BROWN COUNTIES

	Milwaukee		Dane		Brown	
	Respondent N=302	Refusal N=50	Respondent N=179	Refusal N=42	Respondent N=86	Refusal N=19
Median age (in years)	32	32	31	33	36	37
Number of children in home	3.4	3.5	3.4	3.8	3.3	3.2
Marital state						
married	20.9%	36.0%	15.6%	14.3%	14.0%	31.6%
divorced	25.5	26.0	57.0	38.1	62.7	57.8
never married	20.2	24.0	10.6	16.7	2.4	0.0
deserted/separated	31.1	12.0	12.3	21.1	18.6	5.3
widow	2.3	2.0	4.5	9.5	2.3	5.3
	100.0	100.0	100.0	100.0	100.0	100.0
Race						
white	41.1%	42.0%	89.9%	86.0%	97.7%	100.0%
nonwhite	58.9	58.0	10.1	14.0	2.3	
Education[a]						
grade school or less	24.2%	14.3%	15.8%	8.0%	37.3%	18.7%
some high school or high school graduate	74.5	83.3		84.0	60.5	81.3
schooling beyond high school	1.3	2.4	2.8	8.0	2.2	0.0
	100.0	100.0	100.0	100.0	100.0	100.0

[a]Percentages include only those for whom data are available (N = 42 for Milwaukee, 25 for Dane, 16 for Brown).

	Milwaukee		Dane		Brown	
	Respondent	Refusal	Respondent	Refusal	Respondent	Refusal
Length of time in AFDC program						
Less than 1 year	19.9%	14.0%	25.1%	7.1%	26.7%	31.6%
1-2 years	29.1	24.0	31.3	33.3	29.1	31.6
3-4 years	19.9	10.0	20.6	28.6	18.6	15.8
5-6 years	9.6	26.0	7.8	7.1	9.3	10.5
7 years or more	21.4	26.0	15.1	23.8	16.3	10.5
	99.9	100.0	99.9	99.9	100.0	100.0
Does family have mother or relative or other person as payee?						
Mother	87.1%	94.0%	91.6%	95.2%	91.9%	84.2%
Relative/other	12.9	6.0	8.4	4.8	8.1	15.8
Did case close by June 1969?						
Yes	26.4%	32.0%	32.9%	41.5%	54.6%	50.0%
No	73.6	68.0	67.1	59.5	45.4	50.0
Amount of AFDC grant (April 1967)	$173.23	$169.44	$223.09	$217.83	$185.92	$146.99

SECTION I

PROFESSIONAL AND OCCUPATIONAL HISTORY

1. What is your professional or occupational position?   (CIRCLE ONE)

                    Social worker 1 1

                    Social worker 2 2

                    Social worker 3 3

                    Social worker 4 4

                    Social worker 5 5

             Social work supervisor 1 6

             Social work supervisor 2 7

             Student trainee 8

2. Did you have any full time positions before taking your first position

    in the _____ County Department of Public Assistance?

                    Yes 1

                    No 2

    IF YES, would you indicate the full time positions and how many

    years you spent in each position?

Agency	Position	Years

216

3. How long have you worked in _____ County DPW?

Years _____ Months _____

4. Indicate below how many positions you have had since coming to this agency.

Position (merit classification)	Length of Time

5. What would be your realistic guess as to what you will be doing THREE YEARS from now? (CIRCLE ONE) I expect to:

Work in the same job at this agency........... 1

Work in a different county agency............. 2

Work in a state agency........................ 3

Work in a private welfare agency............. 4

Work in a job outside of public assistance ... 5

I shall retire............................... 6

I have no idea............................... 7

6. How long have you been practicing (your profession or occupation)?

Years _____ Months _____

7. List below professional organizations to which you belong and
    indicate how many times per year that you attend meetings.

Organization	Meetings Per Year Attended

8. Do you intend to get further professional training? (CIRCLE ONE)

          Yes................ 1

          No 2

                            SECTION II

                    VIEWS ON CLIENT SERVICES

1. For each of the following statements, please indicate first whether
    you Agree (+) or Disagree (−) with the statement. Second, indicate
    how strongly you feel in your response to each statement. (CIRCLE
    APPROPRIATE SYMBOLS)

                              Agree − Disagree   Strength of Feeling

                                                 Weak ⟵⟶ Strong

                                +   −   1   2   3   4   5

1. It is always best to follow
    uniform procedures when
    servicing clients, regard-
    less of the client's indi-
    vidual needs.   +   −   1   2   3   4   5

4

		Agree – Disagree		Strength of Feeling				
2.	Rules are a necessary part of the operation of the agency, but they often prevent the development of useful services to the client	+	–	1	2	3	4	5
3.	Staff members should spend more time helping clients than trying to get along with one another	+	–	1	2	3	4	5
4.	The client who gets most out of his participation on the program keeps to himself and doesn't get to the other clients	+	–	1	2	3	4	5
5.	In order for services to be effective, staff must first define a standardized service program for the agency	+	–	1	2	3	4	5
6.	Just as long as you do your job well and follow the rules, it is not so important how you feel about the clients	+	–	1	2	3	4	5
7.	If it could have positive results for a client, one should disagree with what his superiors want him to do or how to do it	+	–	1	2	3	4	5
8.	All clients should receive the same kind of service, regardless of their individualities	+	–	1	2	3	4	5
9.	Rules should be flexible guidelines which set standards for clients to achieve rather than standards which staff should enforce	+	–	1	2	3	4	5

5

	Agree – Disagree	Strength of Feeling

10. Order and routine, while important, should be sacrificed for flexibility when working with certain types of clients +   –   1   2   3   4   5

11. The best way for a client to get along in the program is to do what he is told +   –   1   2   3   4   5

12. Rules should be strictly enforced by all agency staff members +   –   1   2   3   4   5

13. The best way to get along on this job is to mind your business and just do as you are told +   –   1   2   3   4   5

14. Regardless of the rules, each staff person should use his own judgment in handling the clients +   –   1   2   3   4   5

15. It is imperative that staff be consistent with one another in their interaction with the clients +   –   1   2   3   4   5

16. Staff should uphold the regulations at all times otherwise the clients go beyond the appropriate limits +   –   1   2   3   4   5

17. Staff should let the clients have freedom to take initiative, but they have to keep a close watch over it. +   –   1   2   3   4   5

18. It is not important whether staff lets clients have the freedom to take initiative +   –   1   2   3   4   5

| | | Agree – Disagree | Strength of Feeling |

19. Staff should not get too close to clients otherwise they lose respect   +   –   1   2   3   4   5

20. Staff has to keep their distance from clients, otherwise the clients are liable to forget that you are a staff member   +   –   1   2   3   4   5

21. Staff should have a close relationship with the clients, so that staff can get to understand them   +   –   1   2   3   4   5

22. It is not important what kind of a relationship staff has with the clients   +   –   1   2   3   4   5

23. When the client and I make plans about how she should conduct her affairs, I am confident they will work all right   +   –   1   2   3   4   5

24. It is not always a good idea to plan too many things with a client, because you never know what the outcome will be   +   –   1   2   3   4   5

25. What happens to the client while she is on my caseload is usually up to her   +   –   1   2   3   4   5

26. What happens to the client while she is on my caseload is usually the result of the service I provide her   +   –   1   2   3   4   5

27. If the client disagrees with me, I sometimes wonder if I am making the best recommendation   +   –   1   2   3   4   5

28. I am nearly always certain that my suggestions to the client will work, even if the client disagrees with me   +   –   1   2   3   4   5

2. The <u>nature of contact</u> which a social worker has with a client can
involve a number of different issues. The issues may look like the ones
listed below. First, indicate whether you feel it is <u>all right</u> to
discuss it with the client and who <u>should take the initiative</u> in handling
the matter (CIRCLE ONE)

	Not All Right to Discuss	All Right to Discuss	All Right to Discuss
		Client Takes Initiative	Staff Takes Initiative
Budget management (how client spends the grant)	1	2	3
Child raising (clothing, diet, school problems, social problems)	1	2	3
Home management (cleanliness, cooking, etc.)	1	2	3
Health problems (medical, dental, mental)	1	2	3
Social life of mother (with family, friends)	1	2	3
Social life of mother (with men including dating, marriage or reconciliation with husband)	1	2	3
Employment possibilities (supplementary income, retraining, vocational placement)	1	2	3

8

	Not All Right to Discuss	All Right to Discuss	All Right to Discuss
		Client Takes Initiative	Staff Takes Initiative
Religious life of the client	1	2	3
Social or personal problems of client (delinquency, drinking promiscuity)	1	2	3
Involvement in other community social service programs (YWCA, counseling, etc.)	1	2	3

3. Now, for each of these issues, could you indicate how often they

   come up in your contact with the clients? (CIRCLE ONE)

	Very Often	Not So Often	Infrequently	Never
Budget management (how the client spends the grant)	4	3	2	1
Child raising (clothing, diet, school problems, social problems)	4	3	2	1
Home management (cleanliness, cooking, etc.)	4	3	2	1
Health problems (medical, dental, mental)	4	3	2	1
Social life of mother (with family, friends)	4	3	2	1
Social life of mother (with men including dating, marriage, or reconciliation with husband)	4	3	2	1

	Very Often	Not So Often	Infrequently	Never
Employment possibilities (supplementary income, retraining, vocational placement	4	3	2	1
Religious life of the client	4	3	2	1
Social or personal problems of client (delinquency, drinking, promiscuity)	4	3	2	1
Involvement in other community social service programs (YWCA, counseling etc.)	4	3	2	1

4. Finally, for each of the issues, could you weigh them according to how important you think a discussion of them is in helping the client to independence.

	Most Important				Least Important
	5	4	3	2	1
Budget management (how the client spends the grant)	5	4	3	2	1
Child raising (clothing, diet, school problems, social problems)	5	4	3	2	1
Home management (cleanliness, cooking, etc.)	5	4	3	2	1
Health problems (medical, dental, mental)	5	4	3	2	1
Social life of mother (with family, friends)	5	4	3	2	1
Social life of mother (with men including dating, marriage, or reconciliation with husband)	5	4	3	2	1

	Most Important			Least Important	
Employment possibilities (supplementary income, retraining, vocational placement)	5	4	3	2	1
Religious life of the client	5	4	3	2	1
Social or personal problems of client (delinquency, drinking, promiscuity)	5	4	3	2	1
Involvement in other community social service programs (YWCA, counseling etc.)	5	4	3	2	1

5. From time to time changes in methods, practices and procedures are introduced into the service programs of the agency. Listed below are some of the different kinds of things that may be done. Please indicate how you feel about each.   (CIRCLE ONE FOR EACH STATEMENT)

	Should Definitely Be Done	Would Not Mind Seeing It Done	Would Be Against It
Provide legal services	1	2	3
Increase vocational rehabilitation plans	1	2	3
Provide homemaker assistance to client	1	2	3
Allow clients to add more to budget through earned income exemption	1	2	3
Provide welfare assistance when father is in the home	1	2	3

	Should Definitely Be Done	Would Not Mind Seeing It Done	Would Be Against It
Support children through completion of college	1	2	3
Provide birth control information to client	1	2	3
Provide a minimum income to all people below the "poverty line"	1	2	3
Intensify service to the client over a shorter period of time	1	2	3

SECTION III

SOCIAL STRUCTURE OF AGENCY

In this section, we are going to ask you about staff relations in the agency. To assist you, we have provided two information sheets which we will call Information Sheet 1 and Information Sheet 2 for convenience.

On Sheet 1, there are a list of columns which correspond to the questions below. Simply record your impressions according to the directions provided by the question.

Col. 1. Please write in the initials of all of the professional persons in your agency.

Col. 2. Please write in the position which they have in the agency.

Col. 3. On matters of agency policy, how much <u>weight</u> do you

attach to the <u>opinions</u> of each person listed. (Let 10

be highest weight and 1 lowest weight; the same weight

may be given to different persons.)

Col. 4. Though you may weigh the opinions of your co-workers

differently, you may find it <u>easier to go</u> to some more

than others for advice on agency matters. Indicate how

easy you find it to go to each person. (Let 10 be easy

———> 1 least easy; the same weight may be given to

different persons.)

Col. 5. We say that people are <u>close</u> to us or <u>distant</u> from us

in how they view situations. Please indicate how close

you and the persons see eye to eye on the way services

should be provided to the client. (Let 10 be close and

1 distant; the same weight may be given to different

persons.)

Col. 6. How many times a week do you come into contact with

each person? (Record number of times.)

Col. 7. Indicate the nature of your contact with each person.

(Let A represent contact over <u>agency centered</u> issues,

C--contact over client centered issues, S--contact

over <u>socially centered issues</u>. Circle as many as apply.)

Col. 8.   Indicate whether you like the person (+), dislike the
person (−), or are neutral to him/her (0).

Col. 9.   Indicate whether you generally agree with the person on
matters of agency policy; agree (+), disagree (−), both (+).

Col. 10. Indicate how much or the intensity with which you agree,
disagree, or both with each person on agency policy.
(Weak 1 2 3 4 5 Strong)

Col. 11. Indicate how much weight each person has in determining
the affairs of the agency. (10 most weight, 1 least weight;
the same weight may be given to different·persons.)

12. On Information Sheet II, you will find a circle with a point in
the center. Let the circle represent the agency and the point
represent you. Locate each person, in any area of the circle,
according to how close you see eye to eye on the way services
should be provided to the client. (Put the number of the person
beside the point where you locate him/her.

SECTION IV

WORK ACTIVITIES

1. On the average, how large is your monthly caseload?

Number of cases _____

2. What proportion of your caseload is made up of the following client service areas?

> AFDC-U _____
>
> Child Welfare _____
>
> Disabled and Blind _____
>
> General Relief _____
>
> Old Age _____
>
> Other _____

3. Please weight your <u>preferences</u> for working in these different client areas.

	Most Preferable			Least Preferable	
AFDC-U	5	4	3	2	1
Child Welfare	5	4	3	2	1
Disabled and Blind	5	4	3	2	1
General Relief	5	4	3	2	1
Old Age	5	4	3	2	1
Other _____	5	4	3	2	1

4. Please indicate how "difficult" it is to work within these different client areas.

	Most Difficult			Least Difficult	
AFDC-U	5	4	3	2	1
Child Welfare	5	4	3	2	1
Disabled and Blind	5	4	3	2	1
General Relief	5	4	3	2	1
Old Age	5	4	3	2	1
Other _____	5	4	3	2	1

5. On the average, how often do you see your clients?

> Less than once a month....... 1
>
> At least once a month........ 2
>
> Usually twice a month........ 3
>
> At least once a week......... 4

6. How routine would you say the work processes are in the agency?

> Very routine 1
>
> Routine...................... 2
>
> Not so routine............... 3
>
> Hectic....................... 4

7. A person in a welfare agency has to do a number of different things
    in the course of a work week. On an average work week, list in the
    spaces below (1) the <u>different</u> activities that you do and (2) <u>check</u>
    whether you perform these activities by yourself or with the help
    of other persons in your agency.

<u>Activity</u>   <u>Perform by Self</u>   <u>Perform with Someone Else</u>

8. It is commonly said that a person has to devote a lot of time <u>and</u>
    energy in order to accomplish something in his work. In the average
    work week, how much (1) <u>of your time</u> and (2) <u>of your energy</u> is
    absorbed by the following activities. (Assume you have 100 "units"
    of time and 100 "units" of energy.)

<u>Activity</u>	<u>Units of Time</u>	<u>Units of Energy</u>
<u>Your activity with the clients</u> (e.g., visiting them at home, in the office, reviewing their records, etc.)		
<u>Your activity with staff members of this agency</u> (e.g., <u>attending meetings</u>, discussing problems of the clients, seeking information and advice, small talk)		
<u>Your activity with staff members in other agencies and services in the</u> community (e.g., referrals, collateral contacts, etc.)		
	100	100

9. Assume that there are 100 units of pressure that can be used to
    control how you do your work in this agency. On the average, how
    much of this pressure comes from the following sources?

	<u>Units of Pressure</u>
State Department of Welfare (rules, regulations, policies)	_____
County Department of Welfare (rules, regulations, policies)	_____
The general "climate" of the community—county in which your agency is located	_____
Your self-initiative and discretion as need arises	_____
	100

10. How satisfied are you with the <u>results of your efforts</u> in the

     following areas? (CIRCLE ONE)

	Very Satisfied	Satisfied	Not Satisfied
Dealings with the clients	3	2	1
Dealings with staff members of this agency	3	2	1
Dealing with other agencies in the community on common problems	3	2	1

11. When you think of the other types of jobs that you could have

     in areas other than social work, how important to you is the social

     welfare work that you are doing now?

Very Important	Important	Not So Important	Unimportant
4	3	2	1

12. How consistent in this agency's definition of the work with your

     conception of what has to be done?

Very Consistent	Fairly Consistent	Not Very Consistent	Not Consistent At All
4	3	2	1

SECTION V

FAIR HEARING

     As you probably know, the state welfare regulations provide for the

right to appeal and a fair hearing for any welfare recipient who feels that

the department has acted wrongly or unfairly in his case.

1. a. What proportion of this agency's clients do you think are generally

        aware of their right to appeal welfare department actions? _____%

b. How are your clients usually informed of this right? _____

_____

2. Has any client of yours ever suggested that he might appeal some action
you or the welfare department has taken? Yes _____ No _____
(IF YES)

    a. With about how many different clients has this happened in
        the last 3 years?

                    One   ___
                    Two to five ___
                    Five to ten ___
                    More than ten ___

3. Have you ever suggested to a client, when the client objected to something done by you or the department, that he (or she) should appeal the
action? Yes _____ No _____
(IF YES)

    a. About how many times has this happened in the last 3 years?

                    Once   ___
                    Two to five times ___
                    Five to ten times ___
                    More than ten times ___

    b. Why did you suggest that the client appeal? (IF MORE THAN ONE,
        ASK FOR TWO MOST RECENT)

        1. _____

        2. _____

4. Has any client of yours ever actually filed an appeal with the state
department? Yes ___ No ___
(IF YES)

    1. How many different times has this happened?

                    Once _____   Three times _____
                    Twice _____   Four or more _____

2. What was the appeal about? (IF MORE THAN ONE, ASK FOR MOST
    RECENT) _____

    _____

3. What was the final result? (IF MORE THAN ONE, ASK FOR MOST
    RECENT) _____

    _____

5. How effective do you think the fair hearing process is as a protection
    for the welfare recipient from an unfair or incorrect action taken by
    the welfare department or a caseworker?

                                    Very effective   ____
                                    Fairly effective   ____
                                    Not too effective   ____
                                    Not at all effective ____

6. Do you think that a client who objects to a department decision is
    wise to appeal and request a hearing? Yes ____ No ____

    a. Why do you feel this way? _____

        _____

7. What do you think is the general attitude of other caseworkers and
    supervisors in your department toward the fair hearing process?

    _____

    _____

SECTION VI

BACKGROUND INFORMATION

1. What is the <u>highest</u> level of education you have reached?

    (CIRCLE ONE)

                          High school graduate................. 1

                          Some college........................ 2

                          College graduate.................... 3

                          Some graduate or professional work... 4

                          Graduate or professional degree...... 5

2. What is your age?   _____ years

3. What is your sex?   (CIRCLE ONE)   Male........ 1

                                              Female...... 2

4. What is your predominant national background?

    (CIRCLE ONE)

                          Western, Northern European........... 1

                          Central, Eastern European........... 2

                          Southern European................... 3

                          American Negro...................... 4

                          Latin American...................... 5

                          Other 6

5. What is your feeling about the area which agency serves?

    (CIRCLE ONE)

        I feel that I am a real part of the community as an

        individual, not just as a staff member at this county

        agency... 1

21

I feel that I am a part of the community,
but mainly as a staff member at the county
agency... 2

I do not feel that I am really a part of
the community in any sense, but I would
like to be... 3

I think of the community as just a place
where I happen to be working......................... 4

THANK YOU FOR YOUR COOPERATION

UNIVERSITY EXTENSION

The University of Wisconsin
905 University Avenue, Room 401
Madison, Wisconsin 53706
Telephone: 262-3122 (Area Code 608)

Wisconsin Survey Research Laboratory

Summer, 1967

Dear Madam:

The University of Wisconsin is making a study of ADC families and the various problems they often face. We are interested both in the needs of ADC families for lawyers (for problems such as divorce, non-support, creditors, landlords and so forth) and also in their experience with the ADC program. These are important matters, but we have little first-hand information. We would like to ask you what your own feelings and experiences have been. We are planning to interview several ADC families like your own.

A professional interviewer of our research staff will call on you to interview you. The interview is entirely voluntary on your part. It will be in your home and will take an hour or an hour and a half. What you say in the interview will be kept secret. Your name will be known only to the research staff and nothing you say will ever be made available to the welfare department.

To compensate you for the time, we will pay you two dollars for granting us an interview. This money would be considered as incidental income and you will not have to report it to the welfare department.

We hope that you will cooperate with us. It is very important for our study. If you do not wish to cooperate, tear off the bottom part of the letter, sign it, and return it to me in the self-addressed envelope. If you want to co-operate, we will get in touch with you later to arrange an appointment. If you decide that you do not want to be interviewed, but have not mailed back the bottom part of the letter, then please tell the member of our staff when she gets in touch with you to arrange an appointment, or call me collect. My telephone number is 262-3122 (area code 608).

Thank you.

Sincerely,

Mina C. Hockstad

Mina C. Hockstad
Associate Director

MCH/djg
P-306

237

UNIVERSITY EXTENSION

The University of Wisconsin
905 University Avenue, Room 401
Madison, Wisconsin 53706
Telephone: 262-3122 (Area Code 608)

Wisconsin Survey Research Laboratory

Summer, 1967

Dear Madam:

A short time ago we wrote to you asking for permission to interview you with
regard to your ADC experience and your need for lawyers for other types of
matters, and you wrote back indicating that you did not wish to be interviewed.
I am writing again to ask if you won't please reconsider your decision.

We have now completed interviews with over 500 ADC families in various parts of
Wisconsin with a high degree of success. We have obtained a great deal of useful information about the families, and our interviewers have reported that many
mothers have enjoyed taking part in this study. Nevertheless, in order to make
our results truly representative and the study accurate, it is important that
we interview as many people as we can on the original mailing lists.

As stated in our first letter, a professional interviewer of our research staff
will call on you to interview you. The interview is entirely voluntary on your
part. It will be in your home and will take an hour or an hour and a half. What
you say in the interview will be kept secret. Your name will be known only to
the research staff and nothing you will say will ever be made available to the
welfare department.

To compensate you for the time, we will pay you three dollars for granting us an
interview. This money would be considered an incidental income and the welfare
department has said that you will not have to report it.

We hope that you will cooperate with us. It is very important for our study.
If you still do <u>not</u> wish to cooperate, tear off the bottom part of the letter,
sign it, and return it to me in the self-addressed envelope. If you want to
cooperate, we will get in touch with you later to arrange an appointment. If
you decide that you do not want to be interviewed, but have not mailed back the
bottom part of the letter, then please tell the member of our staff when she
gets in touch with you to arrange an appointment, or call me collect. My
telephone number is 262-3122 (area code 608).

Won't you please reconsider?

Thank you.

Sincerely,

Mina C. Hockstad

Mina C. Hockstad
Associate Director

MCH/djg
P-306

                I still do not wish to participate in the study.

                Signature: _____

UNIVERSITY EXTENSION

The University of Wisconsin
905 University Avenue, Room 401
Madison, Wisconsin 53706
Telephone: 262-3122 (Area Code 608)

Wisconsin Survey Research Laboratory

Dear Madam:

Some time ago an interviewer on our research staff talked to you about your experiences in the ADC program. Similar interviews have now been completed with over 800 ADC families in various parts of Wisconsin. Because of the excellent cooperation of women such as yourself, we have been able to gather a great deal of useful information about welfare services and problems in this state.

We understand that you left the ADC program. I am writing to you to ask you to take part in a second stage of our study even though some of the ladies may have found it necessary to apply again for ADC benefits. We are contacting women like yourself, and asking to hold a second interview, because we are interested in your impressions of the program as you look back on it. Everything you say in the interview will, of course, be kept strictly confidential.

This interview will be much shorter than the first. We are willing to pay a fee of $5.00 to compensate you for your time. A member of our interviewing staff will call upon you in the near future.

We think that this study is very important. Much is known about what case-workers and other welfare personnel think about the ADC program but almost nothing about what people like yourself, who have taken part in the program, think. We hope that by talking to you and to others who left the program, we can better tell the other side of the story.

We are enclosing a postage paid self-addressed post card with space provided for you to indicate any change of name or address. Please fill this out and mail it back to us. This will make it easier for our interviewer to contact you.

Sincerely,

Mina C. Hockstad
Associate Director

MCH/map
P-325

SURVEY OF WISCONSIN ADC FAMILIES

1. First, I'd like to ask some questions about you and your family. To start...how many years have you lived in Wisconsin?

   /All life/, or _____ (# YRS)
   (TO Q 2)

   1a. In what state were you born? /Wisconsin/, or _____
       (TO Q 2)

       1b. Why did you come to Wisconsin? _____
       _____

2. For most of your life before 16, did you live on a farm or in a rural area, in a small town of less than 10,000, in a city of 10,000 to 50,000, in a city of 50,000 to 100,000, or in a larger city?

/Farm or/ / rural /	/Less than/ / 10,000 /	/10,000 to/ / 49,999 /	/50,000 to/ / 99,999 /	/Larger/ / city/

   2a. How many years have you lived in this community (city)? _____ (# YRS)

3. In what year were you born? 19____

4. What was the highest grade of school you completed? _____

   4a. Have you had any other schooling, such as vocational courses?

       /Yes/   /No/
                               (TO Q 5)

       4b. What schooling was this? _____
       _____

5. Are you now married, divorced, separated, deserted, widowed, or have you never married?

   /Married/   /Divorced/   /Separated/   /Deserted/   /Widowed/   /Never married/

   5a. How many times, in all, have you been married?

   5b. How many years have you been married (to your most recent husband)?

       _____

   5c. On what basis are you eligible for ADC? _____
   _____
                               (TO Q 6)

   5d. How many times, in all, have you been married?
       _____

   5e. How many years were you married (to your most recent husband)?
                               (TO Q 6)

   5f. Do you main-
       tain your ow
       household, o
       are you livi
       with other
       people?

       /Own/ /Other/
              (TO Q 11)

Interviewer's Name: _____   Sample #: _____

Date: _____   Time Started: _____

240

2.

6. How old were you when you were (first) married? _____(AGE)

7. What was the highest grade of school your (most recent) husband completed? _____(GR)

8. What was your (most recent) husband's usual kind of work?

_____

9. Did he work regularly? /Yes/   /Usually/   /No/

10. What was his usual weekly take home pay? $_____PER WEEK

11. What are the ages of the children you have had? (RECORD BELOW)

12. Which of these children are now living with you? (RECORD BELOW)

13. Which of these children are going to school? (RECORD BELOW)

AGES OF CHILDREN	√ IF LIVING WITH R	√ IF IN SCHOOL	WHAT IS CHILD BETWEEN 5 AND 17 DOING, IF NOT IN SCHOOL
____	____	____	_____
____	____	____	_____
____	____	____	_____
____	____	____	_____
____	____	____	_____
____	____	____	_____
____	____	____	_____
____	____	____	_____
____	____	____	_____

IF ANY CHILD BETWEEN 5 AND 17 YEARS OLD IS NOT IN SCHOOL, ASK Q 13a.
13a. Why is your child aged _____ not in school? (RECORD ABOVE)

14. Are you the actual (biological) mother of all of the children you support here in your home?

　　　　　　　　/Yes/　　　　　/No/
　　　　　　　(TO Q 15)

14a. How do you happen to have those children who are not your own?

_____

_____

15. Speaking only of your own children, was there just a single father or do different children have different fathers?

/One father/　　　/More than one/　　　/Inap; R not mother/

16. Were you raised--or mostly raised--by <u>both</u> your mother (or stepmother) and
    your father (or stepfather) when you were growing up; that is, between the
    years 6 and 16?
    /Yes/   /No/
    (TO Q 17)

    16a. By whom were you mostly raised during these years--6 to 16? _____
    _____

    16b. Why was it that both of your parents weren't present
         in your home between the ages of 6 to 16?   _____
    _____

17. What kind of work did your father do during the time
    you were growing-up?
    _____   /Don't know/   /No father/
                                                                        (GO TO Q 20)

18. Did your father work regularly then? /Yes/   /Usually/   /No/

19. What was the highest grade of school your father finished?

    _____(GRADE)   /Don't know/
    (TO Q 20)

    19a. Had he had either some high school or some grade school education?

    /High school/   /Grade school/   /Neither/   /Don't know/

IF R's FATHER NOT PRESENT IN HOME WHILE R GROWING-UP, ASK BOXED Q's

20. In your home during most of the time while you were growing up was
    there a grown man, an adult, living with the family who was like the
    head of the household?
    /Yes/   /No/
                     (TO Q 21)

    20a. Who was this man? _____

    20b. What kind of work did he do during this time?
    _____   /Don't know/

    20c. Did he work regularly? /Yes/   /Usually/   /No/   /Don't know/

21. Did your mother work--other than as a housewife--while
    you were growing up?

    /Yes/   /No/   /Don't know/   /No mother/
                         (TO Q 22)   (TO Q 22)   (TO Q 23)

    21a. What kind of work did she usually do? _____

22. What was the highest grade of school she finished? _____(GRADE OF SCHOOL)

23. How would you describe the living conditions in your home
    while you were growing-up...would you say the home was
    very crowded, fairly crowded, or not crowded?

    /Very/   /Fairly/   /Not crowded/   /R in institution/
                                                     (TO Q 28)

24. Did you have enough to eat at all times, most of
    the time, or often not have enough to eat?

             /All/   /Most/   /Often not enough/

25. How frequently was there enough money
    for special treats for you...often, sometimes,
    very rarely, or never?

             /Often/   /Sometimes/   /Very rarely/   /Never/

26. How well did your parents--or other adults in the
    home--get along together when you were growing up
    ...very well, fairly well, poorly, or very poorly?

    /Very well/   /Fairly well/   /Poorly/   /Very poorly/

27. Did your family receive any public or private welfare aid
    or assistance during the time you were growing up?

             /Yes/   /No/   /Don't know/
                         (TO Q 28)   (TO Q 28)

    27a. What welfare program or welfare aid did your family receive?

    _____

    _____

    27b. For how many years during the time you were growing up
          did your family receive welfare aid?

                              _____(# YRS)   /Don't know/
                              (GO TO Q 28)

          27c. Was it for longer than one year?

                  /Yes/   /No/   /Don't know/

Now I have some questions about the ADC program and your experience with it.

28. Have you ever been on an ADC program before this time?

    /Yes/   /No/
                 (TO Q 29)

28a. How many different times <u>before this one</u> were you on ADC? _____(#)

28b. How many years were you on ADC the first (second, third, fourth)
     time <u>before this one</u>? (RECORD BELOW)

28c. Why did you leave the program the first (second, third, fourth)
     time <u>before this one</u>? (RECORD BELOW)

TIMES ON ADC BEFORE PRESENT	Q 28b. # YRS. ON ADC	Q 28c. REASON FOR LEAVING
1	_____	_____
2	_____	_____
3	_____	_____
4	_____	_____

29. Now, as to your present experience on the ADC program...how long have
    you been on it this time?
                    _____(# YEARS)   _____(# MONTHS)

30. How much time passed between when you became eligible for ADC and when you
    actually applied for ADC? _____(# YEARS)   _____(# MONTHS)

31. DID MORE THAN 4 MONTHS PASS BETWEEN ELIGIBILITY AND APPLICATION?

    /Yes/   /No/
                 (GO TO Q 32)

31a. What was your main source of support--that is, how did you live--during
     this time before you went on the program? _____

     _____

     _____

31b. What happened to make you decide to go on the ADC program?

     _____

     _____

     _____

6.

32. At the time of your <u>first interview</u> with the welfare department (for most recent ADC experience), did the caseworker ask you a lot of questions about...

		Yes	No	Q32a Bothered?	Q32b Personal?
A.	Your financial resources and property?	___	___	_____	_____
B.	The care you give to your children?.	___	___	_____	_____
C.	Any possible marriage plans you had?	___	___	_____	_____
D.	The possibility of a job for either you or your children?.	___	___	_____	_____
E.	The possibility of financial support by your parents or relatives? .	___	___	_____	_____

ASK BOXED QUESTIONS FOR EACH "YES"; RECORD ANSWERS ABOVE.

32a. To what degree were you bothered or annoyed by the questions on _____...very much, moderately, only slightly, or not at all?

32b. Do you feel that any of the questions on _____ were about personal matters that should not concern the agency?

IF R NOT WIDOWED, ASK Q 33. IF WIDOWED, SKIP TO Q 34.

33. In order to qualify for aid, did you have to have an interview with someone in the <u>district attorney's office about child support payments</u> from the father of the children?

/Yes/   /No/
                (TO Q 34)

33a. What did he have you do? _____

_____

_____

_____

_____

_____

_____

_____

_____

33b. To what degree were you bothered or annoyed by what you were asked to do... very much, moderately, slightly, or not at all?

/Very much/   /Moderately/   /Slightly/   /Not at all/

34. Now I would like to ask you about your experience with the ADC program. For the
following questions, please think just about what has happened while on the ADC
program during the last three years--or since first coming on the program if that
was within the last three years. We are interested in anything that has happened
from 1964 to the present while you were receiving ADC support. First of all, does
your caseworker ever discuss your budget with you?

/Yes/   /No/
(TO Q 35)

34a. To what extent do you find these discussions on your budget helpful...are
they very helpful, usually helpful, of some help, or not helpful at all?

/Very/   /Usually/   /Some/   /Not at all/

34b. To what extent does it bother you to have your caseworker discuss your
budget...very much, moderately, slightly, or not at all?

/Very much/   /Moderately/   /Slightly/   /Not at all/

35. At the present time, are you able to manage pretty well on your budget?   /Yes/   /No/

36. Have you ever asked a caseworker for extra money for special needs?

/Yes/   /No/

36a. Have you asked your caseworker   36d. Why haven't you asked your
for extra money for...   caseworker for extra money?

YES	NO		
___	___	A. Clothing	_____
___	___	B. Household goods, including appliances	_____
___	___	C. Day care help	_____
___	___	D. Telephone	_____
___	___	E. Transportation	(GO TO Q 37)
___	___	F. Educational or employment retraining needs	
___	___	G. Extra or special food, including a restaurant allowance	
___	___	H. Home necessities--utilities, rent, heat, etc.	
___	___	I. School needs for your children	
___	___	J. Other (SPECIFY): _____	

36b. Which--if any--of these requests were refused or otherwise not granted?
(RECORD LETTER)
_____, _____, _____, _____, _____, _____   /None refused/

36c. In general, how fair do you think your caseworker and the welfare agency
have been in granting or refusing requests...always fair, usually fair,
usually unfair, or always unfair?

/Always fair/   /Usually fair/   /Usually unfair/   /Always unfair/

8.

37. Did your caseworker ever express disapproval of the way you spent any of your money, either for yourself or for your children?

/Yes/   /No/
                   (TO Q 38)

37a. How often has this happened? _____ (# TIMES)

37b. What was it the caseworker disapproved of? _____

_____

_____

37c. To what extent have you found such comments helpful...are they very helpful, usually helpful, of some help, or not helpful at all?

/Very/   /Usually/   /Some/   /Not at all/

37d. Do you feel you have to follow your caseworker's advice on such matters all of the time, most of the time, not very often, or not at all?

/All the time/   /Most of the time/   /Not very often/   /Not at all/

37e. To what extent does it bother you to have your caseworker discuss such matters...very much, moderately, slightly, or not at all?

/Very much/   /Moderately/   /Slightly/   /Not at all/

38. Has the amount of your basic aid grant been changed since you first went on the program?

/Yes/   /No/
                   (TO Q 39)

38a. About how many times in the last three years--or since coming on the program if entrance within three years--has this basic aid grant been changed?

/None/, or   _____ (#)
(TO Q 39)

38b. Has your caseworker told you the reasons for these changes?   /Yes/   /No/

38c. Have you usually understood why the changes were made?   /Yes/   /No/

38d. Were all of these changes more or less automatic or did you have to bring special facts to the attention of the caseworker?

/All more or less automatic/   /R requested some/
(GO TO Q 39)

38e. How many of these changes resulted from such requests from you?
_____ (#)

39. Has your caseworker ever discussed your children with you?

          /Yes/   /No/
            | (TO Q 40)
            ↓

    39a. What has your caseworker discussed with you about your children?
          Have you discussed...

          YES   NO

          ____   ____   A. General upbringing, nothing in particular?

          ____   ____   B. Health problems?

          ____   ____   C. How they were clothed and fed?

          ____   ____   D. Specific school problems?

          ____   ____   E. General plans about their future education or employment?

          ____   ____   F. Employment -- about a present job?

          ____   ____   G. Employment -- where they should take a part-time job?

          ____   ____   H. Other (SPECIFY): _____

                        _____

                        _____

    39b. Do you generally have discussions about your children every time you see
          your caseworker, on more than half of the caseworker's visits, on half or
          less of the visits, or quite rarely?

          /Every time/   /More than half/   /Half or less/   /Quite rarely/

    39c. To what extent do you find these discussions about your children
          helpful...are they very helpful, usually helpful, of some help,
          or not at all?
                        /Very/   /Usually/   /Some/   /Not at all/

    39d. Do you feel you have to follow advice that your caseworker offers
          concerning your children (child) all of the time, most of the time,
          not very often, or not at all?

          /All the time/   /Most of the time/   /Not very often/   /Not at all/

    39e. To what extent does it bother you to have your caseworker discuss
          your children...very much, moderately, slightly, or not at all?

                /Very much/   /Moderately/   /Slightly/   /Not at all/

10.   Project 306

40. Has your caseworker ever discussed with you how to take care of your house?

                    /Yes/   /No/
                                            (TO Q 41)

    40a. Has your caseworker talked about...

          YES   NO
          ____   ____   A. Keeping the house clean?
          ____   ____   B. Cooking, nutrition, diet, etc.?
          ____   ____   C. General problems of home management?
          ____   ____   D. Other (SPECIFY): _____

    40b. To what extent do you find these discussions helpful?

          /Very helpful/   /Usually helpful/   /Some help/   /Not at all/

    40c. To what extent does it bother you to
          have your caseworker discuss this?   /Very much/ /Moderately/ /Some/ /Not at all/

    40d. Do you feel you have to follow any advice your caseworker offers in such matters
          all the time, most of the time, not very often, or not at all?

          /All/   /Most/   /Not very/   /Not at all/

41. Has your caseworker ever discussed with you health problems, such as medical
     or dental treatment, or mental or psychiatric help, for either you or
     your children?
                    /Yes/   /No/
                                            (TO Q 42)

    41a. Has your caseworker talked about...

          YES   NO
          ____   ____   A. Medical care?
          ____   ____   B. Dental care?
          ____   ____   C. Mental health problems?
          ____   ____   D. Other (SPECIFY): _____

    41b. To what extent do you find these discussions helpful?

          /Very helpful/   /Usually helpful/   /Some help/   /Not at all/

    41c. Do you feel you have to follow any advice your caseworker offers in such
          matters all of the time, most of the time, not very often, or not at all?

          /All the time/   /Most of the time/   /Not very often/   /Not at all/

    41d. To what extent does it bother you to have your caseworker discuss this?

          /Very much/   /Moderately/   /Some/   /Not at all/

(IF R MARRIED AND LIVING WITH HUSBAND, SKIP TO Q 43)

42. Has your caseworker ever discussed with you your social life, specifically your relationship with men--whether you are dating or whether you have any plans for marriage (IF RESPONDENT DIVORCED OR DESERTED; or reconciliation with your husband)?

/Yes/   /No/
                 (TO Q 43)

42a. What has your caseworker talked about? (Anything else?) _____

_____

_____

_____

_____

42b. To what extent do you find these discussions helpful?

/Very helpful/   /Usually helpful/   /Some help/   /Not at all/

42c. To what extent does it bother you to have your caseworker discuss this?

/Very much/   /Moderately/   /Some/   /Not at all/

42d. Do you feel you have to follow any advice your caseworker offers concerning such matters all of the time, most of the time, not very often, or not at all?

/All the time/   /Most of the time/   /Not very often/   /Not at all/

43. Has anyone in the welfare agency contacted the children's father about his relationship with the children?

/Yes/   /No/   /Don't know/

44. Now I have a few questions about the jobs you've had. Forgetting for the moment the three-year time limit, could you tell me the four jobs (or fewer, if that's all) you've held for the longest periods since leaving school? (LIST BELOW)

/Never had job/
(GO TO Q 45)

JOBS	YEAR STARTED	LENGTH OF TIME HELD
1. _____	19____	_____
2. _____	19____	_____
3. _____	19____	_____
4. _____	19____	_____

44a. Could you tell me the year you started each job and how long you held each? (LIST ABOVE)

12.

For the following questions, we will again be concerned with anytime in the last three years when you have been on the ADC program.

45. Do you presently have a job?

/Yes/   /No/
                (GO TO Q 46)

45a. What is your job? _____

_____

45b. How much do you earn per week? $_____

45c. Did the caseworker suggest that you get the job or help you find the job, or did you get your job without the caseworker's help?

/Caseworker helped/   /Without caseworker's help/
        (GO TO Q 49, NEXT PAGE)

(ASK Q's 46 - 48 IF R NOT NOW WORKING; OTHER R's GO TO Q 49)
46. Have you had a job within the last three years--or since coming on the ADC program if that was within the last three years?

/Yes/   /No/

46a. What was your job(s)?   46d. Have you tried to get
                                         work in this period?

_____   /Yes/   /No/
_____   (GO TO Q 47)
_____
_____   46e. What kind of work?

46b. How much did you earn per   _____
     week when you stopped (most   _____
     recent job)?   _____
                   $_____

                                    46f. Why weren't you able to
46c. Why did you stop working?   get a job? _____

_____   _____
_____   _____
_____   _____
_____   _____
_____   _____
_____   _____
_____   _____

47. Has your caseworker ever discussed a job for you or tried to find you a job?

/Yes/   /No/

47a. What happened?   47e. Have you ever asked your
                                                       caseworker to find you
_____   a job?
_____   /Yes/   /No/
_____   (GO TO Q 48)

47b. To what extent do you find
     these discussions helpful?   /Very/ /Moderately/ /Somewhat/ /Not at all/

47c. To what extent does it bother
     you to have your caseworker
     discuss this?   /Very/   /Moderately/   /Somewhat/   /Not at all/

47d. Do you feel you have to follow any advice your caseworker offers concerning
     jobs and employment all of the time, most of the time, not very often, or
     not at all?   /All the time/ /Most of the time/ /Not very often/ /Not at all/

48. If good babysitting or day care for your children were available, to what extent
    would you like to have at least a part-time job...very much, somewhat, not
    especially, or not at all?
                       /Very much/ /Somewhat/ /Not especially/ /Not at all/

ALL RESPONDENTS

49. As you understand it, how does the welfare department treat money you might
    make from a job you might hold--that is, do they let you keep all that you
    make or do they lower the amount of your aid grant and, if so, by how much;
    or what do they do?   _____

    _____

    _____

    _____

50. Do you believe that this is the best policy?   /Yes/   /Not sure/   /No/

51. Why do you feel this way?   _____

    _____

    _____

    _____

    _____

52. I would now like to ask some questions about your contacts with your caseworker.
    First, how many caseworkers have you had in the last three years (or since coming
    on the ADC program, if less than three years)?   _____(#)

14.   Project 306

53. How many months have you had your present caseworker? _____(# MOS), or _____(# YRS)

54. And, how many months did you have your previous caseworker?

     /Had only one/, or _____(# MOS), or _____(# YRS)

55. The following questions concern your present caseworker (unless he is too new--
     then speak of next most recent). First, how often do you usually see your case-
     worker...would it be more than once a month, once every month or two, once every
     three months, a few times a year, or less often?

     /More than once mo./ /Once/mo. or two/ /Once/3 mos./ /Few year/ /Less/

     55a. Do you feel that this is often enough? /Yes/ /Not sure/ /No/

56. To what extent do you feel your caseworker is someone you like, can trust,
     talk to, and discuss your problems with...would it be very much, fairly
     much, not really, or not at all?
                                  /Very/   /Fairly/   /Not really/   /Not at all/

57. How many minutes does your caseworker usually
     stay when he or she comes to your home?
                                     _____(# MINUTES)

58. Have you ever tried to call or contact your caseworker at a time other than
     his or her regular visit?
                            /Yes/   /No/
                                         (GO TO Q 59)

     58a. About how many different times have you done this? _____(#)

     58b. Were you (usually) able to contact your caseworker? /Yes/ /Some/ /No/

     58c. What things have you contacted your caseworker about? _____

     _____

     _____

     _____

     _____

59. How often do you make a special effort to stay on good terms with your caseworker...
     always, usually, once in a while, or never?

          /Always/   /Usually/   /Once in a while/   /Never/

60. To what extent do you feel your caseworker has a good reason for what he or she
     does...always, usually, not very often, or never?

          /Always/   /Usually/   /Not very often/   /Never/

61. Thinking of the 3 year period (or since entering the ADC program), has your caseworker ever talked to you about, or tried to interest you in special programs offered for you or your children by the welfare department or some other community agency--job training, Head Start, special schooling, etc.?

/Yes/   /No/
(TO Q 62)

61a. Did you or your children ever take part in any? /Yes/   /No/
(TO Q 61c)

61b. Which ones? _____

_____

61c. Has your caseworker ever suggested that you or your children participate in some such program that you didn't want to participate in?

/Yes/   /No/
(TO Q 62)

61d. Can you explain what happened? _____

_____

_____

62. Did you ever ask your caseworker about any such programs for either you or your children before he mentioned them? /Yes/   /No/
(TO Q 63)

62a. Which ones? _____

_____

62b. What did your caseworker do? _____

_____

63. At the present time, do you or any of your children have any problems or continuing difficulties other than money problems?

/Yes/   /No/
(TO Q 64)

63a. What kinds of problems or difficulties are these? _____

_____

_____

_____

63b. Have you discussed these problems with your caseworker?

/Yes/   /No/
(TO Q 64)

63c. Has your caseworker been able to help you in any way? /Yes/   /No/

16.

64. Do you think there are things that your caseworker--possibly
   if he had more time or freedom to act--could do to help you
   that he isn't now doing?

   /Yes/   /Not sure/   /No/
                                (TO Q 65)

   64a. What is it you think he could do? _____

   _____

   _____

   _____

   _____

65. Does your caseworker usually call at your home unannounced or does
   he get in touch with you first to let you know that he is coming?

   /Unannounced/   /Gets in touch/   /Both/

66. Do you think it is all right for caseworkers to call unannounced
   or do you think that they should notify clients in advance?

                                        /All right/   /Notify/

67. Should a welfare client have the right to
   refuse to let in a caseworker who calls unannounced? /Yes/   /Not sure/   /No/

68. So far we have talked about several possible problem spots in your
   relations with your caseworker and the welfare agency. Have there
   been times when you have complained to your caseworker about some
   action he took or didn't take, or about some question he asked or
   about anything else that might have bothered you?

        /Yes/   /No/
                    (TO Q 69)

   68a. About how many times have you complained to
        your caseworker about something he or the agency
        has done...would it be many times, quite a lot,
        just a few times, or only once?

        /Many/   /Quite a lot/   /Just a few/   /Only once/

   68b. What are four specific things you have complained about?

        1. _____

        2. _____

        3. _____

        4. _____

69. Suppose your caseworker made a decision in your case that you
    thought was wrong or unfair and you wanted to change the decision.
    How would you go about it?
                            /Have no idea/, or
                             (TO Q 71)

    _____
    _____
    _____
    _____

70. Has this ever happened to you?   /Yes/   /No/
                                                 (TO Q 71)

    70a. Would you say this has happened many times,
          quite a lot, just a few times, or only once? /Many/ /Lot/ /Few/ /Once/

    70b. How long ago was the last time this happened? _____(# MOS), _____(# YRS)

    70c. What, specifically, did your caseworker decide that
          you thought was wrong or unfair then? _____

    _____
    _____

    70d. Did you talk to the caseworker's supervisor about it? /Yes/   /No/

    70e. What (else), specifically, did you do? _____

    _____
    _____
    _____

71. Did you know before my telling you now that you have a right to
    appeal decisions you don't like and to get a hearing on your
    objection before an official of the state welfare department
    (called the Appeal and Fair Hearing Process)?
                                        /Yes/   /No/
                                                   (TO Q 72)

    71a. How did you find out about this? _____

    _____
    _____

    71b. How would you go about making an appeal? _____

    _____
    _____

    71c. Would it do someone any good to make an appeal? /Yes/   /Depends/   /No/

18.

72. Has your experience with the welfare agency been very satisfactory in
view of what you needed, satisfactory, unsatisfactory, or very unsatisfactory?

/Very satisfactory/   /Satisfactory/   /Unsatisfactory/   /Very unsatisfactory/

73. What have been the good points of your experience, if any? (Anything else?)

_____
_____
_____
_____
_____
_____

74. What have been the bad points of your experience, if any? (Anything else?)

_____
_____
_____
_____
_____
_____

75. What are some things about the welfare program you would like
to see changed, if any? (Anything else?)

_____
_____
_____
_____
_____
_____

76. How much do you think you have benefited from the services other
than the basic financial aid, which your caseworker and the welfare
agency have provided...have you greatly benefited, moderately benefited,
benefited very little, or not at all?

/Greatly benefited/   /Moderately benefited/   /Very little/   /Not at all/

77. Do you think that the rules and regulations of the county welfare
department are fair and reasonable?
                              /Yes/   /Not sure/   /No/

Now I would like to ask you a few questions about some of your general feelings
about the ADC program. In each of these questions, I'm going to give you two
sentences. Choose the one that comes closest to telling the way you feel about
the ADC program. Be sure the one you choose tells the way you actually feel,
not the way you'd like them to be. Let me read both sentences in each group
before you select the one that best says what you think.

78. CHECK ONE

_____ A. When my caseworker and I make plans, I am confident they
          will work out all right. OR,

_____ B. It is not always a good idea to plan things with your
          caseworker because the plans usually won't work out.

79. _____ A. What happens to me while I'm in the welfare program is
               usually up to me. OR,

_____ B. What happens to me while I'm in the welfare program is usually
          the result of what my caseworker does for me.

80. _____ A. If my caseworker disagrees with me, I sometimes wonder if
               I am right. OR,

_____ B. I am nearly always certain that my plans will work, even
          if my caseworker disagrees with me.

81. _____ A. I usually feel pretty sure that the welfare program is a
               good thing for me and my family. OR,

_____ B. There are times when I think the welfare program
          is doing more harm than good for me and my family.

Now I have a few questions about your home and community life.

82. Do you have a radio in your home? /Yes/   /No/

83. ...a television? /Yes/   /No/

84. ...a telephone? /Yes/   /No/

85. ...an automobile? /Yes/   /No/

86. In an average week, how many times are you able to get out of the house
     (IF R WORKING: other than for work)?
                                        _____(# PER WEEK)

87. In an average week, how many times are you able to get out of the house
     for just social trips--excluding things like trips to the grocery store,
     the doctor's, and so forth?
                         _____(# PER WEEK)

20.   Project 306

IF R MARRIED, SKIP TO Q 88, BELOW

87a. Do you ever date--that is, have a social life involving men?

/Yes/   /No/
             (GO TO Q 88)

87b. How many dates do you usually have? _____ (#)

88. How many families in your community do you know who are in the ADC program?

/None/, or _____ (#)
(TO Q 89)

88a. How many of these would you consider good friends
whom you see fairly often?
/None/, or _____ (#)
(TO Q 89)

88b. Thinking of the two families on ADC (or one, if that's all)
who you know best...how many times in an average month do
you visit, or go out and do things, with the first (second)
family? (RECORD BELOW)

88c. How many times in an average month do you visit with the
first (second) family over the telephone? (RECORD BELOW)

88d. Do you ever talk over welfare problems with the first
(second) family? (RECORD BELOW)

88e. Do you ever talk over other problems with
the first (second) family? (RECORD BELOW)

	Q 88b. # VISITS IN MONTH	Q 88c. TELEPHONE VISITS/MONTH	Q 88d. TALK WEL- FARE PROB.?	Q 88e. TALK OTHER PROBLEMS
1st FAMILY	_____	_____	_____	_____
2nd FAMILY	_____	_____	_____	_____

89. How many relatives of yours live in this community or in nearby
communities?
_____ (#)   /None/
            (GO TO Q 90)

89a. How often, in an average month, do you visit, or go out and
do things, with your relatives?
_____ (#)

89b. How often, in an average month, do you talk with your relatives
over the telephone? _____ (#)

89c. Do you ever talk over welfare problems with your relatives? /Yes/   /No/

89d. Do you ever talk over other problems with your relatives? /Yes/   /No/

90. How many other families or individuals in your
     community do you know at all well?

                              /None/, or _____ (#)
                              (TO Q 91)

     90a. How many of these would you consider good
           friends whom you see fairly often?

                              /None/, or _____ (#)
                              (TO Q 91)

           90b. Thinking of the two (or one, if that's all) whom you know
                 best...how many times in an average month do you visit, or
                 go out and do things, with the first (second) family? (RECORD BELOW)

           90c. How many times in an average month do you visit with the
                 first (second) family over the telephone? (RECORD BELOW)

           90d. Do you ever talk over welfare problems with the first
                 (second) family? (RECORD BELOW)

           90e. Do you ever talk over other problems with the first
                 (second) family? (RECORD BELOW)

	Q 90b. # VISITS PER MONTH	Q 90c. TELEPHONE VISITS/MONTH	Q 90d. TALK WEL-FARE PROB.?	Q 90e. TALK OTHER PROBLEMS
1st FAMILY				
2nd FAMILY				

91. Have any of the friends we've discussed as being your good friends been
     some of your immediate neighbors; that is, some of the people who live
     in the homes right around your own?

                              /Yes/   /No/
                              (TO Q 92)

     91a. Not counting the families we've discussed, are you fairly good
           friends with any of the families in the immediate neighborhood? /Yes/ /No/

92. Have you or your children had any difficulties or
     disagreements with any of your immediate neighbors?   /Yes/   /No/
                                                                       (TO Q 93)

     92a. What was (were) the problem(s)? _____

     _____

     92b. How often have such problems occurred...only once
           or twice, several times, or fairly often? /Once or twice/ /Several/ /Fairly often/

     92c. Do you think any of these problems (or the problem) resulted fully or in part
           because you are a welfare recipient? (IF YES: Please explain why you think
           so.) /No/, or _____

     _____

93. In general, how do you think people in this community feel about people like yourself who are in the ADC program? Would you say they feel very understanding, fairly understanding, indifferent, fairly hostile, or very hostile?

/Very / /Fairly / /Indifferent/ /Fairly / /Very hostile/ /Don't know/
/understanding/ /understanding/ /hostile/

94. Have you or your children had any difficulties or problems with people or businesses in the community that you think happened because you are a welfare recipient?

/Yes/   /No/   /Don't know/
         (GO TO Q 95)

94a. What was it that happened and why do you think it was related to your welfare experience? _____

_____

_____

_____

95. Every community has a city council or a county government that works on local problems. Have you had any contact with your local government around here--other than the welfare department--either in trying to get the local officials to do something, or to object to some action they have taken?

/Yes/   /No/
             (TO Q 96)

95a. What kind of contact have you had? _____

_____

_____

96. For various reasons many people were not able to vote in the elections held this last November--those for governor and other state and county officials. Did you vote then?

/Yes/   /No/
(TO Q 97)

96a. Are you registered to vote?   /Yes/   /No/

97. Are any of your relatives or friends in this community active in local politics or city affairs or in some way involved with such groups as the city council, the school board, or local political parties?

/Yes/   /No/
           (TO Q 98)

97a. In what ways are they active? _____

_____

_____

_____

98. Within the last three years, have you attended your local PTA?

/Yes/   /No/   /No children in school/
                (TO Q 99)   (TO Q A99)

  98a. Do you attend your local PTA fairly regularly?   /Yes/   /No/

99. Within the three years, have you gone to a parents' program at school to meet your child's (children's) teacher(s)?

/Yes/   /No/
              (TO Q A99)

  99a. How often do you do this...would you say every time there is such a program, for just some of the programs, or for only a few of the programs?

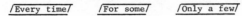

/Every time/   /For some/   /Only a few/

A99. Some ADC mothers have said that when they are with friends or other people not on ADC, they feel embarrassed or uncomfortable about receiving welfare support. Other ADC mothers say they don't feel this way at all. How do you feel when you are with people who don't receive ADC...would you say you are never embarrassed or uncomfortable, sometimes embarrassed or uncomfortable, often embarrassed or uncomfortable, or always embarrassed or uncomfortable?

/Never/   /Sometimes/   /Often/   /Always/

100. Have any of your children participated in any of the "War on Poverty" youth programs such as Head Start, the Job Corps, the Neighborhood Youth Corps, or any of the others that have been offered?

/Yes/   /No/
                (TO Q 101)

  100a. Which programs did they participate in?   (LIST BELOW)

                                                                  Q100b

A. _____   _____
B. _____   _____
C. _____   _____
D. _____   _____
E. _____   _____
F. _____   _____
G. _____   _____

ASK Q BELOW FOR EACH PROGRAM; RECORD ABOVE.

  100b. How long did they participate in the _____ programs--that is, did they complete an entire term or did they go for a while and drop out, or did they just go a couple of times and drop, or what ever?

24.

IF R HAS <u>ANY</u> <u>CHILDREN</u> <u>OVER</u> <u>5</u> <u>YEARS</u> <u>OLD</u>, ASK Q's ON THIS PAGE; IF NOT, SKIP TO NEXT PAGE.

101. Now I shall read to you a list of groups or organizations that children often
      belong to, or participate in. Please tell me if, within the last three years,
      any of your children have participated in any of these.

			I Q 101a	II Q 101b	III Q 101c
YES	**NO**				
___	___	A.	A youth group like the Boy Scouts, the Girl Scouts, the Campfire Girls, or the 4-H.		
___	___	B.	Community groups like the YMCA, YWCA, or the Boy's Club.		
___	___	C.	Any community or school sports team.		
___	___	D.	Any church clubs or organizations.		
___	___	E.	School clubs or organizations.		
___	___	F.	Are there any other groups or organizations your children may have belonged to? (SPECIFY)		

ASK BOXED QUESTIONS ABOUT EACH "YES" CHECKED ABOVE

> 101a. What is the name of the _____ group? (COLUMN I, ABOVE)
>
> 101b. While involved with _____, how often <u>in an average month</u>
>   did your child (children) participate? (<u>COLUMN II</u>)
>
> 101c. Does your child still participate in _____? (COLUMN III)

102. Now, I shall read to you a list of different groups and organizations that many
people belong to or participate in. Please tell me if, within the last three
years, you have participated in, or belonged to, any organizations of these types.

YES	NO		I Q102a	II Q102b	III Q102c	IV Q102d
___	___	A. A labor union.				
___	___	B. A political group--like a political party, or the NAACP or CORE, or any other group concerned with political problems.				
___	___	C. Any of the groups connected to the national "War on Poverty" like a neighborhood task group or a Head Start mothers' group or any other groups or meetings associated with the "War on Poverty".				
___	___	D. A fraternal group like the Elks, the Moose, or the Masons.				
___	___	E. A social group or sports group like a card club, a birthday club, a bowling team, or any other informal group that meets fairly regularly.				
___	___	F. A social group like "Parents without Partners" that has parties and does other things together.				
___	___	G. As a leader for some young people's group like the Cub Scouts, the Girl Scouts, or the 4-H Club.				
___	___	H. Are there any other groups or organizations that you have participated in during the last three years? (SPECIFY)				

ASK BOXED QUESTIONS ABOUT EACH "YES" CHECKED ABOVE; IF NO MEMBERSHIPS, GO TO NEXT PAGE.

102a. What is the name of the _____ group? (COLUMN I, ABOVE)

102b. While involved with _____, how often, in an average month, did you
participate? (COLUMN II)

102c. Do you still participate in _____? (COLUMN III)

102d. Did you participate in _____ before coming on the ADC program? (COLUMN IV)

26.

103. Are there any other groups or organizations like those I've mentioned that you
      participated in during the years just before you entered the ADC program that
      you no longer participate in?

                          /Yes/   /No/
                           | (GO TO Q 104)
                           ↓

      103a. What groups are these? (Any others?) _____

      _____
      _____
      _____

104. What is your religious preference, if any?

      /Protestant/   /Catholic/   Other: _____   /None/
           | (TO Q 104b)   (TO Q 104b)   (TO Q 104b)
           ↓

      104a. What denomination is that? _____

104b. How often--if ever--do you go to church...at least once a week, a few times
      a month, once a month, less often, or never?

      /Once a week/   /Few/month/   /Once a month/   /Less often/ /Never/
           | | | (GO TO Q 105)
           ↓   ↓   ↓

      104c. Do you ever take part in church activities other than Sunday services?

                          /Yes/   /No/
                           | (GO TO Q 105)
                           ↓

          104d. What church activities do you take part in?

          _____
          _____
          _____
          _____

105. Do any of your children attend either church or Sunday school?   /Yes/   /No/

106. Have you ever sought help from a church or church official on any of your problems?

                          /Yes/   /No/
                           | (GO TO Q 107)
                           ↓

      106a. Over the last three years, what problems have you sought help on from
             a church?
             _____
             _____
             _____
             _____

Now, I'd like to ask you a few questions about some of your general feelings about life--not just about your experiences with the ADC program. In each of these questions, I'm going to give you two sentences. Choose the one that comes closest to telling the way you feel things <u>actually are</u> in life. Be sure it's the way you think things <u>actually are at this point in your life</u>, <u>not</u> the way you'd like them to be. Let me read both sentences in each series <u>before</u> you select the one that best represents what you think.

CHECK ONE

107. _____ A. When I make plans, I am almost certain that I can make them work. OR,
     _____ B. It is not always a good idea to plan too far ahead, because many things turn out to be a matter of good or bad luck anyway.

108. _____ A. I've usually felt pretty sure my life would work out the way I want it to.   OR,
     _____ B. There have been times when I haven't been very sure that my life would work out the way I want it to.

109. _____ A. When people disagree with me, I sometimes start to wonder whether I'm right. OR,
     _____ B. I nearly always feel sure of myself, even when people disagree with me.

110. _____ A. I often have trouble making up my mind about important decisions. OR,
     _____ B. I don't have much trouble making up my mind about important decisions.

111. _____ A. When I make plans ahead, I usually get to carry things out the way I expected.   OR,
     _____ B. Things usually come up to make me change my plans.

112. _____ A. I feel I'm a person who gets his share of bad luck.   OR,
     _____ B. I feel I have mostly good luck.

Now I'd like to ask you about some problems often faced by people. Please tell me which of them--if any--have happened to you. Again I'm interested in what has happened to you within the last three years but for these questions, answer for the entire three years, from 1964 on, regardless of whether you were on ADC for the whole period. Some we might have already discussed, but I have a few more questions to ask about them.

IF R MARRIED AT ANY TIME IN LAST THREE YEARS, GIVE BOXED INSTRUCTION.
IF NOT, SKIP TO Q 113.

> Some of these questions will also ask about your husband. I only want to know about problems that happened to him while he was living with you in the home-- and not about things that happened to him while you were not together.

113. First, what difficulties--if any--have you had with your landlord over the three years? I mean with the landlord of any building you have lived in <u>other than public housing</u>.

/None/, or   RECORD BELOW
(TO Q 114)

	I, Q113a	II, Q113b	III, Q113c
A. _____	___	___	___
B. _____	___	___	___
C. _____	___	___	___
D. _____	___	___	___

<u>ASK BOXED Q's ABOUT EACH PROBLEM MENTIONED ABOVE, THEN ASK Q113d</u>

> 113a. Did you speak to anyone--other than a lawyer--whom you thought could help you with _____? (COLUMN I)
>
> (IF YES)
> 113b. To whom did you speak about _____? (COLUMN II)
>
> 113c. Did (he; these people) help you about _____? (COLUMN III)

113d. Did you ever speak with a lawyer about any of these problems?

/Yes/   /No/
                         (TO Q 114)

113e. Which one(s) did you speak to a lawyer about? ___, ___, ___ (LETTERS)

113f. Which problem did you most recently see a lawyer about? ___ (LETTER)

113g. Were you satisfied with what the lawyer did? /Yes/   /No/

113h. What did the lawyer charge then and who paid his bill?

/Nothing/, or $_____, paid by: _____

114. IS R NOW LIVING IN PUBLIC HOUSING? (IF UNSURE, ASK R, "IS THIS PUBLIC HOUSING?")

/Yes/   /No/

114a. Within the last 3 years, have you ever
       lived in public housing?
                              /Yes/   /No/
                                         (TO Q 116)

115. Within the last 3 years, what difficulties--if any--have you had with the public
      housing authorities...such as attempts to evict you, or broken utilities, dirty
      conditions, lack of heat, and so forth?   _____
                                       /None/, or RECORD BELOW
                                       (TO Q 116)

	I, Q 115a	II, Q115b	III, Q115c
A.			
B.			
C.			

ASK BOXED Q's ABOUT EACH PROBLEM MENTIONED ABOVE, THEN ASK Q115d

115a. Did you speak to anyone--other than a lawyer--whom you thought
       could help you with _____? (COLUMN I)

(IF YES)
115b. To whom did you speak about _____? (COLUMN II)

115c. Did (he; these people) help you about _____? (COLUMN III)

115d. Did you ever speak with a lawyer about any of these problems?

           /Yes/   /No/
                            (TO Q 116)

115e. Which one(s) did you speak to a lawyer about? ___, ___, ___ (LETTERS)

115f. Which problem did you most recently see a lawyer about? ___(LETTER)

115g. Were you satisfied with what the lawyer did? /Yes/   /No/

115h. What did the lawyer charge then and who paid his bill?

          /Nothing/, or $_____, paid by: _____

30.

116. Within the last three years, have you ever been turned down on an application
for public housing or in some other way been unsuccessful in applying for public
housing?

/Yes/   /No/
                 (GO TO Q 117)

116a. Why--as far as you know--was your application for public housing
turned down? _____

_____

_____

_____

_____

_____

116b. Have you had more than one
application for public housing turned down?   /Yes/   /No/

116c. Have you ever spoken to a lawyer about this problem?

/Yes/   /No/
                 (GO TO Q 116g)

116d. Were you satisfied with what the lawyer did?   /Yes/   /No/

116e. What did the lawyer charge then?

/Nothing/, or $_____
(TO Q 116g)

116f. Who paid the lawyer's bill then? _____

116g. Did you ever speak to anyone else whom you thought could do something?

/Yes/   /No/
                 (TO Q 117)

116h. What other kinds of people did you speak to about this?

_____

116i. Did (he; these people) help?   /Yes/   /No/

117. Apart from your landlord or public housing authorities...over the last three years have there ever been situations where government or city employees, such as garbage collectors, or building inspectors and so forth, have bothered you unfairly or asked you to do something you didn't want to do or where you asked them to do something and they refused?

/Yes/   /No/
              (GO TO Q 118)

117a. What sorts of problems with city or government people have you had over the last three years? (Anything else?)

_____
_____
_____
_____
_____

117b. Did you ever speak to anyone--other than a lawyer--whom you thought could do something to help you?

/Yes/   /No/
              (GO TO Q 117e)

117c. Whom did you speak to about this? _____

_____

117d. Did (he; these people) help you?   /Yes/   /No/

117e. Have you ever spoken to a lawyer about this problem?

/Yes/   /No/
              (TO Q 118)

117f. Which problems did you speak to a lawyer about?

_____
_____

117g. Were you satisfied with what the lawyer did?   /Yes/   /No/

117h. What did the lawyer charge then?

/Nothing/, or $_____
(TO Q 118)

117i. Who paid the lawyer's bill then? _____

32.

118. During the last three years, have you ever been contacted by the police or the
school authorities about any trouble your children have gotten into or been
accused of? This trouble could have been minor and involved only slight misdeeds
or more serious where the children (child) was accused of some crime. (IF YES:
What things like this have happened?)

/No/, or   RECORD BELOW
(TO Q 119)

	I, 118a	II, 118b	III, 118c	IV, 118d

A. _____

B. _____

C. _____

D. _____

ASK BOXED Q's ABOUT EACH PROBLEM, THEN ASK Q118e

> 118a. Was your child accused of a crime and brought into court for _____? (COL. I)
>
> 118b. Did you speak to anyone--other than a lawyer--whom you
> thought could help you with _____? (COLUMN II)
>
> (IF YES)
> 118c. To whom did you speak about _____? (COLUMN III)
>
> 118d. Did (he; these people) help you about _____? (COLUMN IV)

118e. Have these sorts of problems happened several times, or just once? /Sev./ /Once/

118f. Did you ever speak with a
lawyer about any of these problems? /Yes/   /No/
                                     (TO Q 119)

118g. Which one(s) did you speak to a lawyer about? ___, ___, ___ (LETTERS)

118h. Which problem did you most recently see a lawyer about? ____(LETTER)

118i. Were you satisfied with what the lawyer did? /Yes/   /No/

118j. What did the lawyer charge then and who paid his bill?

/Nothing/, or $_____, paid by: _____

119. During the last 3 years, have you (or your husband) ever been in any trouble with the police or contacted by the police? (IF YES: What types of troubles have you been in?)

/No/, or RECORD BELOW
(TO Q 120)

	I, 119a	II, 119b	III, 119c	IV, 119d
A.				
B.				
C.				
D.				

ASK BOXED Q's ABOUT EACH PROBLEM, THEN ASK Q119e

119a. Were you (or your husband) accused of a crime and brought into court for _____? (COLUMN I, ABOVE)

119b. Did you speak to anyone--other than a lawyer--whom you thought could help you with _____? (COLUMN II)

(IF YES)
119c. To whom did you speak about _____? (COLUMN III)

119d. Did (he; these people) help you about _____? (COLUMN IV)

119e. Have these sorts of problems happened several times, or just once? /Sev./ /Once/

119f. Did you ever speak with a lawyer about any of these problems? /Yes/ /No/
(TO Q 120)

119g. Which one(s) did you speak to a lawyer about? ___, ___, ___ (LETTERS)

119h. Which problem did you most recently see a lawyer about? ____(LETTER)

119i. Were you satisfied with what the lawyer did? /Yes/ /No/

119j. What did the lawyer charge then and who paid his bill?

/Nothing/, or $_____, paid by: _____

34.   Project 306

120. Have you or anyone in your family here had any other dealings with the
     police during the last 3 years that we haven't talked about yet? (IF YES:
     What other things have happened to bring you into contact with the police?)

           /No/, or   RECORD BELOW
           (TO Q 121)

                                    I, Q120a   II, Q120b   III, Q120c

     A. _____   _____   _____   _____

        _____   _____

        _____

     B. _____   _____   _____   _____

        _____   _____

        _____

     C. _____   _____   _____   _____

        _____   _____

        _____

     D. _____   _____   _____   _____

        _____   _____

        _____

ASK BOXED Q's ABOUT EACH PROBLEM MENTIONED ABOVE, THEN ASK Q120d

120a.	Did you speak to anyone--other than a lawyer--whom you thought could help you with _____? (COLUMN I)
	(IF YES)
120b.	To whom did you speak about _____? (COLUMN II)
120c.	Did (he; these people) help you about _____? (COLUMN III)

120d. Did you ever speak with a lawyer about any of these problems?

           /Yes/   /No/
                            (TO Q 121)

120e. Which one(s) did you speak to a lawyer about? ___, ___, ___ (LETTERS)

120f. Which problem did you most recently see a lawyer about? ___ (LETTER)

120g. Were you satisfied with what the lawyer did? /Yes/   /No/

120h. What did the lawyer charge then and who paid his bill?

      /Nothing/, or $_____, paid by: _____

121. During the last 3 years, have you (or your husband) had any problems involving
mental illness or other emotional problems? (IF YES: What sorts of problems have
these been?)

/No/ , or   RECORD BELOW
(TO Q 122)

	I, Q121a	II, Q121b	III, Q121c
A. _____	_____	_____	_____
B. _____	_____	_____	_____
C. _____	_____	_____	_____
D. _____	_____	_____	_____

ASK BOXED Q's ABOUT EACH PROBLEM MENTIONED ABOVE, THEN ASK Q121d

121a. Did you speak to anyone--other than a lawyer--whom you thought
could help you with _____? (COLUMN I)

(IF YES)
121b. To whom did you speak about _____? (COLUMN II)

121c. Did (he; these people) help you about _____? (COLUMN III)

121d. Did you ever speak with a lawyer about any of these problems?

/Yes/   /No/
(TO Q 122)

121e. Which one(s) did you speak to a lawyer about? ___, ___, ___ (LETTERS)

121f. Which problem did you most recently see a lawyer about? ___ (LETTER)

121g. Were you satisfied with what the lawyer did? /Yes/   /No/

121h. What did the lawyer charge then and who paid his bill?

/Nothing/, or $_____, paid by: _____

36.   Project 306

122. During the last three years, have any of your children had any problems
     involving mental illness, or retardation--that is, slow learning, or any
     other emotional problems? (IF YES: What problems have your children had?)

        /No/, or   RECORD BELOW
        (TO Q 123)

                                            I, Q122a   II, Q122b   III, Q122c

A. _____   _____ _____ _____
   _____   _____ _____
   _____   _____
   _____

B. _____   _____ _____ _____
   _____   _____ _____
   _____   _____
   _____

C. _____   _____ _____ _____
   _____   _____ _____
   _____   _____
   _____

D. _____   _____ _____ _____
   _____   _____ _____
   _____   _____
   _____

ASK BOXED Q's ABOUT EACH PROBLEM MENTIONED ABOVE, THEN ASK Q122d

---
| 122a. Did you speak to anyone--other than a lawyer--whom you thought could help you with _____? (COLUMN I)
|
| (IF YES)
| 122b. To whom did you speak about _____? (COLUMN II)
|
| 122c. Did (he; these people) help you about _____? (COLUMN III)

122d. Did you ever speak with a lawyer about any of these problems?

              /Yes/   /No/
                ↓   (TO Q 123)

122e. Which one(s) did you speak to a lawyer about? ___, ___, ___ (LETTERS)

122f. Which problem did you most recently see a lawyer about? ___(LETTER)

122g. Were you satisfied with what the lawyer did? /Yes/   /No/

122h. What did the lawyer charge then and who paid his bill?

      /Nothing/, or $_____, paid by: _____

123. During the last 3 years, what problems--if any--have you (or your husband) had with getting unemployment or welfare benefits?

/None/, or   RECORD BELOW
(TO Q 124)

	I, 123a	II, 123b	III, 123c	IV, 123d
A.				
B.				
C.				
D.				

ASK BOXED Q's ABOUT EACH PROBLEM MENTIONED ABOVE, THEN ASK Q123e

123a. Did the problem about _____ involve the ADC program during the present period of your participation with the program? (COLUMN I ABOVE)

123b. Did you speak to anyone--other than a lawyer--whom you thought could help you with _____? (COLUMN II)

(IF YES)
123c. To whom did you speak about _____? (COLUMN III)

123d. Did (he; these people) help you about _____? (COLUMN IV)

123e. Did you ever speak with a lawyer about any of these problems?

/Yes/   /No/
(TO Q 124)

123f. Which one(s) did you speak to a lawyer about? ___, ___, ___ (LETTERS)

123g. Which problem did you most recently see a lawyer about? ___ (LETTER)

123h. Were you satisfied with what the lawyer did? /Yes/   /No/

123i. What did the lawyer charge then and who paid his bill?

/Nothing/, or $_____, paid by: _____

38.   Project 306

124. During the last three years have you (or your husband) suffered any
     personal injuries either on or off the job? (IF YES: Where and how
     were these injuries suffered?)
                              /No/, or   RECORD BELOW
                         (TO Q 125)

                                    I, Q124a   II, Q124b   III, Q124c

A. _____   _____   _____   _____

   _____   _____

   _____   _____

B. _____   _____   _____   _____

   _____   _____

   _____   _____

C. _____   _____   _____   _____

   _____   _____

   _____   _____

D. _____   _____   _____   _____

   _____   _____

   _____

ASK BOXED Q's ABOUT EACH PROBLEM MENTIONED ABOVE, THEN ASK Q124d

124a. Did you speak with anyone--other than a lawyer--whom you thought could help you about _____ and the possibilities for getting some payment from insurance, a personal injury court suit, etc., to cover medical expenses or other financial losses? (COLUMN I) (IF YES) 124b. To whom did you speak about _____? (COLUMN II) 124c. Did (he; these people) help you about _____? (COLUMN III)

124d. Did you ever speak with a lawyer about any of these problems?

             /Yes/   /No/
               | (TO Q 125)
               ↓

     124e. Which one(s) did you speak to a lawyer about? ___, ___, ___ (LETTERS)

     124f. Which problem did you most recently see a lawyer about? ___ (LETTER)

     124g. Were you satisfied with what the lawyer did? /Yes/   /No/

     124h. What did the lawyer charge then and who paid his bill?

           /Nothing/, or $_____, paid by: _____

125. Have you (or your husband) ever had any trouble collecting on insurance over the last 3 years? (IF YES: What kinds of insurance have you had trouble collecting on?)

/No/ , or   RECORD BELOW
(TO Q 126)

	I, 125a	II, 125b	III, 125c	IV, 125d
A.				
B.				
C.				
D.				

ASK BOXED Q's ABOUT EACH PROBLEM MENTIONED ABOVE, THEN ASK Q 125e

125a. Was the amount involved in the _____ insurance under $500, $500 to $1,000, or over $1,000? (COLUMN I)

125b. Did you speak to anyone--other than a lawyer--whom you thought could help you with _____? (COLUMN II)

(IF YES)
125c. To whom did you speak about _____? (COLUMN III)

125d. Did (he; these people) help you about _____? (COLUMN IV)

125e. Did you ever speak with a lawyer about any of these problems?

/Yes/   /No/
(TO Q 126)

125f. Which one(s) did you speak to a lawyer about? ___, ___, ___ (LETTERS)

125g. Which problem did you most recently see a lawyer about? ___ (LETTER)

125h. Were you satisfied with what the lawyer did? /Yes/   /No/

125i. What did the lawyer charge then and who paid his bill?

/Nothing/, or $_____, paid by: _____

40.   Project 306

126. During the last three years, have you (or your husband), or any of your
      children ever had any trouble collecting wages owed? (IF YES: What was
      the trouble you had collecting wages?)
                                          /No/, or   RECORD BELOW
                                    (TO Q 127)

                                          I, Q126a   II, Q126b   III, Q126c

A. _____ _____ _____ _____

   _____   _____

   _____

B. _____ _____ _____ _____

   _____   _____

   _____

C. _____ _____ _____ _____

   _____   _____

   _____

D. _____ _____ _____ _____

   _____   _____

   _____

ASK BOXED Q's ABOUT EACH PROBLEM MENTIONED ABOVE, THEN ASK Q126d

126a. Did you speak to anyone--other than a lawyer--whom you thought could help you with _____? (COLUMN I)
(IF YES) 126b. To whom did you speak about _____? (COLUMN II)
126c. Did (he; these people) help you about _____? (COLUMN III)

126d. Did you ever speak with a lawyer about any of these problems?

            /Yes/   /No/
              ↓   (TO Q 127)

126e. Which one(s) did you speak to a lawyer about? ___, ___, ___ (LETTERS)

126f. Which problem did you most recently see a lawyer about? ___ (LETTER)

126g. Were you satisfied with what the lawyer did? /Yes/   /No/

126h. What did the lawyer charge then and who paid his bill?

       /Nothing/, or $_____, paid by: _____

127. During the last three years, have you (or your husband) had any difficulties
in collecting other money that people owed you? (IF YES: How much money was
owed and who owed it to you...a relative, a friend, or who?)

/No/, or   RECORD BELOW
(TO Q 128)

	I, Q127a	II, Q127b	III, Q127c
A.			
B.			
C.			
D.			

ASK BOXED Q's ABOUT EACH PROBLEM MENTIONED ABOVE, THEN ASK Q127d

127a. Did you speak to anyone--other than a lawyer--whom you thought
could help you with _____? (COLUMN I)

(IF YES)
127b. To whom did you speak about _____? (COLUMN II)

127c. Did (he; these people) help you about _____? (COLUMN III)

127d. Did you ever speak with a lawyer about any of these problems?

/Yes/   /No/
(TO Q 128)

127e. Which one(s) did you speak to a lawyer about? ___, ___, ___ (LETTERS)

127f. Which problem did you most recently see a lawyer about? ___ (LETTER)

127g. Were you satisfied with what the lawyer did? /Yes/   /No/

127h. What did the lawyer charge then and who paid his bill?

/Nothing/, or $_____, paid by: _____

128. Still within the last three years, have you ever purchased anything "on time"--for example, furniture, clothing, a washing machine, a car, or other items which you agreed to pay for in installments?

/Yes/   /No/
                         (TO Q 129, PG 44)

128a. What are three of the more important items you've purchased on time?

1. _____

2. _____
   _____

3. _____
   _____

128b. Have you had any difficulties with people trying to collect money from you for such sales, including repossessing of any of the items?

/Yes/   /No/
                    (TO Q 129, PG 44)

128c. What problems have you had? (Anything else?)

	I, 128d	II, 128e	III, 128f	IV, 128g
A. _____	$_____	_____	_____	_____
_____			_____	
_____			_____	
_____				
_____				
B. _____	$_____	_____	_____	_____
_____			_____	
_____			_____	
_____				
_____				

Project 306   43.

	I, 128d	II, 128e	III, 128f	IV, 128g

C. _____ $ _____ _____ _____ _____

D. _____ $ _____ _____ _____ _____

E. _____ $ _____ _____ _____ _____

ASK BOXED QUESTIONS ABOUT EACH PROBLEM MENTIONED ABOVE, THEN ASK 128h

128d. How much was owed at the time of the dispute about _____ ? (COLUMN I)

128e. Did you speak to anyone--other than a lawyer--whom you
thought could help you with _____ ? (COLUMN II)

(IF YES)
128f. To whom did you speak about _____ ? (COLUMN III)

128g. Did (he; these people) help you about _____ ? (COLUMN IV)

128h. Did you ever speak with a lawyer about any of these problems?

　　　　　　　　/Yes/　　　　/No/
　　　　　　　　　　　　　　(TO Q 129)

128i. Which one(s) did you speak to a lawyer about? ___, ___, ___, ___(LETTERS)

128j. Which problem did you most recently see a lawyer about? ___ (LETTER)

128k. Were you satisfied with what the lawyer did? /Yes/   /No/

128l. What did the lawyer charge then and who paid the bill?

/Nothing/, or $_____, paid by: _____

44.

129. During the last 3 years, have you ever had any other difficulties with stores, markets or some other business involving something you bought or tried to buy? (IF YES: What difficulties have you had?)

/No/, or   RECORD BELOW
(TO Q 130)

	I, 129a	II, 129b	III, 129c	IV, 129d
A. _____	$_____	_____	_____	_____
_____			_____	
_____				
B. _____	$_____	_____	_____	_____
_____			_____	
_____				
C. _____	$_____	_____	_____	_____
_____			_____	
_____				

ASK BOXED Q's ABOUT EACH PROBLEM MENTIONED ABOVE, THEN ASK Q129e

129a. What was the purchase price of the merchandise involved in the problem about _____? (COLUMN I)

129b. Did you speak to anyone--other than a lawyer--whom you thought could help you with _____? (COLUMN II)

(IF YES)
129c. To whom did you speak about _____? (COLUMN III)

129d. Did (he; these people) help you about _____? (COLUMN IV)

129e. Did you ever speak with a lawyer about any of these problems?

/Yes/   /No/
(TO Q 130)

129f. Which one(s) did you speak to a lawyer about? ___, ___, ___ (LETTERS)

129g. Which problem did you most recently see a lawyer about? ___ (LETTER)

129h. Were you satisfied with what the lawyer did?   /Yes/   /No/

129i. What did the lawyer charge then and who paid his bill?

/Nothing/, or $_____, paid by: _____

Project 306   45.

130. Have your (or your husband's) wages been attached or garnished, or have you
     (or your husband) gone through bankruptcy in the last 3 years? (IF YES:
     What sorts of things have happened?)
                                           /No/, or   RECORD BELOW
                          (TO Q 131)

                                      I, Q130a   II, Q130b   III, Q130c

A. _____   _____   _____   _____
   _____   _____
   _____
B. _____   _____   _____   _____
   _____   _____
   _____
C. _____   _____   _____   _____
   _____   _____
   _____
D. _____   _____   _____   _____
   _____   _____
   _____

ASK BOXED Q's ABOUT EACH PROBLEM MENTIONED ABOVE, THEN ASK Q130d

---

130a. Did you speak to anyone--other than a lawyer--whom you thought
       could help you with _____? (COLUMN I)

       (IF YES)
       130b. To whom did you speak about _____? (COLUMN II)

       130c. Did (he; these people) help you about _____? (COLUMN III)

130d. Did you ever speak with a lawyer about any of these problems?

              /Yes/   /No/
                ↓   (TO Q 131)

130e. Which one(s) did you speak to a lawyer about? ___, ___, ___ (LETTERS)

130f. Which problem did you most recently see a lawyer about? ___ (LETTER)

130g. Were you satisfied with what the lawyer did? /Yes/   /No/

130h. What did the lawyer charge then and who paid his bill?

       /Nothing/, or $_____, paid by: _____

46.

131. Have you (or your husband) borrowed any money in the last three
      years from a bank, a loan company or any other such place?

                    /Yes/   /No/
                                   (TO Q 132, PG 48)

      131a. From what types of businesses--banks, loan companies or what--did
             you borrow this money? (LIST 4 MOST RECENT)

             A. _____
                _____
             B. _____
                _____
             C. _____
                _____
             D. _____
                _____

      131b. Have you had any difficulties with people trying to collect
             this money?
                         /Yes/   /No/
                                      (TO Q 132, PG 48)

             131c. What kinds of difficulties and with whom did you have
                    these difficulties?

                                        I, 131d   II, 131e   III, 131f   IV, 131g

      A. _____ $_____   _____   _____   _____
         _____
         _____   _____
         _____

      B. _____ $_____   _____   _____   _____
         _____
         _____   _____
         _____

Project 306

	I, 131d	II, 131e	III, 131f	IV, 131g
C. _____	$_____	_____	_____	_____
			_____	
D. _____	$_____	_____	_____	_____
			_____	
E. _____ _____	$_____	_____	_____	_____
			_____	

ASK BOXED Q's ABOUT EACH PROBLEM MENTIONED ABOVE, THEN ASK Q131h

131d. What was the amount of the loan in the problem with _____? (COLUMN I)

131e. Did you speak to anyone--other than a lawyer--whom you thought could help you with _____? (COLUMN II)

(IF YES)
131f. To whom did you speak about _____? (COLUMN III)

131g. Did (he; these people) help you about _____? (COLUMN IV)

131h. Did you ever speak with a lawyer about any of these problems?

            /Yes/   /No/
                ↓   (TO Q 132)

131i. Which one(s) did you speak to a lawyer about? ___, ___, ___ (LETTERS)

131j. Which problem did you most recently see a lawyer about? ___ (LETTER)

131k. Were you satisfied with what the lawyer did? /Yes/   /No/

131l. What did the lawyer charge then and who paid his bill?

      /Nothing/, or $_____, paid by: _____

132. Still within the last 3 years, have you had any difficulties concerning
     a child of yours that was born out of wedlock or concerning the adoption
     of children? (IF YES: What problems of this sort have you had?)

            /No/, or   RECORD BELOW
     (TO Q 133)

                                    I, Q132a   II, Q132b   III, Q132c

A. _____   _____ _____ _____
   _____   _____
   _____   _____
   _____

B. _____   _____ _____ _____
   _____   _____
   _____   _____
   _____

C. _____   _____ _____ _____
   _____   _____
   _____   _____
   _____

D. _____   _____ _____ _____
   _____   _____
   _____   _____
   _____

ASK BOXED Q's ABOUT EACH PROBLEM MENTIONED ABOVE, THEN ASK Q132d

---

132a. Did you speak to anyone--other than a lawyer--whom you thought
       could help you with _____? (COLUMN I)

       (IF YES)
       132b. To whom did you speak about _____? (COLUMN II)

       132c. Did (he; these people) help you about _____? (COLUMN III)

132d. Did you ever speak with a lawyer about any of these problems?

            /Yes/   /No/
              | (TO Q 133)
              ↓
       132e. Which one(s) did you speak to a lawyer about? ___, ___, ___ (LETTERS)

       132f. Which problem did you most recently see a lawyer about? ___ (LETTER)

       132g. Were you satisfied with what the lawyer did? /Yes/   /No/

       132h. What did the lawyer charge then and who paid his bill?

              /Nothing/, or $_____, paid by: _____

133. Have you had any difficulties in collecting child support payments from the father of the children during the last three years? (IF YES: What problems of this sort have you had?)

/No/, or   RECORD BELOW
(TO Q 134)

	I, Q133a	II, Q133b	III, Q133c
A. _____	_____	_____	_____
B. _____	_____	_____	_____
C. _____	_____	_____	_____
D. _____	_____	_____	_____

ASK BOXED Q's ABOUT EACH PROBLEM MENTIONED ABOVE, THEN ASK Q133d

---

133a. Did you speak to anyone--other than a lawyer--whom you thought could help you with _____? (COLUMN I)

(IF YES)
133b. To whom did you speak about _____? (COLUMN II)

133c. Did (he; these people) help you about _____? (COLUMN III)

133d. Did you ever speak with a lawyer about any of these problems?

/Yes/   /No/
         (TO Q 134)

133e. Which one(s) did you speak to a lawyer about? ___, ___, ___ (LETTERS)

133f. Which problem did you most recently see a lawyer about? ___ (LETTER)

133g. Were you satisfied with what the lawyer   /Yes/   /No/

121h. What did the lawyer charge then and who paid his bill?

/Nothing/, or $_____, paid by: _____

50.

134. IS R <u>NOW OR EVER MARRIED?</u>   /YES/   /NO/
                                                      (TO Q 135)

   134a. Now forget for the moment the three-year limitation and think of all the
          time since you were first married. Which of the following marriage
          difficulties have happened to you?

<u>YES</u> <u>NO</u>   I, Q134b   II, Q134c   III, Q134d   IV, Q134e   V, Q134f

___ ___   A. Divorce. . . .   _____   _____   _____   _____   _____

___ ___   B. Annulment. . .   _____   _____   _____   _____   _____

___ ___   C. Separation . .   _____   _____   _____   _____   _____

___ ___   D. Desertion. . .   _____   _____   _____   _____   _____

ASK BOXED Q's FOR EACH "YES"; THEN ASK Q134g. IF ALL Q's CHECKED "NO", GO TO Q 135.

   134b. Has _____ occurred within the last three years?   (COLUMN I)

   134c. Did _____ happen more than once? (COLUMN II)

   134d. Did you speak to anyone--other than a lawyer--
          whom you thought could help you with _____?   (COLUMN III)

          (IF YES)
          134e. To whom did you speak about _____?   (COLUMN IV)

          134f. Did (he; these people) help you about _____?   (COLUMN V)

   134g. Did you ever speak with a lawyer about any of these problems?

                         /Yes/   /No/
                                         (TO Q 135)

   134h. Which one(s) did you speak to a lawyer about?

                ____, ____, ____, ____ (LETTERS)

   134i. Which problem did you most recently see a lawyer about? ____(LETTER)

   134j. Were you satisfied with what the lawyer did? /Yes/   /No/

   134k. What did the lawyer charge then and who paid the lawyer's bill?

          /Nothing/, or $_____   Paid by: _____

135. Now thinking again of the last three years, have you had any contact
with a lawyer, either one representing you or someone else, other
than in the situations we have already discussed?

/Yes/   /No/
                    (TO Q 136)

135a. Could you explain what happened to cause you to have this contact
with the lawyer? _____

_____

_____

_____

_____

_____

_____

_____

_____

_____

135b. Have any of these things happened more than once?   /Yes/   /No/

135c. Was the lawyer you used most recently representing you? That is, was he
hired by you or by someone for you, or was he representing someone else?

/Representing R/   /Someone else/   /Both/
                     (TO Q 136)

135d. Were you satisfied with what your lawyer did?   /Yes/   /No/

135e. What did the lawyer charge then and who paid his bill?

/Nothing/, or $_____; Paid by: _____

136. DID R HAVE ONE OR MORE PROBLEMS AND CONSULT A LAWYER AT ALL FOR ANY PROBLEM
DISCUSSED TO THIS POINT?
                          /YES/   /NO/
                    (TO Q 137, NEXT PAGE)

136a. DID R HAVE ONE OR MORE PROBLEMS, BUT NOT CONSULT A LAWYER FOR ANY
PROBLEM DISCUSSED TO THIS POINT?
                                    /YES/   /NO/
                              (TO Q 142,   (TO Q 152,
                               PAGE 53)   PAGE 55)

52.

Q's FOR R's WHO HAVE CONSULTED A LAWYER.

137. Why specifically did you see a lawyer for some of the problems you mentioned
      and not for some of the other serious ones we have discussed?

      /R saw lawyer for all problems/, or _____
      _____
      _____
      _____

138. How many different lawyers have you used in dealing with the problems we have
      discussed here?
                          /One only/, or _____ (#)
                          (TO Q 139)

      138a. Why did you use more than one lawyer? _____
             _____
             _____
             _____
             _____

      138b. How did you find--that is, get in touch with--the lawyer you used just before
             the most recent lawyer you have worked with? _____
             _____
             _____
             _____

139. How did you find--that is, get in touch with--the (most recent) lawyer you have used?
      _____
      _____
      _____

141. In general, how satisfied have you been with your lawyer(s)...very satisfied,
      satisfied, dissatisfied, or very dissatisfied?

             /Very satisfied/ /Satisfied/ /Dissatisfied/ /Very dissatisfied/
             (TO Q 152, PAGE 55)

      141a. Why have you been dissatisfied with your lawyer(s)? _____
             _____
             _____
             _____
             _____

                          (TO Q 152, PAGE 55)

Q's FOR R's WHO HAVE HAD PROBLEMS, BUT HAVE <u>NOT</u> CONSULTED A LAWYER.

142. Now I'd like you to think about what you consider to be the most serious problem you've had among those we have discussed. Which one do you feel was the most serious?

_____

_____

_____

_____

143. Were you satisfied that this problem worked out as well as could be expected...that is, do you think there was really nothing else you could have done to make it turn out better?

/Yes/   /No/   /Don't know/

144. At the time this problem arose, did you consider consulting a lawyer?

/Yes/   /No/

144a. Why did you decide not   144b. Why didn't you consider
       to consult a lawyer?   consulting a lawyer?

_____

_____

_____

_____

_____

_____

_____

145. Of all the problems we've discussed, which one do you consider as the second most serious?

/No second serious problem/
(GO TO Q 148)

_____

_____

146. Were you satisfied that this problem worked out as well as could be expected... that is, do you think there was really nothing else you could have done to make it turn out better?

/Yes/   /No/   /Don't know/

(GO ON TO QUESTION 147)

54.   Project 306

Q's FOR R's WHO HAVE HAD PROBLEMS, BUT HAVE <u>NOT</u> CONSULTED A LAWYER (Continued)

147. At the time this problem arose, did you consider consulting a lawyer?

            /Yes/   /No/

147a. Why did you decide not   147b. Why didn't you consider
       to consult a lawyer?   consulting a lawyer?

_____

_____

_____

_____

_____

_____

_____

_____

_____

_____

_____

148. Looking back at these problems do you think that you should
      have consulted a lawyer--that is, you might have gotten a
      better result if you had?
                            /Yes/   /No/   /Don't know/

149. Do you think that you would have consulted a lawyer if the welfare agency
      would pay the expenses?
                            /Yes/   /No/   /Don't know/

150. Would you have consulted a lawyer on the welfare agency staff, if
      one were made available for your problems?
                                      /Yes/   /No/   /Don't know/

151. Do you know any lawyers in this community?

            /Yes/   /No/
        (TO Q 152)

151a. Do any of your friends or relatives know any lawyers?   /Yes/   /No/

                                            (GO ON TO NEXT PAGE)

ALL RESPONDENTS

152. People have various opinions about lawyers. I would like to ask you about your opinions. First, how honest do you think most lawyers are in their dealings with their clients? Would you say very honest, fairly honest, fairly dishonest, or very dishonest?

/Very honest/ /Fairly honest/ /Fairly dishonest/ /Very dishonest/ /Don't know/

153. Do you think the amount of money lawyers charge for their services is much too high, fairly high, or reasonable?

/Much too high/ /Fairly high/ /Reasonable/ /Don't know/

154. Finally, I would like to ask you about your future plans. First, do you see sometime in the future when you think assistance from ADC or other welfare programs will no longer be necessary for you?

/Yes/ /Uncertain/ /No/ /Don't know/
                      (TO Q 155) (TO Q 155)

154a. Do you presently have any plans which, if successful, will make the ADC program unnecessary for you?

/Yes/ /No/
      (TO Q 155)

154b. What are your plans? _____

_____

_____

_____

_____

_____

_____

_____

_____

155. DOES R HAVE ANY SONS? /YES/ /NO/
                                 (TO Q 156)

155a. How far would you like to see your sons go in school?

_____

155b. Do you expect that your sons will get most of the schooling or training you would like them to get? /Yes/ /Not sure/ /No/ /Don't know/

155c. What occupation would you like to see your sons in?

_____

56.   Project 306

156. DOES R HAVE ANY DAUGHTERS?   /YES/   /NO/
                                                   (TO Q 157)

   156a. How far would you like to see your daughters go in school?

   _____

   156b. Do you expect that your daughters will get most of the schooling or training
          you would like them to get?
                              /Yes/   /Not sure/   /No/   /Don't know/

   156c. After your daughters finish school, what would you like to see them do?

   _____

157. IS R DIVORCED, SEPARATED, OR DESERTED?   /YES/   /NO/
                                                              (TO Q 158)

   157a. Do you have any plans or hopes of reconciliation with your
          (husband; ex-husband)?
                              /Yes/   /No/
                                           (TO Q 158)

          157b. Are you making any attempts for a reconciliation?   /Yes/   /No/
                                                                      (END)

                                          157c. Would you like to
                                                 do this?

                                                 /Yes/   /No/
                                          (END OF INTERVIEW)

158. IS R NEVER MARRIED, DIVORCED, OR WIDOWED?   /YES/   /NO/
                                                                 (END)

   158a. Do you have any plans to get married?   /Yes/   /No/
                                                              (END)

          158b. What are these plans? (Why haven't you gone ahead already?)

          _____
          _____
          _____
          _____
          _____

                              (END OF INTERVIEW)

Project 325
1968

University Extension
The University of Wisconsin
Survey Research Laboratory

A

A FOLLOW-UP SURVEY OF ADC FAMILIES

1. On about what date did you first leave the ADC program after April, 1967?

    _____(MONTH), 19 ____

2. When you were first interviewed, were you in the ADC program, or had you already left it?

    /In program/   /Already left/

3. We have found that people have many reasons for leaving the ADC program. Could you tell me in your own words the reasons why you stopped receiving aid from the ADC program? (Anything else?) _____

    _____

    _____

    _____

    _____

    _____

    _____

    _____

    _____

4. Were you receiving ADC benefits for a child or children of a relative, or a foster child or children only and not for your entire family, or were the benefits for your own children, or for both?

    /Foster child/   /Own children/   /Both/
                         (TO Q 5)

4a. Does the foster child (Do the foster children) still live here?

    /Yes/   /No/   /Some of them: #/

    IF RESPONDENT WAS RECEIVING AID ONLY FOR FOSTER CHILDREN, TELL HER
    THAT SOME OF THE QUESTIONS MAY SEEM AWKWARD TO HER, BECAUSE THE
    INTERVIEW WAS DESIGNED ALSO FOR PEOPLE RECEIVING AID FOR THEIR
    OWN CHILDREN. ASK THROUGH QUESTION 8 AND THEN FOLLOW SKIP DIRECTIONS.

5. How are you supporting yourself (and your children) now? _____

    _____

    _____

Interviewer's Name: _____   Int. No.: _____

Date: _____   Time Started: _____

2.   Project 325

6. Are you married, separated, widowed, divorced, deserted, or have you never
    married?
    /Married/   /Separated/   /Widowed/   /Divorced/   /Deserted/   /Never married/

7. Did you notify the agency that you no longer were eligible for ADC benefits,
    or did they tell you that you no longer qualified, or what happened?

    /R notified agency/   /Agency notified R/

    OTHER: (Specify) _____

8. Did your caseworker or the welfare agency say that you would have to leave the
    ADC program even though you did not think you should have to leave?

                /Yes/   /No/
                  | (GO TO Q 9, OR
                  ↓   Q 17 IF ONLY FOR
    8a. Why did the agency say that   FOSTER CHILDREN)
         you could no longer receive
         ADC support?
         _____
         _____
         _____

    8b. Why did you think you should not have to leave the program?
         _____
         _____
         _____

    8c. Did you complain to the agency or to your caseworker about losing
         ADC support?   /Yes/   /No/
                            | (TO Q 8e)
                            ↓
         8d. What did they do when you complained? _____
              _____
              _____

    8e. Did you consider appealing the agency's decision to someone higher in
         the welfare department?
                            /Yes/   /No/
                          (TO Q 8g) |
                                                       ↓
         8f. Why didn't you? _____

                  (TO Q 9, OR Q 17 IF FOR FOSTER CHILDREN ONLY)

    8g. Did you finally appeal their decision?   /Yes/   /No/
                                                 (TO Q 8i) |
                                                                  ↓
         8h. Why didn't you appeal?   _____

                  (TO Q 9, OR Q17 IF FOR FOSTER CHILDREN ONLY)

8i. Who did you appeal to? _____

_____

_____

8j. What happened? _____

_____

_____

_____

INTERVIEWER: IF R RECEIVED AID ONLY FOR FOSTER CHILDREN, SKIP TO QUESTION 17 AT
THIS POINT.

9. HAS R MARRIED OR REMARRIED A DIFFERENT HUSBAND, OR IS SHE GETTING MARRIED?
(IF NOT CLEAR FROM Q 3, ASK: Have you married a man to whom you were not
married before, or are you planning to get married?)

/Yes/   /No/
(TO Q 10)

9a. Did your caseworker or the agency play any part in your getting married
(or remarried)?   /Yes/   /No/
(TO Q 9c)

9b. What did they do? _____

_____

_____

9c. What kind of job does your (new husband; husband-to-be) have?

_____

9d. Does he work regularly?   /Yes/   /Usually/   /No/

9e. What is his usual weekly take home pay? $_____ PER WEEK

9f. Does your (new husband; husband-to-be) have children of his own?

/Yes/   /No/
(TO Q 10)

9g. Will (Do) these children live with you?   /Yes/   /Some will,/   /No/
(TO Q9j)   /some won't/

9h. Does (Will) your (new husband; husband-to-be) contribute to the
support of these children not living with you?

/Yes/   /No/
(TO Q 9j)

9i. About how much (does)(will) he pay? $_____ PER _____

9j. Does he plan to legally adopt (or has he adopted) any of your children?

/Yes/   /No/   /Undecided/

4.

10. IS R RECONCILED OR OTHERWISE BACK TOGETHER WITH HER HUSBAND? (IF NOT CLEAR
     FROM Q 3, ASK: Are you reconciled or otherwise back together with your husband?)

                         /Yes/   /No/
                                           (TO Q 11)

     10a. Did the welfare agency or your caseworker play any part in getting you
           and your husband back together?
                                           /Yes/   /No/
                                                      (TO Q 10c)

           10b. What did they do? _____

           _____

           _____

     10c. What kind of job does your husband now have? _____

           _____

     10d. Does he work regularly? /Yes/   /Usually/   /No/

     10e. What is his usual weekly take home pay? $_____ PER WEEK

11. WAS R's HUSBAND PREVIOUSLY DISABLED BUT IS NOW ABLE TO WORK, OR FOR OTHER
     REASONS, NO LONGER ELIBIBLE FOR DISABLED AID? (IF NOT CLEAR FROM Q 3, ASK:
     Was your husband previously disabled but is now able to work, or for other
     reasons no longer eligible for disabled aid?)
                                           /Yes/   /No/
                                                        (TO Q 12)

     11a. Is your husband now working? /Yes/   /No/
                                               (TO Q 12)

           11b. What kind of job does your husband now have? _____

           _____

           11c. Does he work regularly? /Yes/   /Usually/   /No/

           11d. What is his usual weekly take home pay?

                 $_____ PER WEEK

12. DOES R HAVE, OR IS SHE GETTING, A JOB? (IF NOT CLEAR FROM Q 3, ASK: Do you
     now have a job or are you getting a job?)
                                           /Yes/   /No/
                                                      (TO Q 13)

     12a. What is (will be) your job? _____

           _____

12b. What kind of work does (will) that involve? _____

_____

_____

12c. How many hours a week do (will) you usually work? _____(HOURS)

12d. What is (will be) your usual <u>weekly</u> take home pay? $_____ PER WEEK

12e. Do you work (Will you work) regularly? /Yes/ /Usually/ /No/

12f. Was there anything the welfare agency did for you, or some program you
participated in, while on ADC which made you better able to get a job--
vocational schooling or job counseling, for instance?

/Yes/   /No/
                (TO Q 12h)
↓

12g. What was it that you feel was helpful? _____

_____

_____

_____

12h. Which of the following statements would you say is most true of your
caseworker's attitude toward your getting a job? Let me read all three
statements before you decide.

(a) Your caseworker did not want you to get a job.
                                            (TO Q 12k)

(b) Your caseworker did not care whether you got a job or not.
                                                (TO Q 12k)

(c) Your caseworker suggested you get a job or expected
you to try to get a job.
                    (TO Q 12i)

/Matter never discussed/
      (TO Q 12k)

12i. Why did (she, he) say you should get a job? _____

_____

_____

12j. How did you, yourself, feel about getting a job? _____

_____

_____

6.

12k. Did your caseworker help you get your job?   /Yes/   /No/
                                                  (TO Q 12m)   ↓

    121. How did you get your job? _____

    _____

    _____
                                  (TO Q 12n)

12m. What did your caseworker do to help you?   _____

    _____

    _____

12n. What else did you have to do to find a job? _____

    _____

    _____

12o. Would you say it was easy or difficult to find your job?

              /Easy/   /Difficult/

12p. Why do you say it was (easy, difficult)? _____

    _____

    _____

12q. Does (Will) someone take care of your children while you work?

          /Yes/   /No/   /Not necessary/
            ↓   (TO Q 13)   (TO Q 13)

    12r. Who (will) take(s) care of your children? _____

    _____

    12s. Do (Will) you have to pay for this?   /Yes/   /No/

                        (GO ON TO NEXT PAGE)

13. HAVE R's CHILDREN GROWN TOO OLD AND THUS BECOME INELIGIBLE? (IF NOT CLEAR FROM Q 3, ASK: Have your children grown too old and thus become ineligible?)

/Yes/   /No/
(TO Q 13c)

13a. HAVE R's CHILDREN LEFT HOME, QUIT SCHOOL, OR OTHERWISE BECOME INELIGIBLE? (IF NOT CLEAR FROM Q 3, ASK: Have your children quit school or otherwise become ineligible?

/Yes/   /No/
(TO Q 14)

13b. Why did your children become ineligible for aid? _____

_____

_____

13c. Are the children that are now ineligible still living at home?

/Yes/   /No/
(TO Q 14)

13d. How many of these children (at home) are you still supporting?

/None/, or _____ (#)

13e. What are these children (at home) doing now--are they working, looking for work, or what? (PUT EACH CHILD ON A SEPARATE LINE)

1. _____

2. _____

3. _____

4. _____

14. HAS OTHER FINANCIAL SUPPORT BECOME AVAILABLE SO THAT R NO LONGER NEEDS, OR IS NO LONGER ELIGIBLE FOR, SUPPORT FROM THE ADC PROGRAM? (IF NOT CLEAR FROM Q 3, ASK: Has other financial support become available so that you no longer need or are no longer eligible for support from the ADC program?)

/Yes/   /No/
(TO Q 15)

14a. What support became available so that you no longer need (or are eligible to receive) support from the ADC program?

_____

_____

_____

14b. Did your caseworker or the welfare agency play a part in getting
      this support?

             /Yes/   /No/
                             (TO Q 15)

      14c. What did the welfare agency do? _____

            _____

            _____

            _____

15. Were you accused of breaking some rule or of some other conduct that made
     you ineligible?

             /Yes/   /No/
                             (TO Q 16)

     15a. What did the welfare agency say you did that made you ineligible
           for further aid? _____

           _____

           _____

           _____

           _____

           _____

     15b. Was what they said correct--that is, had you done what they said?

                 /Yes/   /No/
                 (TO Q 16)

     15c. Could you tell me what actually happened? _____

           _____

           _____

           _____

           _____

           _____

16. Are you now receiving any other financial support that we haven't discussed so
     far, such as retirement, pensions, help from relatives, child support from
     children's father, or something like that?

                                   /Yes/   /No/
                                                   (TO Q 17)

     16a. What support is this? _____

           _____

           _____

     16b. How much does this amount to? $_____ PER _____

17. DID ADC GRANT STOP BECAUSE FOSTER CHILD(REN) OR CHILD(REN) OF A RELATIVE LEFT
    THE HOME, WAS (WERE) ADOPTED BY R, OR BECAME INELIGIBLE BECAUSE OF AGE, FOR
    INSTANCE? (IF NOT CLEAR FROM Q 3, ASK: Did your ADC grant stop because your
    foster child(ren) or child(ren) of a relative became ineligible or left home?)

    /Left home/   /Ineligible/   /No/
                           (TO Q 17b)   (TO Q 18)

17a. Where did the child(ren) go? _____

_____

_____
                              (GO TO Q 17f)

17b. Why did your child(ren) become ineligible? _____

_____

_____

17c. Is (Are) the child(ren) continuing to live with you?   /Yes/   /No/

17d. Are you supporting this (these) child(ren)?   /Yes/   /No/   /In part/

17e. What is (are) the child(ren) doing--working, looking for work, or what?

_____

_____

17f. Do you expect to have any more foster children or children of relatives
     in your home who will be eligible for ADC?
                                           /Yes/   /No/
                                                      (TO Q 18)

    17g. Whose children would they be? _____

_____

_____

(GO ON TO NEXT PAGE)

10.

18. Now I would like some information about the people who live here in your
household. Will you please list everyone who lives here according to
their relationship to you? (RECORD IN COLUMN I, BELOW)

18a. What is (his; her) sex? (RECORD IN COLUMN II, BELOW)

18b. What is (his; her) age? (RECORD IN COLUMN III, BELOW)

18c. (ASK ONLY FOR SONS, DAUGHTERS, AND OTHER CHILDREN)
Is _____ your own (biological) child? (RECORD "YES" OR "NO" IN
COLUMN IV, BELOW)

I Relationship to R	II Sex	III Age	IV Biologically R's?
1. R E S P O N D E N T			XXXXXXXX
2.			
3.			
4.			
5.			
6.			
7.			
8.			
9.			
10.			
11.			
12.			

Project 325

Now I would like to ask you a few questions about how you look at the ADC program.

19. During the past three years while in the ADC program, did your children participate in any programs or activities or meetings that were recommended, sponsored, or paid for by the welfare agency or your caseworker?

         /Yes/   /No/
                 (TO Q 20)

19a. What activities were these? _____

_____

19b. Do you think these activities were beneficial or useful? /Yes/   /No/
                                                            (TO Q 20)

     19c. In what ways do you think they were beneficial or useful?

          _____

          _____

          _____

20. During the past three years while in the ADC program, did you, yourself, participate in any programs or activities or meetings that were recommended, sponsored, or paid for by the welfare agency or your caseworker?

                                          /Yes/   /No/
                                                    (TO Q 21)

20a. What activities were these? _____

_____

20b. Do you think these activities were beneficial or useful? /Yes/   /No/
                                                            (TO Q 21)

     20c. In what ways do you think they were beneficial or useful?

          _____

          _____

          _____

21. During the last three years while in the ADC program, did you or your children participate in any programs, activities, or meetings that you felt were of little or no benefit or use?

                          /Yes/   /No/
                                   (TO Q 22)

21a. What activities were these? _____

_____

21b. In what ways were they of little or no use? _____

_____

12.

22. During the last three years while you were in the ADC program, did you or
your children receive any medical aid or treatment that was paid for by
the welfare agency?

/Yes/   /No/
(TO Q 23)

22a. What was this medical assistance for? (RECORD BELOW)

TYPE OF MEDICAL ASSISTANCE	HOSPITALIZATION?
1.	
2.	
3.	
4.	
5.	
6.	

22b. (ASK FOR EACH ITEM AND RECORD ABOVE)
Was hospitalization required?

22c. Who usually suggested getting this medical assistance?

_____

23. During the last three years while you were in the ADC program, did you or
your children receive any dental care that was paid for by the welfare agency?

/Yes/   /No/
(TO Q 24)

23a. What was this dental care? _____

_____

23b. Who usually suggested getting the dental care? _____

24. During the last three years while on ADC, did you or your children receive any
help with mental or emotional problems that was paid for by the welfare agency?

/Yes/   /No/
(TO Q 25)

24a. What kind of help did you or your children receive? _____

_____
_____

24b. Who usually suggested getting this help? _____

_____

25. Was there any time in the last three years when you were in the ADC program when your caseworker suggested that you or your children get some medical or dental help, or help with mental or emotional problems, but you didn't?

/Yes/   /No/
               (TO Q 26)

25a. What help was suggested to you? _____

_____

_____

25b. Why didn't you get the help? _____

_____

_____

26. In the last three years while in the ADC program was there any time you thought you or your children needed care (medical care, dental care, or help with mental or emotional problems), but you, for one reason or another, did not ask for it?

/Yes/   /No/
            (TO Q 27)

26a. What kinds of help did you need? (RECORD BELOW)

HELP NEEDED	REASON DIDN'T ASK FOR HELP
1. _____	1. _____
2. _____	2. _____
3. _____	3. _____
4. _____	4. _____

26b. Why didn't you ask for it? (RECORD ABOVE)

27. Was there any time while in the ADC program in the last three years when
    you requested some help for yourself or your children with medical, dental,
    or mental health problems, but the request was turned down by the welfare
    agency or your caseworker?

                    /Yes/   /No/
                      ↓   (TO Q 28)

   27a. What help did you request, which was refused? (RECORD BELOW)

HELP REQUESTED	REASON HELP REFUSED
1. _____	1. _____
2. _____	2. _____
3. _____	3. _____

   27b. Now for each of these requests you made, but which were not granted, will
        you please tell me what your caseworker or the welfare agency told you--
        that is, why did they say you couldn't have the help? (RECORD ABOVE)

28. While you were in the ADC program in the last three years, were you visited
    by a homemaker or someone other than your caseworker from the welfare depart-
    ment who made suggestions about housekeeping, cooking, nutrition, or child
    care--or who helped you with some of these things?

                    /Yes/   /No/
                      ↓   (TO Q 29)

   28a. How often? _____

   28b. What kinds of help did she provide? _____

        _____

        _____

29. Now I'd like to ask you a few questions about your caseworker(s) in the last
     three years. Can you think of several things your caseworker(s) did for you
     or your family while you were on the program that you thought were helpful?
     Such things could be services they performed, things they arranged, or perhaps
     just advice they gave? Are there three or four things you could mention?

     /Nothing to mention/, or 1. _____
          (TO Q 30)   _____

                              2. _____
                                  _____

                              3. _____
                                  _____

                              4. _____
                                  _____

30. In general, how helpful do you feel your caseworkers were in seeing that you and
     your family got the most good out of the ADC program during the past three years--
     would you say they were very helpful, moderately helpful, slightly helpful, or
     not at all helpful? (IF R SAYS SHE CANNOT GENERALIZE, ASK HER TO RATE THE CASE-
     WORKER SHE HAD FOR THE LONGEST TIME.)

     /Very helpful/ /Moderately helpful/ /Slightly helpful/ /Not at all helpful/

31. Can you think of some things your caseworkers might have done to help you or
     your family during the last three years that they didn't do?

     /Nothing/, or _____
                    _____

32. Would you say that during the last three years while you were in the ADC program
     you saw your caseworker too often, somewhat too often, about often enough, or
     not often enough?
                    /Too often/   /Somewhat/   /About often enough/   /Not often/
                                                                      /enough   /

33. What kinds of discussions did you have with your caseworker--were they just
     general or did the caseworker try to suggest to you how you should do things
     or did she try to find ways that she could help you, or what?

               /General/   /Suggested/   /Tried to find/
                                                    /ways to help /

34. As you recall, what things did you and your caseworker(s) discuss <u>most often</u>? (Anything else?)

1. _____

_____

2. _____

_____

3. _____

_____

35. While on the ADC program, how much were you bothered by the questions asked by your caseworkers about you and your children's lives and by other information you had to give--would you say you were not at all bothered, only slightly bothered, moderately, or very much bothered?

/Not at all/   /Slightly/   /Moderately/   /Very much/
(TO Q 36)

35a. What were the things that bothered you most? _____

_____

_____

36. In general, how fairly do you think you were treated by the welfare agency and your caseworkers--would you say you were treated always fairly, usually fairly, usually unfairly, or always unfairly?

/Always fairly/   /Usually fairly/   /Usually unfairly/   /Always unfairly/
(TO Q 37)

36a. Could you tell me of any times in particular when you felt you were treated unfairly? _____

_____

_____

37. Was your experience with the welfare agency very satisfactory in view of what you needed, satisfactory, unsatisfactory, or very unsatisfactory?

/Very satis./   /Satisfactory/   /Unsatisfactory/   /Very unsatis./

38. How much do you think you benefited from the services other than the basic financial aid, which your caseworker and the welfare agency provided--would you say you greatly benefited, moderately benefited, benefited very little, or benefited not at all?

/Greatly benefited/   /Moderately/   /Very little/   /Not at all/

39. Looking at your entire experience with the ADC program, what do you think
     was the <u>one</u> <u>most</u> <u>beneficial</u> <u>thing</u> for you and your family?

     /Nothing beneficial/, or _____
        (TO Q 40)   _____
                               _____
                               _____
                               _____

     39a. Were there any other things you could mention that you thought were
           fairly beneficial? _____

     _____
     _____
     _____
     _____

40. What were the worst parts, or those least beneficial, of your experience
     with the ADC program? _____

     _____
     _____
     _____
     _____
     _____

41. How long before the time when you left the ADC program had you seen the
     change coming and had been planning to leave the program?

     _____(YEARS)   OR   _____(MONTHS)   /Had not planned/
                                                 / to leave   /

18.

USE FOR MILWAUKEE COUNTY ONLY

42. Have you ever participated in the food stamp program?

/Yes/   /No/

42a. Why haven't you participated in the food
      stamp program?

      _____

      _____

                        (SKIP TO Q 44)

42b. During the last year while in the ADC program, did you use food stamps
      every month, every other month, a few times, just once, or didn't you
      use them at all in the year?

      /Every month/   /Every other month/   /A few times/   /Once/   /Never/

                        42c. Why didn't you use the food stamps more than you did?

                        _____

                        _____

                        _____

                        _____

42d. How convenient was obtaining and using the food stamps--would you say
      they were very convenient, fairly convenient, fairly inconvenient,
      or very inconvenient?

      /‾ Very ‾/   /‾ Fairly ‾/   /‾ Fairly ‾/   /‾   Very   ‾/
      /convenient/   /convenient/   /inconvenient/   /inconvenient/

42e. Did you ever have any problems with the way people treated you
      when you were using food stamps?

                /Yes/   /No/
                          (SKIP TO Q 44)

42f. What problems did you have?   _____

      _____

      _____

      _____

                        (SKIP TO Q 44)

| USE FOR BROWN, DANE, DODGE, AND SAUK COUNTIES |

43. Have you ever participated in the food commodities program?

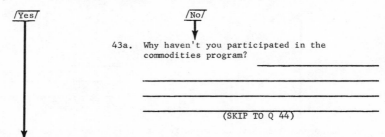

/Yes/   /No/

43a. Why haven't you participated in the
      commodities program? _____

      _____

      _____

      _____
                              (SKIP TO Q 44)

43b. During the last year while you were on the ADC program, how often
      did you participate--every month, every other month, a few times,
      just once, or not at all?

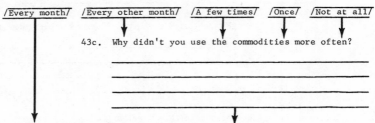

/Every month/ /Every other month/ /A few times/ /Once/ /Not at all/

      43c. Why didn't you use the commodities more often?

            _____

            _____

            _____

            _____

43d. How convenient have you found obtaining and using the commodities--
      would you say they were very convenient, fairly convenient, fairly
      inconvenient, or very inconvenient?

      /   Very   /   / Fairly /   / Fairly   /   /   Very   /
      /convenient/   /convenient/   /inconvenient/   /inconvenient/

(GO ON TO NEXT PAGE)

44. How long were you in the ADC program most recently?

_____(YEARS)   OR   _____(MONTHS)

45. WAS R IN PROGRAM 2 YEARS OR MORE OR FOR A SHORTER TIME?

/TWO YEARS OR MORE/   /LESS THAN TWO YEARS/

45a. How many times did you move   45b. How many times did you move
     during the last two years   during the time you were in
     you were in the ADC program?   the ADC program?

     0 1 2 3 4 or _____(#)   0 1 2 3 4 or _____(#)

45c. Could you tell me the major reason for each of these moves?
     (IF MORE THAN FOUR MOVES, ASK FOR FOUR MOST RECENT)

     1. _____

     2. _____

     3. _____

     4. _____

When we interviewed you before, we asked you a few questions about some of your
general feelings about life, not just your experiences with the ADC program.
(Now that you are no longer on ADC), we're interested in learning whether you
feel differently now than you did before. In each of these questions, I'm
going to give you two sentences. Choose the one that comes closest to telling
the way you feel things actually are in life. Be sure it's the way you think
things actually are at this point in your life, not the way you'd like them
to be. Let me read both sentences in each series before you select the one
that best represents what you think.

CHECK ONE

46. _____   A. When I make plans, I am almost certain that I can
                  make them work. OR,
    _____   B. It is not always a good idea to plan too far ahead,
                  because many things turn out to be a matter of good
                  or bad luck anyway.

47. _____   A. I've usually felt pretty sure my life would work out the
                  way I want it to. OR,
    _____   B. There have been times when I haven't been very sure that
                  my life would work out the way I want it to.

48. _____   A. When people disagree with me, I sometimes start to wonder
                  whether I'm right. OR,
    _____   B. I nearly always feel sure of myself, even when people
                  disagree with me.

Project 325   21.

CHECK ONE

49. _____   A. I often have trouble making up my mind about important
                   decisions.   OR,
    _____   B. I don't have much trouble making up my mind about
                   important decisions.

50. _____   A. When I make plans ahead, I usually get to carry things
                   out the way I expected.   OR,
    _____   B. Things usually come up to make me change my plans.

51. _____   A. I feel I'm a person who gets his share of bad luck.   OR,
    _____   B. I feel I have mostly good luck.

52. In general, how do you think people in this community feel about people
    who are in the ADC program? Would you say they feel very understanding,
    fairly understanding, indifferent, fairly hostile, or very hostile?

    / Very /   / Fairly /   /Indifferent/   /Fairly /   / Very /
    /understanding/ /understanding/   /hostile/   /hostile/

53. What is most different about your life now that you aren't in the ADC program?

    _____
    _____
    _____
                                       ↓
    53a. What other things are different about your life that you have noticed?

          _____
          _____
          _____

54. How do you feel about having left the ADC program? As compared with the time
    spent on the program, do you think you and your family will now be much better
    off, somewhat better off, about the same, or worse off?

    /Much better off/   /Somewhat better off/   /About the same/   /Worse off/

55. Do you plan to continue to live here in _____?   /Yes/   /No/
                                                          (TO Q 56)   ↓

    55a. Where do you plan to move? _____

          _____

    55b. Why would you move there? _____

          _____

    55c. When do you plan to move? _____

56. Do you see any time in the future when you will again need help
    from the ADC program?

    /Yes/   /Unsure/   /No/
                                     (END)

56a. When might this be and why would you need aid then?

    _____
    _____
    _____
    _____

                        (END)

INTERVIEWER'S SUPPLEMENT

A1. Time interview ended: _____

A2. Make sure the data on contacts you have made at this housing unit, including
     the present contact, has been supplied in full on bottom of Cover Sheet.

A3. R's race is: /White/   /Negro/   Other: _____

A4. R's sex is: /Male/   /Female/

A5. R's cooperation was: /Very good/   /Good/   /Fair/   /Poor/

A6. Other persons present at interview were: /None/   /Children under 6/
     /Older children/   /Spouse/   /Other relatives/   /Other adults/
                      (CHECK MORE THAN ONE BOX IF NECESSARY)

A7. This housing unit is in a structure that contains: /One HU only/
     /2-9 HU's/   /10 or more/   /Rooming/
                   /apartments/   / house /   Other: _____

THUMBNAIL SKETCH

_____

_____

_____

_____

_____

_____

_____

_____

_____

_____

_____

INDEX

A 4
B 5
C 6
D 7
E 8
F 9
G 0
H 1
I 2
J 3